Aging and Caring at the Intersection of Work and Home Life

Aging and Caring at the Intersection of Work and Home Life

Blurring the Boundaries

Edited by

Anne Martin-Matthews
Canadian Institute of Health and University of British Columbia, Vancouver

Judith E. Phillips
Swansea University, Wales, UK

New York London

Psychology Press
Taylor & Francis Group
270 Madison Avenue
New York, NY 10016

Psychology Press
Taylor & Francis Group
27 Church Road
Hove, East Sussex BN3 2FA

Printed in the United States of America on acid-free paper
10 9 8 7 6 5 4 3 2 1

International Standard Book Number-13: 978-0-8058-5917-1 (Hardcover)

Library of Congress Cataloging-in-Publication Data

Aging and caring at the intersection of work and home life : blurring the boundaries / edited by Anne Martin-Matthews and Judith Phillips.
p. cm.
Includes bibliographical references and index.
ISBN-13: 978-0-8058-5917-1 (hardcover : alk. paper)
ISBN-10: 0-8058-5917-9 (hardcover : alk. paper)
1. Older people--Services for. 2. Older people--Government policy. 3. Older people--Home care. 4. Population aging. 5. Work and family. I. Martin Matthews, Anne. II. Phillips, Judith (Judith E.)

HV1451.A317 2008
362.6--dc22 2007037016

Visit the Taylor & Francis Web site at
http://www.taylorandfrancis.com

and the Psychology Press Web site at
http://www.psypress.com

For Anne Martin-Matthews:

To Max and Tess Martin,

Adam and Leah Matthews

For Judith E. Phillips:

To the memory of Bridget Phillips

Contents

Foreword

Megatrends That Affect Caregiving Boundaries

Michael A. Creedon

This text brings together research, policy, and program perspectives from various countries on the broad topic of *Aging at the Intersection of Work and Home Life: Blurring the Boundaries.* It should be welcomed by all those concerned with the massive phenomenon of growing life expectancy throughout the world. We all hope for longer, healthier lives, but the sheer numbers of older adults, and their accompanying needs, can place a major strain on tax systems, pension programs, health systems, and of course the family support structures of society. On the family level there can be intense pressures that come from coping with work and caregiving. This text explores the shifting boundaries of caregiving in families. The advent of public sector financial support for caregiving by family members will also affect caregiving patterns, as noted in the text. The changing nature of pension benefits can affect the freedom to rely on that source of income.

In the following paragraphs the growth in demand for older workers in the United States is noted, and the apparent growth among them of willingness to work part-time or full-time, or to establish a microbusiness. So the boundary between work and retirement is likely to blur also, and this may in turn affect caregiving patterns. Another issue that affects the United States and other societies is the growth of legal and illegal immigration to the United States and the European Union and the massive migration from rural to urban areas in China, India, and other countries. Some of these topics are addressed in chapters in this text; others may suggest areas for future work by academic colleagues throughout the world.

A Growing Demand for Older Workers

On November 28, 2006, the chairman of the U.S. Federal Reserve Board, Ben Bernanke, addressed the National Italian American Foundation in New York (Bernanke, 2006). One of his more notable statements was the declaration that the proportion of women available to enter the American workforce has reached a peak, and therefore the demand for retired workers will grow substantially in the years ahead. This suggests that the United States has optimized the use of women workers, at least in the sense that the great majority of women who want jobs now have them (though not always in their preferred fields). This in itself is a major milestone in the United States. But the subsequent statement was also notable: The demand for older workers to stay in the workforce, and for retirees to reenter it on a full-time or part-time basis, is likely to grow in the years ahead. These statements were made in the context of a national 4.4% unemployment rate—in other words, a full employment society. The implications of these trends for work and home life are subjects central to this volume. Bill Novelli, CEO of AARP, in the October 2007 *AARP Bulletin*, cites Bureau of Labor statistics data: in 2006 some 29% of people in the U.S. between 60 and 69 years of age were active in the workforce as were 17% of those 70–74 years of age.

The current average age for retirement in the United States is 61.9, not unrelated to the availability of Social Security at age 62! The leading edge of the U.S. baby boom will reach 62 within 2 years, and this can be expected to substantially increase the number of retirees per year. But it will also increase the number of older workers. Rutgers University, in a 2006 national survey on retirement and work, found that 70% of their respondents want some level of work, for months or for years, full-time or part-time, during their retirement (Reynolds, Ridley, & Van Horn, 2005). Merrill Lynch, in a similar study, found that 75% of their respondents had the same desire (Merrill Lynch, 2005). Quinn and Burkhauser (1990) state that the majority of older adults who work in retirement do so for financial reasons. These studies suggest that, in future, the issue may not be "work or retire," but cycles of work and leisure or the attainment of a balance of work and leisure activities that may shift over time, depending on health, family finances and obligations, and economic opportunity.

Caregiving for Elders

Many of these baby boomers will become caregivers for frail parents, and many will care for frail spouses over time. However, the demand for retiree workers, full-time or part-time, will likely impact on the caregiving availability of many. One possible outcome of increased work participation by retirees, and continued work into later years, may be greater workplace emphasis on eldercare benefits. Another outcome may be a more limited supply of informal caregivers. A recent study conducted by the National Alliance for Caregiving examined the role of children in caring for adult family members. The authors reported that some 1.4 million children are providers of care to adult members of their families, and some of them are the primary caregivers (Hunt, Levine, & Naiditch, 2005). Most studies of working caregivers have focused on adult workers, but one of the by-products of maximization of female participation in the formal workforce is an inevitable increase in caregiving demands on other family members. Several chapters in this text explore the range of caregiving roles that can be carried by family members, relatives, and friends.

I am currently engaged in a project in Appalachia to use high school teenagers as trainers of Alzheimer's caregivers in the use of computers to reach other caregivers, to use chat rooms with other caregivers, and to use Internet search tools for Alzheimer's care information (Maxwell & Creedon, 2003; Mountain Empire Older Citizens, 2006–2007). That project links the local high school, the Area Agency on Aging, the Wired Community Project in the county, and the local campus of the University of Virginia to bring together local teen tutors and older adult caregivers. Teenagers and even younger children can do much to enhance our community care of elders. Of course, there is also a potential for burdening young people and even abusing them. One wonders whether heavy caregiving demands are depriving some youth of the time for study, or of the opportunity to earn pocket money or gather money for college tuition. Previous research on working caregivers found that some 10% of them quit work to provide care—an obvious financial loss. Perhaps we need to quantify the financial impact on youth and the opportunity costs that care of a parent can impose. Thus, Joanie Sims-Gould, Anne Martin-Matthews, and Carolyn Rosenthal's contribution to this text (chapter 4) is very timely, because it calls attention to the variety of caregiving roles within families and broadens the focus to the family as a caring system.

In this society, and in others, caregiving duties may prevent children from leaving home, getting an education, or having a life and a career of their own. Growing up in rural Ireland, I was personally aware of parents refusing to let a daughter marry because they wanted her help with the family farm. On a visit to Japan, I became aware of the caregiving expectations placed on the wife of the oldest son. In Pakistan I visited the only publicly sponsored nursing home for men in Punjab at that time (1984) and realized that their society expected families to be the sole caregivers for elders. This text includes aging studies in various societies. Thus it should heighten the reader's awareness of diversity in cultural expectations regarding retirement and work, but also regarding care-giving roles.

Changing Pension Policies and Business Opportunities

The changing demographics of the United States and the growth plans of American companies may offer more work opportunities to older persons. However, there is also a decreasing likelihood of "defined benefit" pensions that guarantee a pension for life from the company to American workers. More and more workers are being offered "defined contribution" programs (where contributions are made by the company and also the worker to stock funds, only during the years of work for that organization). Such programs transfer the risk of retirement financing to the worker-retiree, and may cause many to delay retirement or to work part-time in retirement. Thus pension policies may contribute to the blurring of the boundary between retirement and work in the United States, and impact particularly on the availability of spouses and siblings for care-giving tasks.

Societies such as Japan, whose baby boom occurred earlier (before World War II), may offer different lessons. Japan has just come out of a decade-long recession that provided little workplace demand for older workers. I was very impressed during a 2-year Dialogue Between U.S. and Japanese Legislators on Policies for Aging Societies (sponsored by the National Conference of State Legislators) by the number of older Japanese who started a microbusiness in retirement. In the United States, currently it is estimated that 8.4% of the workforce are self-employed and that self-employment increases with age (Blanchflower, 1998). In the Merrill Lynch survey on work and retirement (2005) some 13% of respondents said they wanted to have a business of some kind in retirement. There are indications that the rate of entrepreneurship among older Americans is going up. For example, at Johns Hopkins University (with which I am associated), 50% of the current participants in an entrepreneurship program are midlife and older women. Likewise, retirement workshops that I have conducted for federal employees consistently reveal that a number of participants already have a microbusiness. Self-employment offers greater opportunities to control the use of time than does employment by public or private sector organizations. The present text does not explore the relationship between self-employment roles and caregiving, but the future is likely to witness a substantial growth in self-employment among retirees.

Rural-Urban Migration and International Migration

Another worldwide trend, of enormous consequence for work–family dynamics, is the massive migration of peasant populations from rural areas to major urban communities. In China this migration is affecting many millions of families. As the teenagers and young adults leave for work opportunities far from home, inevitably the availability of caregivers for the family elders weakens. Perhaps the financial contributions of such migrant workers can enable elderly relatives to survive and even to hire caregivers. The huge transfers of money to relatives in Mexico, Honduras, and other Caribbean and Central American nations, by the millions of both documented and undocumented workers in the United States, have been widely recognized (Sura, 2002). Similar large waves of immigration within Europe (Eastern Europeans migrating to countries in Western Europe, Turks migrating to Germany, and people from African nations going to France, Spain, Ireland, etc.) are causing similar financial transfers to parents, spouses, and others back in the home country. The International Fund for Agricultural Development has released a report in October 2007 stating that 150 million migrants are sending more that $300 billion home to there families each year in more than 1.5 billion separate transactions. Such migration patterns, and related financial flows, suggest that a massive shift in caregiving patterns may be occurring in some developing countries: from informal family care to paid caregivers. Mehta and Thang's chapter in this text (chapter 3), on multigenerational care, discusses the increasing presence of paid foreign domestic workers in Singapore. Likewise, Neal, Wagner, Bonn, and Niles-Yokum (chapter 5) discuss the growth of long-distance care in the United States and even intercountry care. The growing demand for retiree workers in the United States, along with the aging of the baby boomers, the massive migration from rural to urban areas in countries like India, China, and Brazil, and the migration of workers from developing countries to more advanced economies, are all affecting work–family dynamics around the world. Much work needs to be done to help us grasp the impact of migration on caregiving.

The Role of Technology in Independent Living and Caregiving

But there are other developments that can also affect work–family and caregiving patterns. One of these is the rapid rise of technologies for the home and technologies for communication. Japan's baby boom occurred in the 1930s. Today Japan has an enormous number of retirees and a dynamic "silver industry" dedicated to meeting the needs of older Japanese. In the United States, "smart houses" are proliferating, offering educational opportunities for professionals and for families, and demonstrating the use of wireless communications in the home, electronically controlled home security, bathrooms with supportive devices, and other supportive features. Family caregivers and professional services can be immediately informed, via the press of a button, if intervention is needed. Neal et al. in their chapter also reflect on the positive contribution of communications technology to the work–caregiving nexus. Dr. Bill Mann and colleagues at the State University of New York at Buffalo tested the use of two-way audiovisual technology between nurses and home-based frail elders. They found that the nurses could provide service to 19 patients per day rather than 6 per day. They also found that the elderly patients were quite happy to receive more frequent contacts of this kind, rather than the traditional weekly home visit, with the assurance that immediate personal visits would occur when necessary (Mann et al., 1999). Such applications could provide similar reassurance to elders and their working caregivers. Research in the workplace has indicated that telephone calls to or from frail family members are a staple of caregiving by workers. But we can expect a burgeoning of such technology applications that provide continued independence for elders and improved monitoring capacity for working caregivers in the coming decade.

Workplace Eldercare Programs

The aging of the United States has increased workplace management awareness of the care-giving responsibilities of workers. Studies on working caregivers have indicated that their average age is 47, just about midcareer for many workers. Back in the 1980s the initial phase of workplace response to eldercare burdens on employees by companies like PepsiCo, IBM, and Stride Rite included handbooks for employee caregivers, workplace workshops on caregiving provided by professionals, and telephone-based counseling on eldercare issues. In the early 1990s the U.S. Department of Defense Office of Family Policy developed an eldercare resource manual for military families along with a briefing book on eldercare for counselors and chaplains (U.S. Department of Defense, 1992). Today, the number of companies offering such resources has reached at least 25% of American companies. Studies undertaken by some of the authors of this text have helped to provide the economic justification for such workplace programs. For example, the fact that 10% of working caregivers leave the workforce because of care-giving duties, and that many others are tardy to work or make excessive use of the phone during work hours, translates into significant impacts on productivity (Creedon, 1995).

Public Policies

Of course, public policies on retirement, on older workers' rights and protections, on childcare and eldercare support, and on housing and transportation have an enormous impact on aging societies. In the United States, for example, there has been little or no federal government activity regarding low- and moderate-income housing in recent years. This surely affects the options for lower-income elders. About 75% of older Americans own their own homes. Approximately one third of these houses are recent structures, one third are 20–40 years old, and one third are older—some quite old. Because of the increase in housing values in the past decade, particularly on the East and West coasts, many elders have substantial assets locked up in their houses. Older Americans, seeing the home as something to be handed on to their heirs, have been very reluctant to embark on such ways of releasing the value of their homes as reverse mortgages. But a reverse mortgage can provide the cash that allows an older person or couple to repair a home, pay for ordinary expenses, and remain independent in their own home longer. The house is sold after they leave, or after death, and the loan is repaid at that point. In the United States and in many other countries, the public policies on housing can have a major impact on the ability of elders to carry on with satisfying lives in the homes and neighborhoods they know and prefer. Keefe, Glendinning, and Fancey, in chapter 10, discuss a number of approaches to financial compensation of family caregivers by government, adopted in the United Kingdom, Australia, Canada, and Germany. Public services for frail elders vary greatly in both availability and intensity in different societies. One of the significant contributions of this text is the exploration of the relationships that can emerge between family caregivers and both professional and paraprofessional providers of care.

This foreword has focused on a few issues that currently affect the quality of life for older Americans as well as elders in other societies: the blurring of the line between retirement and work; the massive migration of workers from rural to urban areas, and from developing to developed countries; and the reality that children and teenagers as well as adults may be heavily engaged in caregiving. Other dynamics may offer very positive perspectives for an aging world, such as the increasing availability of communications technologies and home electronic technologies, the boom in housing values in the United

States and elsewhere, and the rise in microbusiness involvement by older workers and retirees. The changing policies, technologies, and labor force configurations, discussed in this text, offer much hope for elders and will surely result in enhanced care-giving strategies for families.

References

Bernanke, B. (2006, November 28). The economic outlook (speech given to the National Italian American Foundation, New York). Retrieved September 3, 2007, from http://www.federalreserve.gov/boarddocs/speeches/2006/20061128/default.htm

Blanchflower, D. G. (1998, September 24–26). Self-employment in OECD countries. International Conference on Self-Employment, Burlington, Ontario, Canada. Retrieved from http://cerf.mcmaster.ca/papers/seconf/OECD.pdf

Creedon, M. A. (1995). Eldercare research in the United States (paper presented at the European Foundation for Work and Social Wellbeing Conference on Work and Eldercare, Bonn, Germany). Dublin, Ireland: European Foundation.

Hunt, G., Levine, C., & Naiditch, L. (2005). *Young caregivers in the United States: Findings from a national survey.* Bethesda, MD, and New York: National Alliance for Caregiving and United Hospital Fund.

International Fund for Agricultural Development (2007, October). Sending money home: Worldwide remittance flows to developing countries. Remittances @ IFAD.org

Mann, W. C., Ottenbacher, K. J., Fraas, L., Tomita, M., & Granger, C. V. (1999). Effectiveness of assistive technology and environmental interventions in maintaining independence and reducing home care costs for the frail elderly: A randomized controlled trial. *Archives of Family Medicine*, *8*(3) 210–217.

Maxwell, M. P., & Creedon, M. A. (2003). *Using the Internet for Alzheimer's care: The challenge for elders and service organizations.* Big Stone Gap, VA: Mountain Empire Older Citizens.

Merrill Lynch. (2005). *Harris interactive, age wave: The new retirement survey at Merrill Lynch.* Retrieved September 3, 2007, from http://www.ml.com/index.asp?id=7695_7696_8149_46028_46503_46635

Mountain Empire Older Citizens. (2006–2007). *Students/Alzheimer's care givers technology project: An intergenerational initiative to benefit all involved.* Big Stone Gap, VA: Author.

Novelli, B. (2007). Staying on the job. *AARP Bulletin*, October 2007, *48*(9) 36.

Quinn, J. F., & Burkhauser, R. V. (1990). Work and retirement. In R H. Binstock, & L. K. George (Eds.), *Handbook of aging and the social sciences* (pp. 303–327). San Diego, California: Academic Press.

Reynolds, S., Ridley, N., & Van Horn, E. (2005, August). *A work-filled retirement: Workers' changing views on employment and leisure*. Retrieved September 3, 2007, from http://www.heldrich.rutgers.edu/Resources/Publication/191/WT16.pdf

Sura, R. (2002). *Billions in motion: Latino immigrants, remittances and banking*. Washington, DC: Inter-American Development Bank.

U.S. Census Bureau. (1990, December). Homeownership trends in the 1980s. In *Current Housing Reports* (Series H-121, No. 2). Washington, DC: Author.

U.S. Department of Defense. (1992). *Department of Defense eldercare handbook*. Washington, DC: Office of the Assistant Secretary of Defense for Force Management and Personnel.

Acknowledgments

The production of this book is the result of extensive interaction and a history of relationships and collaborations amongst the editors and contributors over time and across continents. Michael A. Creedon was the catalyst for many of these relations and collaborations, and we thank him sincerely for the pivotal role he played in introducing Anne Martin-Matthews and Judith E. Phillips, the coeditors of this volume, to one another in 1992. Michael was also instrumental in introducing Judith and Anne to Margaret B. Neal and her colleagues at a time when their industry-partnered research served to inform the Canadian Aging Research Network (CARNET) studies on work and eldercare being initiated in Canada. Subsequently, Judith E. Phillips and Miriam Bernard adapted some of the CARNET research instruments for use in their UK studies, and these in turn were used by Sally Keeling and Judith Davey in their New Zealand studies of workers and their managing of employment and care responsibilities. And over time, several of the doctoral students who worked on CARNET data (e.g., Janice Keefe and Joanie Sims-Gould) have benefited from these international connections and developed their own research agendas on issues of work–home life balance. All this is the result of Michael's inveterate network building and urging of early collaborations. Thank you, Michael!

National and international workshops and conferences over the past decade have also furthered the connections amongst the coauthors of this book, and provided opportunities for us to hear from and learn from one another and thereby refine and advance our thinking about these issues. A preconference workshop at the annual meetings of the British Society of Gerontology in Stirling in 2001 was particularly catalytic. More recently, a symposium organized by the coeditors at the annual meeting of the Gerontological Society of America in Orlando, Florida, in 2005 enabled us to invite other authors and our PhD students to share methodologies and explore ideas on the issues discussed in these pages. Over the course of time, the boundaries between our professional and personal relationships with one another have become blurred as well, and that too has been important to the development of this book!

We also wish to recognize the funders of the research reported in this volume. The range of national governments, funding agencies, foundations, and private-sector partners who have supported these studies attests to the perceived relevance and importance of issues of work and home life balance for employees across nations and in a wide variety of public and social policy contexts. The list below is not exhaustive but identifies and acknowledges the major funders of our research: The Government of Canada's Networks of Centres of Excellence Funding to CARNET funded Anne Martin-Matthews' research. The collaboration between Anne and Judith in the development of this proposal was furthered during Anne's visiting professorship, supported by the British Academy, in September 2004.

Research reported in chapter 1 by Catherine Ward-Griffin was funded by the Canadian Institutes of Health Research (CIHR) and the Social Sciences and Humanities Research Council of Canada (SSHRC).

The funding for Atiya Mahmood's postdoctoral fellowship (chapter 2) came from the CIHR through its support for Anne Martin-Matthews' research project "Home Care in Canada: Aging at the Nexus of the Public and Private Spheres."

Joanie Sims-Gould held a doctoral fellowship funded by the SSHRC while completing the research that forms the basis of chapter 4.

In the United Kingdom, research by Judith E. Phillips and Miriam Bernard (chapter 5) was supported by the Joseph Rowntree Foundation.

Analysis conducted in chapter 6 by Margaret B. Neal, Donna L. Wagner, Kathleen J.B. Bonn, and Kelly Niles-Yokum was supported by the Alfred P. Sloan Foundation for their study "Dual-Earner Couples in the Sandwiched Generation."

Research reported in chapter 7 by Sally Keeling and Judith Davey was supported by the Future of Work Fund, Department of Labour, New Zealand.

Preparation of chapter 9 by Norah Keating, Donna Dosman, Jennifer Swindle, and Janet Fast was supported by the SSHRC and the Research Data Centres program of Statistics Canada.

A portion of the research on which Janice Keefe, Caroline Glendinning, and Pamela Fancey's chapter 10 is based was funded by the SSHRC.

Research reported in chapter 12 by Julia Twigg was funded by the Economic and Social Research Council (ESRC) in the United Kingdom.

We also especially thank Margaret B. Neal for encouraging this project and for facilitating contact for us with Anne Duffy, at that time an editor with Lawrence Erlbaum and Associates. Anonymous reviewers of the original prospectus provided many helpful comments. Support staff based at the University of British Columbia also provided valuable assistance. Andrea Cosentino ably assisted with editorial work and in attending to the myriad details getting all the components of a book together. Many thanks, Andrea. Marian Chong-Kit and Jessica Patterson also provided administrative and research assistance.

Anne Martin-Matthews acknowledges the support of Ralph Matthews and Adam Matthews as she took time away from home life to write and reflect on issues of work and home life balance. Anne dedicates this volume to the "up" and "down" generations who blur her professional and personal boundaries, enhance her understanding of aging, and enrich her life: her parents, Max and Tess Martin, and her young adult children, Adam and Leah Matthews. Judith E. Phillips dedicates the book to the memory of her mother, Bridget Phillips, wife, mother, comptometer operator, secretary of the women's guild, carer, and diarist who throughout her life effectively juggled work and care.

Introduction

Anne Martin-Matthews and Judith E. Phillips

The 30 years since Rosabeth Moss Kanter wrote *Work and Family in the United States* (1977), a pioneering book that challenged the sociological myth of "separate worlds" of work and family life, have seen the development of "the sociology of work and family ... as a major subfield within the discipline" (Hood, 1993). Although much of the early work on the intersection of work and family roles focused on issues of a single family member (typically a woman) balancing or "juggling" these two life spheres, more recent research has examined the complex interplay of multiple roles and multiple players in the dynamics of aging lives at the intersection of work and home life.

This book aims to capture and conceptualize the complexity of the intersection of work and home life as it relates to the provision of assistance and support to older relatives in a variety of "carework" contexts. It explores these issues within a critical framework, rather than from an assumed stress or burden perspective, which dominates current texts on the topic. Throughout the book we challenge such traditional ways of seeing the care world. Such a critical lens, for example, challenges both policies and practices in the workplace and in society that are directed at ameliorating role stress in balancing work and care. As Phillips (2007) noted, care is not a single concept but is characterized by its diversity and "multiple discourses" drawing on feminism, disability studies, legislation, and different organizational interests. It is also socially constructed by all these groups. At the heart of care are relationships, and these are central to our understanding of work and family life; care is an interdependent and connected concept, one that coexists with numerous other roles in an individual's life.

The connections and tensions between work and home life typically involve intersections between the private and the public spheres, between professional and personal responsibilities, and between paid and unpaid work. Each chapter addresses some aspect of these intersections, and the blurring of the boundaries at these points of intersection between work and home life. Viewed through the lens of boundaries that are sometimes (although not necessarily always) blurred, we gain further insight into the management and negotiation of caring and carework at the margins and the intersections between the private and the public, professional and personal, and the paid and unpaid. These include the intersection of home and work life, the limits of a professional care role or geographical constraints on the provision of care.

Readers of this volume will gain a deeper understanding of issues of care provision amongst "networks" of carers and helpers, and of the particular dynamics of care when it is episodic or framed by constraints of space and time as a result of geography. They will become familiar with how intersections and boundaries are viewed and, at times, managed in the process of seeking to attain a work–life balance. They will learn the significance of "locale" in relation to boundaries and intersections, as when "home" is the site of care or when care provision is bounded by proximity or distributed by distance. The notion of geographic context is further underscored here by the range of studies from around the world: from Canada, the United States, the United Kingdom, Singapore, Australia, and New Zealand. This book addresses current thinking in different cultural, social, and economic contexts on issues of work life, family responsibilities, and relationships and carework in aging societies.

In addition, in each chapter the authors address issues of diversity with sensitivity to gender, race, and ethnicity. A critical gerontological perspective is taken throughout the chapters, challenging assumptions, stereotypes, and constructions of aging and care. Although the focus of this discussion is on issues of aging at the intersection of work and home life, some chapters adopt a life course perspective by considering the interconnection between different parts of the life course as well as the intersection of individual, family, and historical time and intergenerational issues. Other chapters address work and care in the context of "space" and "place."

About the Book

In chapter 1, Catherine Ward-Griffin examines the intersections of the public and the private, the professional and the personal, and the paid and the unpaid caring work of female health professionals in Canada. Her focus is on the ways in which nurses, physiotherapists, physicians, and social workers caring for aging relatives negotiate the boundaries between their professional and personal care-giving roles within the context of changes to Canada's health care system. This chapter calls attention to the invisibility of this unique group of unpaid professional caregivers among their employers and their professional associations.

In chapter 2, Atiya Mahmood and Anne Martin-Matthews draw on qualitative data from Canada to examine the development and negotiation of relationships between home care workers and elderly clients, family members of clients, and employer agencies. The focus is primarily on women employed in the "nonprofessional" end of home care, providing services often described as *social care*. The isolation, variability, and invisibility of their work are challenges to boundary management for workers. For elderly clients, boundary management is challenged by the entry of a public service into the private sphere of the home. This chapter develops a conceptual model of the social, spatial, temporal, and organizational contexts of the home care experience for elderly clients, family caregivers, and paid care workers.

In chapter 3, Kalyani K. Mehta and Leng Leng Thang argue that the principle of "interdependence" permeates the multigenerational family care system in Singapore, with the roles of caregivers and care recipients changing over the life course of the family. Care for older members not only involves the immediate family but sometimes includes a foreign domestic worker as well. The paid worker lives within the family home, and provides many services traditionally performed by women in the family. Filial piety beliefs drive adult children to continue caring for elder relatives within the family home, resulting in a juggling of care of dependents within the family, bound by the spatial and economic constraints and boundaries drawn by national ideology and policies.

In chapter 4, Joanie Sims-Gould, Anne Martin-Matthews, and Carolyn J. Rosenthal stress the relational nature of family caregiving, viewing carework as a group effort typically involving family members in a variety of roles. They examine the intersections and overlaps between and within helping and caregiving. The chapter highlights the importance of not only the number of individuals involved in family caregiving and the nature of their contributions to the care of their older relative, but also the ways in which they care for one another. The authors examine the distinction between direct help provided to the older person(s) requiring care and assistive help provided to other helpers and caregivers.

In chapter 5, Judith E. Phillips and Miriam Bernard build from the premise that the "spatial context" in which care is provided has become an important issue for many families juggling work with caring responsibilities. They argue that, as more dual-income families juggle work and care and often commute in different directions, the spatial dimensions of caregiving and work location are increasingly complex issues to be considered. This chapter makes the case that despite developments of postmodernity and globalization, geography remains important. Distance and space still have to be considered in geographically bounded, absolute, and relative terms and lead to a distinct form of caring. In bringing the social and the spatial together, Phillips and Bernard argue that "the feminist ethic of care" should provide a guiding framework.

In chapter 6, Margaret B. Neal, Donna L. Wagner, Kathleen J.B. Bonn, and Kelly Niles-Yokum examine patterns of long-distance caregiving among U.S. employees and the distinct challenges that arise as a result of the separation between the older person in need of assistance and his or her family carer. This chapter explores the factors that may result in spatial or temporal separation between older adults and their carers; differences in the nature of care provided depending on the amount of separation; the issues involved in providing long-distance care in families of different social, economic, and cultural backgrounds; and strategies used by families to manage the separation. Contemporary support options, such as the use of assistive technology and professional care, are reviewed and discussed as to their effect on family ties.

In chapter 7, Sally Keeling and Judith Davey explore how employees of two large city councils in New Zealand manage their roles as working carers of older people. This chapter discusses their negotiations within and between several boundary areas: boundaries between their working (public) lives and their eldercare (private) roles, boundaries relating to their family networks, and those with the older family member. And, finally, these workers' eldercare roles can be placed at the boundary of informal care and public sector service delivery in their local communities. This chapter offers comparative insights on the intersection of formal and informal care, and on the definitions of local zones of care, and it applies a sociological analysis of public and private to research on care and support systems for older people.

In chapter 8, Jane Mears and Elizabeth A. Watson reanalyze data from 20 years of studies in Australia to examine carers' constructions of care and caring. They argue that, in theorizing about care and in developing good policies, it is important to consider whether theory and policy responses resonate with those doing the caring. They consider how carers and care workers construct the various parts of their lives and the meaning they attach to what they do: their responsibilities to family and to employers and work colleagues, their notions of what constitutes good care and good professional care practice, the place of empathy and personal connectedness in care, and how caring changes over time and with what impact. The chapter addresses how, where, and why carers construct boundaries around their care and the rest of their lives and the nature of those constructs.

In chapter 9, Norah Keating, Donna Dosman, Jennifer Swindle, and Janet Fast outline how work is shared among family members and friends through the development of profiles of care networks illustrating patterns of paid and unpaid work among groups of people providing care. The understanding of network types that may be typified by high labor force demands moves us beyond a focus limited to care dyads toward a more comprehensive view of the complexity of ways in which paid and unpaid work are shared. The chapter discusses the caring capacity of these networks in light of the small size of most networks and the competing demands of employment.

In chapter 10, Canadian researchers Janice Keefe and Pamela Fancey collaborate with UK researcher Caroline Glendinning to examine the various forms of financial compensation initiatives as a public policy option in the United Kingdom, Australia, Canada, and

Germany. Each country's approach is embedded in its traditions, ideologies, and social policy debates that change over time. This chapter examines each country's respective approach to financial compensation initiatives for family caregivers and the impact of such changes on caregivers in each national context. The drivers of these changes are discussed, as are current issues and debates surrounding payment of family members within each of the countries.

In chapter 11, Maria Evandrou and Karen Glaser move to a more macro focus on issues of aging at the intersection of work and home life. They examine changes in the extent of economic and social role occupancy across the life course between cohorts in Britain, through a focus on the factors associated with multiple role occupancy amongst women and men in midlife. This chapter sheds light on the socioeconomic circumstances of individuals who try to manage family care responsibilities with paid employment, and the constraints they face.

In chapter 12, Julia Twigg makes a considered shift to move the analysis of social care away from its current primary location at the level of organizations and policies, toward the front line of provision. She frames the analysis around themes of time and the rival temporal orderings of body, home, and service delivery. She argues that homecare cannot be seen as separated from the world in which it is embedded—that of home, the body, and domesticity. Home and body are enmeshed in complex interpenetrating time frames, so that the coming of care potentially disrupts and disorders these in ways that parallel and intersect with spatiality.

In the final chapter, Judith E. Phillips and Anne Martin-Matthews reflect on the concepts, issues, and themes that cross-cut the chapters of this book, linking personal and professional interests for the editors. We draw on policy perspectives and consider new directions for research in this area.

Intersections of Work and Home Life: Speaking From Experience

For many of the contributors to this volume, the writing of this book has in itself been a journey of negotiation and management of the intersections of work and home life. In the course of writing, several authors have experienced the serious illness, disability, or death of one or more elderly parents and relatives. Others of us have relocated elderly parents to be closer to our places of employment, or have ourselves changed work and home to be closer to our frail elderly kin. In the provision of assistance to our family members, some of us have come to now utilize the very same employee assistance plans or community-based support services that we had previously studied. Although some authors have, elsewhere, noted how "personal struggles and experiences offer an important touchstone for academic theorizing" (Twigg, 2004, p. 62), or used the process of writing collectively to be more conscious of our own journey of aging (Phillips and Bernard, 2000), or adopted a self-reflexive, autobiographical stance in an explicit examination of the relationship between our scholarly enquiry and our personal biographies of care (Martin-Matthews, 2007), we do not do so in this volume. Although these experiences are not foregrounded in our chapters, we do recognize the implications of our individual efforts to manage the combination of our paid professional work and eldercare work, the challenges of long-distance caring, and the challenges of providing care framed by family dynamics and in conjunction with paid carers in the formal care system. With our perspectives grounded in the realities of individuals and families aging at the intersections of work and home life, the experiences about which we write are far more than "mere" conceptual abstractions or empirical data-derived "observations." They are very real issues that constitute highly salient aspects of our own personal and family biographies. As such, they inevitably and implicitly frame our interpretations and shape our scholarship.

References

Hood, T. (1993). *Men, work, and family.* Newbury Park, CA: Sage.

Kanter, R. M. (1977). Work and family in the United States: A critical review and agenda for research and policy. *New York: Russell Sage Foundation.*

Martin-Matthews, A. (2007). Situating "home" at the nexus of the public and the private spheres: Ageing, gender and home support in Canada. *Current Sociology, 55*(2), 229–249.

Phillips, J. (2007). *Care.* Cambridge: Polity.

Phillips, J., & Bernard, M. (2000). Changing policy, challenging practice. In M. Bernard, J. Phillips, L. Machin, & V. Harding Davies (Eds.), *Women ageing: Changing identities, challenging myths* (pp. 168–177). London: Routledge.

Twigg, J. (2004). The body, gender, and age: Feminist insights in social gerontology. *Journal of Aging Studies, 18*(1), 59–73.

Contributors

Miriam Bernard is professor of social gerontology and director of the recently established Research Institute for Life Course Studies at Keele University, United Kingdom. She is also a long-standing member of Keele's internationally known Centre for Social Gerontology—one of the largest groupings specializing in gerontology in the United Kingdom. Building on a background of innovative work with older people in the voluntary sector (as research officer with the Beth Johnson Foundation), she has 25 years' experience of research and teaching about aging and older people. Her research interests focus primarily on the development of new and healthy lifestyles in later life, and she has a long-standing interest in women's lives as they age. She is the author or editor of 16 books and monographs, over 70 book chapters and journal articles, and many research reports. With Judith E. Phillips, she carried out the first British study of working carers of older adults that explored the use, relevance, and effectiveness of a range of workplace policies and practices operating in one Social Services Department and one National Health Service (NHS) Health Trust. Funded by the Joseph Rowntree Foundation between 2000 and 2002, the resulting publication, *Juggling Work and Care: The Experiences of Working Carers of Older Adults* (Policy Press), won the 2002 Work-Life Balance Trust Award for nonfiction.

Kathleen J.B. Bonn has a master's degree from Lewis and Clark College in counseling psychology and has been a doctoral student in the Urban Studies Program at Portland State University, Oregon, United States, since September 2001. Her interests focus on seniors' support systems, the effects of social interactions on well-being, and the health impacts of social justice. For the past 16 years, she has worked with the elderly in intensive case management. She has served as a graduate research and teaching assistant at the Institute on Aging at Portland State University, working closely with Dr. Margaret Neal, for the past 6 years. She has taught classes in mental health and aging and in families and aging. Kathleen is expected to advance to doctoral candidacy in the spring of 2007.

Michael A. Creedon holds an appointment as professor of geriatric health management at the A. T. Still University of the Health Sciences (Kirksville, Missouri, United States). He was the founding coordinator of the Certificate Program in Aging Studies at Johns Hopkins University (1997–2006) and held the Virginia Prentice Andrews Chair in Gerontology at the University of Bridgeport, Connecticut (1984–1987), where he directed the Bridgeport Eldercare Project and initiated and codirected the first National Conference on Employees and Eldercare (1986). He was director of corporate programs for the National Council on the Aging from 1987 to 1990, and codirected the first National Teleconference on Eldercare and the Workplace (1989). Michael has published widely on long-term care and on aging issues that affect the workplace. His publications include *Selected Readings in Assessment and Case Management*; *The Pepsico Eldercare Handbook*; *Issues for an Aging America: Employees and Eldercare*; *Employees and Eldercare: Designing Effective Responses for the Workplace*; *Eldercare in the Workplace*; *Managing Work and Family Life*; and *A Report to the European Union on Cooperation in Europe in Care of the Elderly*. Dr. Creedon was a delegate and section leader for the White House Conference on Aging in 1995. He keynoted the White House Mini-Conference on Eldercare and the Workplace, and he was comanager of the White House Mini-Conference on Transportation and the Elderly (1995).

Judith Davey was the director of the New Zealand Institute for Research on Ageing and associate professor in social policy at Victoria University of Wellington up to early 2007. Prior to 1991, she was the deputy director of the New Zealand Planning Council and a consultant on social policy and social research in a wide variety of areas. Judith's personal focus for research is the aging of the population and its policy implications. She has researched income, workforce, transport, and housing issues for older people and has published several papers and reports on home equity conversion and intergenerational issues. In addition to her extensive publication record, she has provided advice to numerous policy-making bodies in the public, private, and voluntary sectors.

Donna Dosman is the western regional manager for the Statistics Canada Research Data Center Program and is an adjunct professor in the Department of Human Ecology at the University of Alberta, Canada. Dr. Dosman has recently been examining gaps in our understanding about the challenges families face when managing employment and care giving. She is currently engaged in policy research on the shifting of responsibility of providing care from formal to informal care givers. She also conducts research in the areas of household decision making and unpaid and paid work of family members.

Maria Evandrou is professor of gerontology and director of the Centre for Research on Ageing in the School of Social Sciences at the University of Southampton, United Kingdom. Her research interests include investigating paid work and family care in the United Kingdom over time and across cohorts; examining the implications of long-term care giving over the life course for health, income, pension, and leisure using nationally representative longitudinal UK data; studying the retirement prospects of future generations of elders; and examining the building and use of different types of policy tools for modeling employment, income, pensions, health, incapacity, and care giving amongst older people in the future. She is also director of the MSc gerontology program at the University of Southampton and supervises a number of PhD students.

Pamela Fancey is associate director and research associate, Nova Scotia Centre on Aging, Mount Saint Vincent University, Canada, where she assists with advancing the center's three-part mandate of research, continuing education, and consultation on aging issues. Her research interests include care giver assessment, support for care givers including financial compensation, policies for employed care givers, social isolation of seniors, and specialized programming for persons with Alzheimer's disease and related dementias. As research associate with the University of Alberta–based Hidden Costs/Invisible Contributions Project, she has assisted with the comparative analysis of policies that support family care givers in 10 countries.

Janet Fast is a family and consumer economist who codirects the Research on Aging, Policies, and Practice research program based in the Department of Human Ecology at the University of Alberta, Canada. The program involves a large, international, multidisciplinary team of researchers and policy and practice partners. They are investigating the costs and contributions of older adults and adults with chronic illness and disability, set within social, political, historic, cultural, and literary contexts. On the cost side, the team is examining the consequences of recent health and social policy reform for family and friends who care for frail seniors or other adults with chronic illness and disability. Of particular interest are the economic consequences of having to accommodate employment to care demands. On the contributions side, they are exploring the activities of older adults and adults with chronic illness and disability that contribute to their own well-being and to broader society.

Karen Glaser has a BA in psychology from the University of Michigan, an MA in Latin American studies from the University of Texas, United States, an MSc in demography from the London School of Economics, and a PhD in sociology (specializing in demography) from the Population Studies Center, University of Michigan. She is a senior lecturer in gerontology at the Institute of Gerontology, King's College London, United Kingdom. She has investigated the multiple work and family roles of midlife individuals in Britain and conducted comparative research on co-residence, kin availability, proximity, and the provision and receipt of care among older people. She is currently working on a project investigating the relationship between disruptions in key life course events, in particular family disruption due to divorce, death, or repartnering and social support in later life.

Caroline Glendinning is professor of social policy in the Social Policy Research Unit, University of York, United Kingdom. She has a wide range of research interests and activities including informal care and older people, partnerships and collaboration between health and social care services, the development and management of services for older people, and policies on the funding and delivery of long-term care in the United Kingdom and abroad. She is currently responsible for a research program funded by the English Department of Health; at the core of this is a longitudinal panel study investigating disabled and older people's experiences of choice and control in the context of changing circumstances.

Norah Keating is professor and co-director of Research on Aging, Policies, and Practice (RAPP) in the Department of Human Ecology at the University of Alberta, Canada. Dr. Keating is a family scholar and gerontologist whose expertise is in later-life families and care to older adults. She is senior author on the Statistics Canada book *Eldercare in Canada*, which provided the first national picture of the extent of care to seniors in Canada. Recently she has been examining gaps in our understanding of the structure of families of adults, and the family challenges inherent in managing employment and care giving. She is actively engaged in knowledge transfer through consultations with federal and provincial governments about health and social policy for families, and care to seniors.

Janice Keefe is professor of family studies and gerontology and the Lena Isabel Jodrey Chair in Gerontology at Mount Saint Vincent University, Canada. She is also director of the Nova Scotia Centre on Aging. Professor Keefe also holds a Canada Research Chair in Aging and Caregiving Policy and was awarded funding from the Canada Foundation for Innovation to develop the Maritime Data Centre for Aging Research and Policy Analysis. Her research areas include the rural elderly; social isolation; continuing care policy and care giving, including projecting future needs; work and elder care; care giver assessment; and care giver policy in Canada and internationally.

Sally Keeling has taught and supervised research students in the postgraduate gerontology program of the Christchurch School of Medicine and Health Sciences, New Zealand, since 2000. She is a past president of the New Zealand Association of Gerontology, and has prior senior management experience in community and residential aged care services in the voluntary sector. Her academic background is in social and cultural anthropology, and her research interests are currently in the areas of social support and health of older people. She has contributed to policy and guideline development, at the national level, in the field of health of older people. From early 2007, she continues this work, concurrent with taking over the position of director of the New Zealand Institute for Research on Ageing in the School of Government at Victoria University of Wellington.

Atiya Mahmood is an assistant professor at the Department of Design and Human Environment and a research associate with the Center for Healthy Aging Research, Oregon State University, United States. Her postsecondary education is in architecture and design with a focus on environment–behavior relationships. She received her PhD in architecture from the University of Wisconsin–Milwaukee, United States. Her research interests include topics on health and the built environment with specific focus on senior's housing, health, aging in place, and care giving. Her ongoing projects include research on gerotechnology, aging in place, and care giving; physical activity, the built environment, and aging; the housing and well-being of immigrant older adults; and the built environment's role in staff outcome in long-term care settings.

Anne Martin-Matthews is the scientific director of the national Institute of Aging of the Canadian Institutes of Health Research, and a professor in the School of Social Work and Family Studies at the University of British Columbia in Vancouver, Canada. She holds a PhD in sociology from McMaster University in Canada. Her publications include a book, *Widowhood in Later Life*; three edited volumes (on methodological diversity, bridging policy and research on aging, and Canadian gerontology in an international context) as special issues of the *Canadian Journal on Aging*; and papers on aging and health, intergenerational relations, social support, care giving, work–family balance, and rural aging. She served as editor-in-chief (1996–2000) of the *Canadian Journal on Aging*, and is currently vice president of the Research Committee on Aging of the International Sociological Association. She is a fellow of the Gerontological Society of America and of the Canadian Academy of Health Sciences.

Jane Mears is an associate professor in social policy at the University of Western Sydney, Australia. She has a long history of researching issues of concern to women, such as care work, paid and unpaid. Relevant publications include *Women, Work and Care of the Elderly* (Ashgate, 1999, with Liz Watson). She is particularly interested in utilizing qualitative research methodologies that enable us to listen to and hear women's voices.

Kalyani K. Mehta is an associate professor at the Department of Social Work, National University of Singapore. She has been researching in the field of social gerontology for the past 15 years. Although most of her research is conducted in Singapore, she has extensive knowledge of the Asia Pacific region. Her publications include two books, *Untapped Resources: Women in Ageing Societies Across Asia*, and *Understanding and Counseling Older Persons.* Together with three faculty members from her university, she has published *Ageing in Singapore: Service Needs and the State* (2006). She has contributed chapters in cross-national books—for example, *Who Should Care for the Elderly? An East-West Value Divide*, which won the Australian Association of Gerontology Book Award—and more than 30 articles on the subject of gerontology in well-reputed international and regional journals. Dr. Mehta's research interests include social policies and their impact on older people, older workers and their needs, gender and retirement, the impact of widowhood, and lastly suicide among older persons. She is currently serving as nominated member of Parliament in Singapore. She is first vice president of the Gerontological Society, Singapore.

Margaret B. Neal is director of the Institute on Aging and professor of community health at Portland State University, Oregon, United States. She teaches graduate courses in research methods and gerontology. Her research has focused on the challenges and opportunities faced by individuals who are balancing employment with providing informal care to elders and how the public and private sectors can facilitate work–family integration. She recently completed a book with Leslie Hammer (*Working Couples Caring for Children and Aging Parents*, 2007), and she has written extensively on this and related topics (e.g., *Balancing Work and Care Giving for Children, Adults, and Elders*, 1993; and *Work and Caring for the Elderly: International Perspectives*, edited with Viola Lechner, 1999). Her other research and teaching interests include issues affecting Hispanic elders, global aging, older workers and retirement, and health promotion strategies.

Kelly Niles-Yokum is currently director of the Consortium Gerontology Studies Program, an academic program of the Colleges of Worcester Consortium, Inc., United States. She serves as managing editor for *Gerontology and Geriatrics Education*, the official journal of the Association for Gerontology in Higher Education. Dr. Niles-Yokum holds a doctorate in gerontology from the University of Maryland, Baltimore County, and a master's degree in public administration with a specialty in aging policy from Portland State University. Dr. Niles-Yokum is currently the chair of the Emerging Scholars and Professionals Organization of the Gerontological Society of America (GSA); past president and founding member of Delta Lambda, a chapter of the gerontology honor society of the GSA; and an alumna of the International Field Research Scholars Program, University of Maryland, Baltimore County.

Judith E. Phillips is professor of social work and gerontology and acting head of the School of Human Sciences at the University of Swansea in Wales. She is also director of the Interdisciplinary Research Centre on Ageing and the co-director of the Older People and Ageing Research and Development Network in Wales. Her research interests are in social work and social care, and include housing and retirement communities, family and kinship networks, carework, and older offenders. Her recent publications include *Concepts of Care* (Polity Press), *Social Work With Older People* (Palgrave), *Women Ageing* (Routledge), and *The Family and Community Life of Older People* (Routledge). Judith is Ageing and the Lifecourse series editor for the Policy Press and is president-elect of the British Society of Gerontology.

Carolyn J. Rosenthal is professor emerita, sociology and gerontology, McMaster University, Hamilton, Ontario, Canada. Her research interests have included aging and intergenerational relations, families and aging, balancing paid employment and family responsibilities, and support and care for older adults. Her current research examines family issues related to inheritance. She is a former editor-in-chief of the *Canadian Journal on Aging.*

Joanie Sims-Gould is a postdoctoral research fellow jointly funded by the Nexus Home Care Project at the University of British Columbia, Canada, and the Social and Economic Dimensions of an Aging Population project (McMaster University, Canada). Her doctoral research focused on examining how families mobilize to provide care for aging relatives. Her research emphasized the complexity of family care giving by illustrating the multiple types of assistance extended both to the older relative receiving care and among family members who provide the care. Her research interests include care giving, social support, intergenerational relations, social work practice with older adults, home support, and aging in rural environments. Joanie is on the board of directors for the Care Givers Association of British Columbia and the Canadian Care Giver Coalition.

Jennifer Swindle is a PhD student and member of the Research on Aging, Policies, and Practice (RAPP) group with the Department of Human Ecology, University of Alberta, Canada. She holds a master's degree in gerontology from Keele University, United Kingdom. Her research and teaching interests involve social aspects of aging. Jennifer is interested in the social and supportive relationships of older people in various contexts, including families, long-term care institutions, and rural communities. Her research is supported by a University of Alberta Recruitment Award and a doctoral fellowship from the Social Sciences and Humanities Research Council of Canada.

Leng Leng Thang is a sociocultural anthropologist with research interests in aging, intergenerational relationships, and gender. Her field is Asia, in particular Japan and Singapore. She is currently associate professor and head of the Department of Japanese Studies, National University of Singapore, and also vice chair of the International Consortium for Intergenerational Programmes (ICIP). Her recent publications include *Old Challenges, New Strategies? Women, Work and Family in Contemporary Asia* (2004); *Ageing in Singapore: Service Needs and the State* (2006); "Experiencing Leisure in Later Life: A Study of Retirees and Activity in Singapore," *Journal of Cross-Cultural Gerontology* (2005); and "Defining a Second Career: Volunteering Among Seniors in Japan," in *Work, Employment, and Society in Contemporary Japan: Sociological and Anthropological Perspectives* (2006).

Julia Twigg is professor of social policy and sociology at the University of Kent, United Kingdom. She has written widely on the sociology of social care, addressing issues in relation to family carers, carework, and the provision of personal care. In 2000 she published *Bathing: The Body and Community Care*, which explored the nature of carework as a form of bodywork. Recently she published *The Body in Health and Social Care*, which draws on cultural theorizing in relation to the body. She is actively engaged in critical gerontology, and is currently working on a study of the role of clothing in the constitution of age.

Donna L. Wagner is the founding director of the gerontology programs and a professor of gerontology at Towson University, United States. Dr. Wagner also directs the Center for Productive Aging within the Health Sciences Department. She teaches graduate and undergraduate courses in the gerontology, sociology, and women's studies programs at the university. Her research interests include the intersection of work and family, the aging workforce, community-residing elders, and rural aging. She sits on the national boards of the Older Women's League and the National Alliance for Care Giving, and is a fellow of the Gerontological Society of America. Dr. Wagner has conducted two studies of long-distance care giving, the first with the National Council on the Aging in 1997 and the second in conjunction with MetLife's Mature Marketing Institute and the National Alliance for Care Giving in 2004.

Catherine Ward-Griffin is an associate professor in the School of Nursing, Faculty of Health Sciences, at the University of Western Ontario, Canada. Her program of research focuses on the relationships between health professionals and older adults and their families. She is currently working in the areas of women's health, health promotion, care giving, home care, and social policy. Dr. Ward-Griffin has received peer-reviewed funding from a number of national funding agencies, and is usually part of or leading an interdisciplinary research team. Findings of her research have been widely published in gerontology and nursing research journals.

Elizabeth A. Watson is a member of the School of Social Sciences and the Social Justice and Social Change Research Centre at the University of Western Sydney, Australia. She has a particular interest in the area of women's work, paid and unpaid, and most especially the issue of care and carework. Her earliest research, undertaken with her colleague Jane Mears and funded by the (then) Office of the Status of Women in Canberra, was one of the first Australian studies to examine the lived experience of carers, in this case women caring for both children and/or grandchildren as well as elderly relatives at the same time. Her most recent work on care has been concerned with men's caring work in the context of a long-standing relationship—caring for a partner with multiple sclerosis. Her publications include a study of working carers, *Women, Work and Care of the Elderly* (1999), with Jane Mears.

1

Health Professionals Caring for Aging Relatives

Negotiating the Public-Private Boundary

Catherine Ward-Griffin

Background

As the population continues to age in Canada, there are a number of challenges ahead, one of which includes the care of our most frail older citizens. A number of trends account for this concern. The rising incidence of chronic illness with increasing age has escalated demands for care provision for elderly persons. At the same time, recent changes in patterns of care provision for older people, including the closure of long-term care facilities and underfunding of home care (Armstrong & Kitts, 2004; Aronson, 2004; Chappell, 1999), have led to a decline in the availability of formal homecare services. In Canada, a reduction in the proportion of provincial funds devoted to homecare services has been used as a primary cost-cutting strategy in the current health care reform. Because seniors comprise the majority of users of homecare, this policy decision has had a particularly significant impact on the care of older people (Elder Health Elder Care Coalition, 2005).

Other provincial health care reform strategies, such as shorter hospital stays and early hospital discharge, are based on the assumption that families will look after their relatives at home. Currently it is estimated that between 75 and 85% of all care received by elderly people in Canada comes from family members, with women providing 77% of this care (National Profile of Family Caregivers in

Canada, 2002). Furthermore, as more people are being sent home "quicker and sicker" (National Coordinating Group on Health Care Reform and Women, 2003), women are taking on more family caregiving responsibilities than in the past (Armstrong, 2001; Wuest, 1998). Because women also provide the majority of paid health care (National Coordinating Group on Health Care Reform and Women), health care restructuring and staff layoffs have resulted in increasing workloads and stress for those providing paid health care services (Armstrong, 2001). Thus, the persistent representation of women in both paid and unpaid caregiving roles means that shifts in the delivery of health care from institution to the household in Canada tend to affect women to a greater degree than men (Aronson, 2004; Morris, 2004).

Over 15 years, feminist scholars have questioned the distinction between paid and unpaid caring work (Baines, Evans, & Neysmith, 1991; Hooyman & Gonyea, 1995; Olesen, 2005; Ungerson, 1990) and have proposed that women's caring work is not domain specific but, instead, is interdependent, crossing both public and private domains (Baines, 2004; Grant et al., 2004) Nonetheless, the separation of paid, professional caregiving and unpaid, lay caregiving continues to persist. Based on qualitative findings from two critical feminist studies (Ward-Griffin, 2002; Ward-Griffin, Brown, Vandervoort, McNair, & Dashnay, 2005), the boundaries and intersections between the public and the private, the professional and the personal, and the paid and the unpaid caring work of female health professionals in Ontario, Canada, will be the focus of this chapter. The role of gender is essential to this enquiry. Using a feminist lens, I will describe how health care professionals caring for aging relatives in both institutional and homecare settings negotiate the boundaries between professional and personal caregiving within the context of health care reform and social service cuts, and how the blurring of these boundaries affects their health and well-being. Second, I will briefly discuss the existing practices, programs, and policies within professional organizations that address the issue of blurred boundaries among health care professionals who also care for relatives. Essentially I argue that double-duty caregivers are invisible because they are caught between the public and private domains of caregiving—they are in the "intermediate domain." The conceptualization of an "intermediate domain," first identified by Stacey and Davies (1983, cited in Mayall, 1993), highlights how the complex dimensions of location and social relations are brought together in caring work. It is particularly useful because it facilitates recognition that the family and the state are not separate spheres of interest, but are interconnected in the provision of care to older family members. Ultimately, this chapter is meant to stimulate debate about the blurred boundaries between professional and personal caregiving among health professionals caring for aging relatives, and to suggest policy changes in broader social and political systems.

Existing Research

Although there is increasing empirical investigation of employed caregivers (Davey & Keeling, 2004; Duxbury & Higgins, 2001; Guberman & Maheu, 1999; Phillips, 1995; Phillips, Bernard, & Chittenden, 2002), very little is known about individuals who provide care both at home and at work. It can be argued that the experiences of all employed caregivers may be similar, such as juggling multiple roles and employing management strategies to cope with the stress of engaging in paid and unpaid work; however, the literature suggests that there may be unique characteristics within double-duty caregiving. Most of this existing research on the simultaneous participation in the public and private domains of caregiving has identified high levels of stress (Denton, Zeytinoglu, Webb, & Lian, 1999; Ross, Rideout, & Carson, 1996), powerlessness (Rutman, 1996), and role conflict (Gattuso & Bevan, 2000). Findings from Rutman's qualitative study of five "double-duty caregivers" (home support workers, nurses, and long-term care workers who provided care to elderly relatives) revealed feelings of powerlessness, which were connected to a perceived lack of recognition for caregiving competence, lack of control, and inadequate services and resources to provide quality care. In a multisite, qualitative study, Baines (2004) also reported the blurring of lines between professional and nonprofessional identities of 83 Canadian social service workers. Most of their paid, volunteer, community, and union activist work involved many of the same skills, tasks, and mind-sets. As well, although most workers spoke extensively about the different forms of unpaid service work, unpaid family caregiving was discussed only with prompting. Family caring was "naturalized," and seen as something separate from other unpaid social services work. And yet, double-duty caregivers were experiencing an increase in the amount and intensity of unpaid caring in the family, ranging from childcare to care of elderly relatives. Intensification of childcare work among the social service workers reflected cuts to services as well as a growing shift of the responsibility for educating children from schools to parents. This study highlights the importance of understanding various forms of unpaid caring work that cut across public and private domains, and how family caring work subsidizes an underresourced system.

Empirical studies of health care professionals caring for family members have mainly focused on nurses (Denton et al., 1999; Gattuso & Bevan, 2000; Gottlieb, Kelloway, & Martin-Matthews, 1996; Peterson, Ward-Griffin, & McWilliam, 2001; Ross et al., 1996; Walters et al., 1996; Ward-Griffin, 2004). There is evidence that nurses experience high levels of stress associated with caregiving in both their professional and private lives (Ross et al.). As well, nurses feel a slightly greater sense of control in their work lives than in their home lives. However, nurses, therapists, and those in managerial positions experience work-related stress (Denton et al.), with hospital-based nurses who care for children at home experiencing the most stress (Gottlieb et al., 1996). Other factors predicting the level of stress are family support, perceived organizational support for family life, and perceived workload size. Finally, it is apparent that there are significant gender differences in the area of home demands. The pressures of time and caring for dependent adults are positively related to health problems for female nurses only (Walters et al.). As the population continues to age and health care structuring advances, these demands may increase.

Women in the health professions are described in the literature as needing to develop coping strategies to address the stress of "balancing" or "juggling" two or more roles. We know that this stress expresses itself in feelings of being obligated to assume the caregiver role, providing care constantly, struggling to manage, and expressing emotion (Peterson et al., 2001). Various "management strategies" are used, such as attempting to set boundaries for care. There is also evidence that health professionals providing care to relatives of all ages make continual adjustments and accommodations in order to achieve "equilibrium in their lives" (Guberman & Maheu, 1999), and use work-related knowledge, information, and coping techniques to "buffer" the caregiving demands of older adults (Phillips et al., 2002). Research on the use, relevance, and effectiveness of a range of workplace policies and practices, from the perspectives of working carers of older adults in two British public sector organizations, also contributes to our understanding of the experiences of those with dual, hands-on caring responsibilities at work and at home. At least one in 10 employees in each workforce had caring responsibilities for older adults. Coping techniques revolved around using their own expertise and experience, talking with others, and ensuring that they had time for interests beyond caring. Inflexible work schedules and the pressures of the job were identified as hindrances in juggling competing demands and responsibilities.

Combining similar family and work roles has also been studied in other professional groups, such as psychotherapists-parents (Golden & Farber, 1998). At times, the dual roles complemented one another; however, expectations were seen as ambiguous and unrealistic at times, and as a result, participants learned strategies to cope with and benefit from both roles. Nurses who simultaneously provide care to elderly relatives use a number of strategies to contain increasing caregiving demands and to alleviate stress, such as setting limits and delegating care (Ward-Griffin, 2004). Moreover, family care and nursing care are conceptualized as two different types of caregiving, and these differences separate along the lines of *caring about* and *caring for*, respectively. Although *caring about* involves feelings of affection and love, *caring for* has to do with meeting physical, mental, and emotional needs (Ungerson, 1990). Even though attempts were made to differentiate between the two spheres, it is interesting to note that *caring about* and *caring for* existed in both the nurses' family care and their nursing care. For many, boundaries ceased to exist between *caring for* and *caring about* in family care and in nursing care. The need to explore the interface between professional and personal caring work and the health effects of double-duty caregiving is evident. Echoing the recommendation made by others (Baines, 2004; Guberman & Maheu, 1999; Phillips et al., 2002), policies that challenge the gendered nature of caregiving are needed rather than short-term solutions designed to help women cope with their caregiving roles.

In summary, there is general consensus (Guberman & Maheu, 1999; Phillips et al., 2002; Ward-Griffin, 2004) on the importance of looking beyond personal coping strategies of caregiving to include strategies aimed at changing the structural social conditions of carework of women. Caregiving cuts across public and private domains, and how gender, race, and other contextual factors shape the organization of this caring work. Finally, previous research in the area of double-duty caregiving describes how caring professionally and personally may have a direct impact on health and well-being, suggesting the need for long-term solutions in the form of government and workplace policies. In order to better understand these relationships, an analysis of the unpaid and paid caregiving experiences of double-duty caregivers is overdue.

Double-Duty Caregiving: Women in the Health Professions

One way to understand double-duty caregiving is to examine the ways in which women experienced the provision of care to older relatives as health professionals (nurses, physicians, physiotherapists, or social workers; Ward-Griffin et al., 2005). These four health professions represent a diverse group of women who provide health care across a variety of settings (e.g., home care, acute care, long-term care, and outpatient clinics) within southwestern Ontario, Canada. Specifically, we were interested in how female health professionals described their familial caring work, what contextual factors influenced the provision of care to elderly relatives, what strategies were used to negotiate boundaries between paid and unpaid caring work, and what the health effects of providing familial care were. Overall, this study explored new understandings of the intersection of women's paid and unpaid caring work and identified possibilities of positive social change.

The findings discussed here are based on data from 37 women representing four different health professions (15 nurses, 6 physicians, 7 physiotherapists, and 9 social workers) and ranging in age from 23 to 69 years, with a mean age of 47 years. Most provided care to their parents or parents-in-law. Other eldercare recipients included grandparents, siblings, friends, aunts, and spouses. Approximately one third of the participants provided care to two or more elderly relatives. Participants discussed their double-duty caregiving experiences freely during in-depth interviews; however, only with prompting would they expand on the similarities and contradictions about providing professional care in the private sphere. These individual audiotaped interviews, three focus-group interviews with 21 of the original participants, and the corresponding field notes were transcribed and analyzed. Individual and team data analysis led to the development of a conceptual model of the experience of double-duty caregiving (see Figure 1.1).

Health professionals who assume eldercare responsibilities are located in the intermediate domain of caregiving, negotiating (and renegotiating) the boundaries between professional, paid care and unpaid, family caregiving. There are three inextricably linked components of double-duty caregiving: familial care expectations, supports, and negotiating strategies. Due to their specific knowledge and skills in health care, many health professionals feel that they are expected to assume additional responsibilities, such as advocating on behalf of and supervising the care of their older relative. Years of professional education and experience resulted in high expectations of self as well as expectations from family and other health professionals to provide “professional” care. Moreover, the women usually provided professional care to their relative because often there were no other options and/or they believed that potential harm might come to their relative if they withheld care. As a physician who had been monitoring her parents’ chronic health conditions for years declared, “I think that they [parents] would both be dead now if I wasn’t a health professional, a doctor.” Similarly, a nurse commented

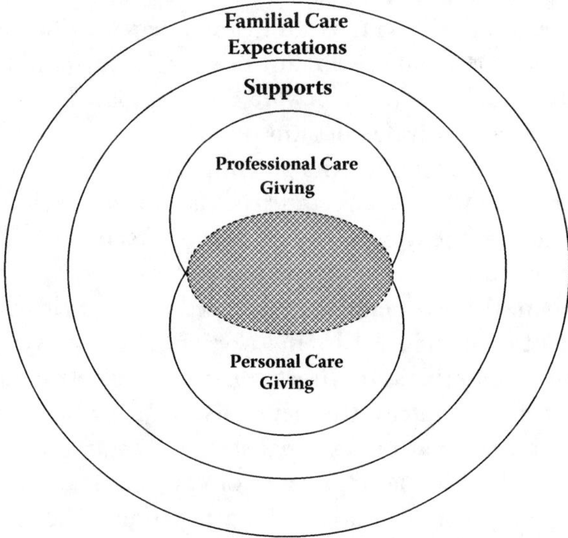

Figure 1.1 Double duty elder caregiving. (From Ward-Griffin, C., Brown, J.B., Vandervoort, A., NcNair, S., Dashnay, I. (2005). Double-duty caregiving: Women in the health professions. *Canadian Journal on Aging*, *24*(4), 379–394. Printed by permission of University of Toronto Press. www.utpjournals.com.)

on how hospital staff expected her to provide care to her bedridden father: "The nurses actually expected a lot from me. I don't mind giving mouth care and I would help them lift him [father] in bed, but it was almost as [if] I did become unpaid help." In short, health professionals were expected to provide unpaid, professional care to their elderly relatives, regardless of the care setting.

In order to manage these additional caregiving demands, family, colleagues, and other professional resources were identified as the primary sources of support, providing emotional, informational, and instrumental assistance. Women who had workplace supports, such as an understanding manager, flextime, and unpaid leaves of absence, considered themselves fortunate. In most cases, however, the current shortage of health professionals prevented them from taking advantage of many of these workplace supports, especially time off work. When asked to identify existing supports within their professional organizations, many had difficulty identifying any programs or policies that would help them address the unique challenges of providing care at work and at home.

Two major strategies, *setting limits* and *making connections*, were reported by the women as being somewhat useful to contain the expectations of elderly relatives, other family members, and health care professionals and/or to expand their supports. Setting limits was premised on the belief that family members who are health care professionals in the public domain of caregiving should not care for their own relatives in the private domain. Based on the notion that the public and private domains of caregiving need to be clearly demarcated, many identified the potential risks and problems associated with caring for family and friends in a professional capacity. Many felt that their respective professional standards of practice prohibited them from caring for relatives. However, the decision of whether to limit care depended on the needs of their elderly relative, the degree of obligation felt by the women, and the availability of quality care from others. In direct contrast, "making connections" was employed as a strategy; this depended on using their knowledge of the system and their professional status to acquire certain types of support, such as homecare service or consultations with specialists who were not readily available. At other times, when inadequate care or unsafe conditions placed their relatives at risk, these health professionals (or double-duty caregivers) used their connections to obtain professional services they knew were available but were often being withheld or denied, which sometimes led to confrontations with paid staff. Regardless of the outcome, the use of this strategy brought the worlds of professional caregiving and familial caregiving closer together. Although these two strategies were somewhat effective in limiting caregiving demands while increasing supports, it is apparent that the source of these demands, the types of caring work involved, and the resulting boundaries of care involved a number of multiple players, both paid and unpaid.

It is important to note that the nature of professional caregiving (nursing, medicine, social work, and physiotherapy) and personal caregiving varied enormously among these caregivers. The majority of caregivers provided care for less than 10 hours a week, whereas others were engaged in more extensive and demanding care for more than one older relative. Depending on the degree of internal and external expectations of familial care, and the availability of supports, the boundary between professional and personal caregiving varied for each participant. As well, three prototypes of double-duty caregiving experiences emerged from the data: "making it work," "working to manage," and "living on the edge" (see Figure 1.2). Although setting limits and making connections were used to manage increasing caregiving responsibilities, it was apparent that, over time or during crises, many women experienced more dramatic blurring or erosion of these boundaries, characterized by feelings of isolation, tension, and extreme physical and mental exhaustion. These findings suggest that women who are double-duty caregivers, especially those with limited time, finances, and other tangible supports, may experience poor health, which warrants further study.

Health Professionals as Caregivers of Elderly Relatives: Practice and Policy Implications

We also examined various supports within professional health care organizations that may influence the double-duty caregiving experiences of health professionals (Ward-Griffin, 2002). In particular, we were interested in learning about the existing practices, programs, or policies within these organizations that address the issue of blurred boundaries among health care professionals who also care for elderly relatives. The impetus for this second study came from the findings described above; although many double-duty caregivers

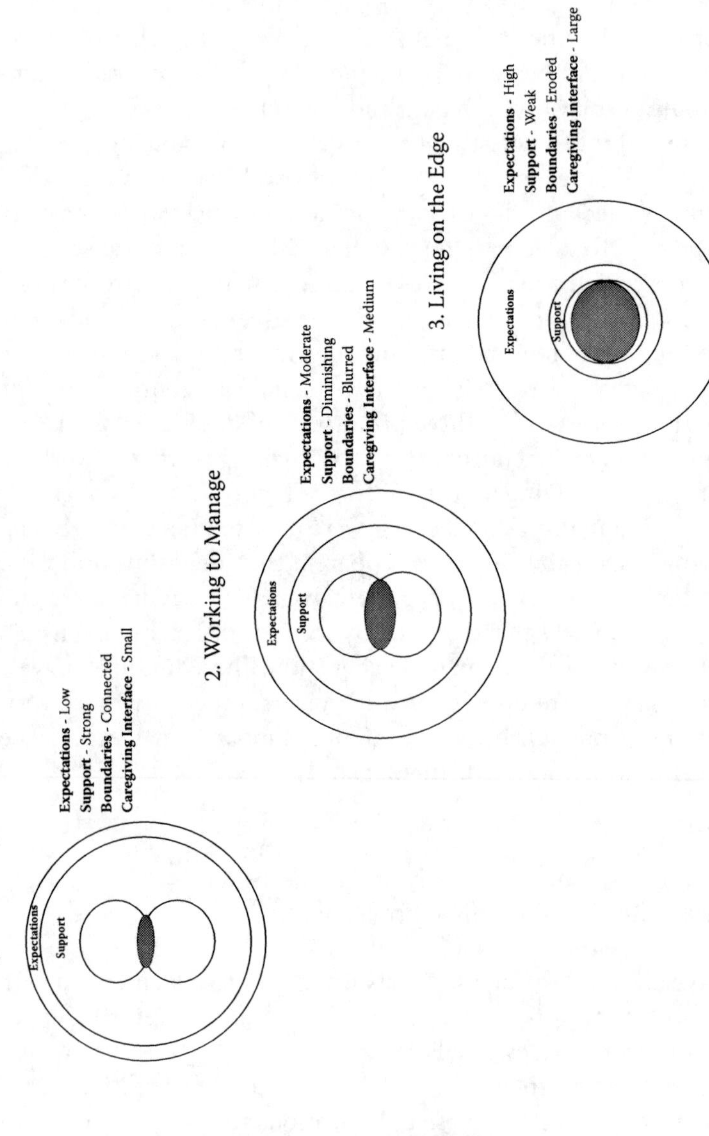

Figure 1.2 Types of double duty caregiving. (From Ward-Griffin, C., Brown, J.B., Vandervoort, A., NcNair, S., Dashnay, I. (2005). Double-duty caregiving: Women in the health professions. *Canadian Journal on Aging*, 24(4), 379–394. Printed by permission of University of Toronto Press. www.utpjournals.com.)

understood that they "should" not provide professional care in their personal lives, it was apparent that they had difficulty delineating the boundary between professional and personal caregiving. To that end, health professionals commented that they would welcome some assistance and leadership from their respective professional health care organizations in addressing this issue.

Eleven provincial health care professional organizations representing the four respective disciplines of nursing, medicine, social work, and physiotherapy were approached to participate in the project. All but one agreed to identify key informants who were knowledgeable about practices, programs, and policies within their organization. As a result, in-depth interviews with a total of 28 key informants were conducted over a 3-month period. All key informants were women, with a mean age of 54 years, ranging from 34 to 70 years. Most of the key informants had graduated from university (n = 22), worked full-time (n = 27), and held various administrative positions within the organization (e.g., policy analysts, executive directors, and department heads). The average number of years worked within one of the specified health care professions was 22.5 years. Nursing was most highly represented (n = 12), followed by physiotherapy (n = 8), social work (n = 4), and medicine (n = 3). In addition, one key informant represented an interdisciplinary gerontological association.

The majority of the interviews were conducted in person (n = 21), either at the informant's office or at a convenient location; the rest were conducted by telephone (n = 5) or by asking for e-mail responses to preformed questions, such as "What supports (if any) are in place to assist members who have elder care responsibilities?" and "What role (if any) does the professional health care association play in assisting members who care for elderly relatives?" (n = 2). At the beginning of each interview, the conceptual model of "double-duty caregiving" was presented to the key informants, and they were asked to comment. In addition, seven key informants representing the four major health disciplines attended a round-table discussion with the goal of sharing information and developing collective strategies to address the issue of double-duty caregiving, as well as serving as a means of member-checking the main findings from the individual interviews. All key informant interviews and the round-table discussion were audiotaped, transcribed, and analyzed. Following the guidelines of Lofland and Lofland (1995), early analysis focused on key phrases and themes that emerged from the data. As common themes emerged, an initial coding system was created. Numerous and varying codes were thus inserted into the text by hand and then entered onto NUD*IST, a software program used to facilitate qualitative analysis.

Two interrelated themes characterized the supports for double-duty caregivers within professional health care organizations. First, the practices, programs, and policies of the health care professional associations reflected an individualistic, gendered view of caring. When asked to identify the current supports available to members who were also providing care to elderly relatives, very few were identified. Those mentioned tended to focus on helping members "cope" with family caregiving, such as individual counseling and employee assistance programs. However, some key informants agreed that more workplace supports, including daycare programs and unpaid leaves without fear of job loss, are needed in the future. Some felt that it was the role of workplaces or the "union" to help those members "manage" the demands of work and family responsibilities. Others indicated that professional associations should take a lead role in helping their members with childcare and eldercare responsibilities, especially those professional groups with a high percentage of female members. Finally, representatives from the nursing and medical professional associations stated that it was important to identify and implement flexible work arrangements, especially with the looming doctor and nurse shortage in Canada; however, limited time, people, and finances have prevented them from assuming a major role. Although supports were identified to help members with dual work and family responsibilities, none mentioned that perhaps caring for someone at home and at work may require different types of supports compared to those for employees who do not work in the "caring" professions.

The second key study finding was that boundary demarcation between professional and personal caregiving was described as the primary responsibility of the individual member. The majority of key informants located family caring performed by health professionals squarely in the private domain. In other words, if a member had caregiving responsibilities within the family, it was a personal issue for the member to solve, not a professional issue of the association. Furthermore, some representatives from the professional associations indicated that they did not think it was appropriate to tell members how to behave in their "personal lives," even though these members were providing "professional" care. In particular, key informants who represented the regulatory professional associations stated that members who provided care to family members fell outside their mandate, which was to serve and protect the public (i.e., patient care). Although there are professional standards that prohibit and reprimand health care professionals from becoming personally involved with their clients-patients, little attention has been paid to the other side of the boundary—health care professionals becoming professionally involved with their family members. In response, key informants did recommend that members with family caregiving responsibilities refer to professional guidelines, such as standards of practice and codes of ethics, in maintaining the boundary between professional and personal caregiving.

However, specific boundary guidelines vary among the regulatory bodies. Some forbid their members from providing care to family members, whereas others require that they follow certain guidelines when providing care to a relative. For instance, according to the College of Nurses in one Canadian province, nurses may be required to provide care to a loved one. In this situation, the nurse is acting not as a paid professional, but as a family member or friend to the person needing care. The person needing care is not the nurse's client. In these instances, the nurse is not concerned with boundary issues, but only with providing competent care. (College of Nurses of Ontario, 2004, p. 13)

On the one hand, caring in the family is conceptualized as different and separate from professional caring (with clearly demarcated boundaries), and yet, on the other hand, nurses are expected to provide "competent [nursing] care." Clearly this guideline not only illustrates the ambiguous position of health professionals who provide family care, but also reflects the ideology of separate spheres within professional health care associations.

Discussion

In this chapter, I have considered the juncture of the private and the public spheres of care by examining issues of double-duty caregiving. Guided by a feminist lens, findings from Canadian research on this topic identified a form of Cartesian dualism in which not only was family care seen as different from professional care, but also attempts were made by both double-duty caregivers and their respective health care associations to separate the private and public spheres of care. Premised on the belief that one cannot provide "objective" professional care within an emotionally close relationship, practice standards within the Colleges of Medicine, Nursing, and Physiotherapy in one Canadian province stipulate that its members should not care for family and friends. This particular directive is most notable in the medical profession. Although the College of Nurses of Ontario, the governing body for registered nurses and registered practical nurses, also supports this belief, it acknowledges certain situations (e.g., working in small communities) where nurses may be placed in a position to care for family members. However, in doing so, nurses are instructed under the "Maintaining the Boundaries" section of the *Therapeutic Nurse-Client Relationship Practice Standard* to "be aware of the boundary between their professional role and personal role" and of the importance of "clarifying that boundary for the client" (College of Nurses of Ontario, 2004, p. 14). This conceptual splitting between professional and personal care poses a false dichotomy by assuming that the nature of the relationship in each sphere is totally different. This is especially problematic for women in the health professions. As evidenced in the narratives of the health professionals whom we interviewed, double-duty caregivers were aware of the professional-personal care boundary. However, neither this awareness nor their attempts to keep these demarcations distinct actually prevented the blurring of boundaries for these women (see also Mears & Watson, chapter 8). Rather, inadequate supports, demanding expectations, and unavailable formal care options influenced the degree of professional care provided to aging family members. If women's caring work as "formal" and "informal" continues to be dichotomized, we will fail to see the interconnections between paid and unpaid care, as well as the strategies that caregivers must use to negotiate these boundaries.

Gender is particularly relevant to our understanding of the blurring of boundaries between family care and professional care. The accounts of study participants reflect the entanglement of gendered caring in the home and in the workplace. For instance, even though recruitment of 28 key informants for the second study was open to both men and women, all were women. As one key informant aptly observed during the round-table discussion, "It is interesting that all of us here are women, but it is not surprising since caregiving is seen as a women's issue." Although Sims-Gould (see chapter 4) found in her study of helpers that there are differences in helping networks of men and women, there are also similarities of care provision to elderly relatives such as comparable patterns in the frequency and type of direct help. However, within families, women have been associated with carework, such as childcare and eldercare, and this gendered association remains when these activities are transferred across the sphere of paid carework. Carework, especially care associated with the body, is gendered work in that it is performed predominantly by women within the private and public spheres (Twigg, 2004, and chapter 12). Some have argued (Dalley, 1996; Gilligan, 1982) that women go into the "caring occupations" because of their natures and because their intertwined capacities for caring for and caring about are thought to suit them well for those jobs. Indeed, some of the study participants, particularly those in the nursing and social work professions, viewed their professional caring work as an extension of their "natural" nurturing abilities, which helped them to cross the boundaries between professional and family care, into the intermediate domain.

The conceptualization of an interface between the private and public domains, the intermediate domain, is particularly useful in helping us understand the experiences of double-duty caregivers. As previously mentioned in this chapter, and as mentioned in others (see Mears & Watson, chapter 8), the convergence of professional and personal boundaries is not a new issue for the health professions. Mandated by the Regulated Health Professions Act (Provincial Government of Ontario, 1991), health professions in Ontario, Canada, must identify and reprimand members whose health care practices cross professional boundaries, such as sexual contact between patients and health professionals. According to our study findings, information on how to avoid these "boundary crossings" is provided to health professionals within their basic training and ongoing education workshops. Similarly, Mears and Watson (see chapter 8) describe how paid care workers transgress these boundaries by becoming "too personal" with their elderly clients, but "breaking the rules" was of less concern to the workers than to their managers, who emphasized the need for setting limits between professional and personal boundaries. However, the failure for managers and other policy makers to see the other "face" of the blurred boundaries—one in which health care workers provide professional care in their personal lives—is troubling. Ignoring this aspect of the public-private boundary between family and professional care among double-duty caregivers and the resulting psychological health effects (Gattuso & Bevan, 2000) not only is shortsighted but also continues to obscure the significance of women's caring work, particularly emotional caring (James, 1989). Although precise boundaries and standard procedures may limit the possibilities for choices and care, the lack of boundaries may also limit choices (Armstrong & Armstrong, 2002). To that end, we do not need to recreate the dichotomies between family and professional caregiving that have so deeply influenced the professional practice guidelines, but instead accept that double-duty caregiving may require a different set of guidelines and supports. For instance, identification of gender-specific health promotion policies and other supports (Ward-Griffin, 2004) may assist double-duty caregivers to participate in making decisions about their own lives.

Prior to the identification of appropriate supports for double-duty caregivers in the management of blurring boundaries, further research is necessary. Based on the qualitative findings from the first double-duty caregiving study, a team of Canadian researchers (Ward-Griffin, Keefe, Martin-Matthews, Kerr, & Brown, 2006) developed an instrument that measures the expectations to provide familial eldercare, supports, negotiating strategies, and the caregiving interface. A survey package that contains this newly developed scale, the Double-Duty Caregiving Scale (Ward-Griffin et al., 2006), along with other instruments that measure role strain, health, and well-being, has been mailed to 800 registered nurses in Ontario. We anticipate that high expectations to provide familial care and low supports will lead to increased blurring of boundaries between professional and personal domains of caregiving. Those double-duty caregivers with large caregiving interfaces will experience greater negative health effects. It is anticipated that the results from this study and others will increase our understanding of the intersections between private and public, professional and personal, and paid and unpaid.

In conclusion, the relationship between professional and family care among double-duty caregivers is complex and merits closer investigation. Examining how boundaries are both demarcated and blurred is central to our understanding of this caregiving interface. Moreover, using the conceptualization of an intermediate domain helps us to understand the process of double-duty caregiving. This model depicts how familial expectations and supports, and the corresponding strategies of setting limits and making connections, shape the provision of care to older relatives of health professionals. Furthermore, it enables us to understand how the blurring of boundaries between private and public may predict poor health outcomes for double-duty caregivers. In the future, findings from qualitative and quantitative investigations of double-duty caregiving could facilitate the recognition and value of care that is provided in the public, private, and intermediate domains. This information would also inform decision makers and other policy personnel about the potential health effects of double-duty caregiving. Understanding those areas where double-duty caregivers may need support would help workplace, professional, and governmental organizations to develop appropriate programs and policies. Ultimately, the quality of caregivers' lives and those of the elders they care for would be greatly enhanced.

References

Armstrong, P. (2001). *Exposing privatization: Women and health care reform in Canada*. Aurora, ON: Garamond Press.

Armstrong, P., & Armstrong, H. (2002). *Thinking it through: Women, work, and caring in the new millennium*. Halifax, NS: Maritime Centre of Excellence for Women's Health.

Armstrong, P., & Kitts, O. (2004). One hundred years of caregiving. In K. Grant, C. Armaratunga, P. Armstrong, M. Boscoe, A. Pederson, & K. Willson (Eds.), *Caring for/caring about: Women, home care and unpaid care giving* (pp. 5–44). Aurora, ON: Garamond Press.

Aronson, J. (2004). "Just fed and watered": Women's experiences of the gutting of home care in Ontario. In K. Grant, C. Amaratunga, P. Armstrong, M. Boscoe, A. Pederson, & K. Willson (Eds.), *Caring for/caring about: Women, home care and unpaid caregiving* (pp. 167–184). Aurora, ON: Garamond Press.

Baines, C., Evans, P., & Neysmith, S. (Eds.). (1991). *Women's caring: Feminist perspectives on social welfare*. Toronto: McClelland & Stewart.

Baines, D. (2004). Seven kinds of work—only one paid: Raced, gendered and restructured work in social services. *Atlantis, 28*(2), 19–28.

Chappell, N. (1999). Editorial: Canadian Association on Gerontology policy statement on home care in Canada. *Canadian Journal on Aging, 18*(3), i–iii.

College of Nurses of Ontario. (2004). *Practice standard: Therapeutic nurse-client relationship* (Pub. No. 41033). Toronto: College of Nurses of Ontario.

Dalley, G. (1996). *Ideologies of caring: Rethinking community and collectivism* (2nd ed). London: MacMillan Education.

Davey, J., & Keeling, S. (2004). Combining work and eldercare: A neglected work-life balance issue (Labour, Employment and Work in New Zealand, Working Paper). Wellington: Victoria University of Wellington.

Denton, M., Zeytinoglu, I., Webb, S., & Lian, J. (1999). Occupational health issues among employees of home care agencies. *Canadian Journal on Aging, 18*(2), 154–181.

Duxbury, L., & Higgins, C. (2001). Work-life balance in the new millennium: Where are we? Where do we need to go? (Report No. CPRN discussion paper W\12). Ottawa: Canadian Policy Research Networks.

Elder Health Elder Care Coalition. (2005). *Towards an elder health framework: A working document.* Toronto: Registered Nurses Association of Ontario.

Gattuso, S., & Bevan, C. (2000). Mother, daughter, patient, nurse: Women's emotion work in aged care. *Journal of Advanced Nursing, 31*(4), 892–899.

Gilligan, C. (1982). *In a different voice: Psychological theory and women's development.* Cambridge, MA: Harvard University Press.

Golden, V., & Farber B. A. (1998). Therapists as parents: Is it good for the children? *Professional Psychology, Research, and Practice, 29*(2), 135–139.

Gottlieb, B. H., Kelloway, K., & Martin-Matthews, A. (1996). Predictors of work-family stress and job satisfaction among nurses. *Canadian Journal of Nursing Research, 28*(2), 99–117.

Grant, K., Amaratunga, C., Armstrong, P., Boscoe, M., Pederson, A., & Willson, K. (Eds.). (2004). *Caring for/caring about: Women, home care and unpaid caregiving.* Aurora, ON: Garamond Press.

Guberman, N., & Maheu, P. (1999). Combining employment and caregiving: An intricate juggling act. *Canadian Journal on Aging, 18*(1), 84–106.

Hooyman, N., & Gonyea, J. (1995). *Feminist perspectives on family care: Policies for gender justice.* Thousand Oaks, CA: Sage.

James, N. (1989). Emotional labour: Skills and work in the social regulation of feelings. *Sociological Review, 37,* 15–42.

Lofland, J., & Lofland, L. (1995). *Analyzing social settings: A guide to qualitative observation and analysis* (3rd ed.). Belmont, CA: Wadsworth.

Mayall, B. (1993). Keeping children healthy: The intermediate domain. *Social Sciences & Medicine, 36*(1), 77–83.

Morris, M. (2004). What research reveals about gender, home care and caregiving: Overview and policy implications. In K. Grant, C. Amaratunga, P. Armstrong, M. Boscoe, A. Pederson, & K. Willson (Eds.), *Caring for/caring about. women, home care, and unpaid care giving* (pp. 91–114). Aurora, ON: Garamond Press.

National Coordinating Group on Health Care Reform and Women. (2003). *Reading Romanow: The implications of the final report of the Commission on the Future of Health Care in Canada for Women.* Winnipeg, MB: Author.

National Profile of Family Caregivers in Canada. (2002). *National Profile of Family Caregivers in Canada: Final report.* Retrieved May 1, 2006, from http://www.hc-sc.gc.ca/hcs-sss/alt_formats/hpd-dgps/pubs/2002-caregiv-interven/2002-caregiv-interven_e.pdf

Olesen, V. (2005). Early millennial feminist qualitative research: Challenges and contours. In N. Denzin & Y. S. Lincoln (Eds.), *The handbook of qualitative research* (3rd ed, pp. 235–278). Thousand Oaks, CA: Sage.

Peterson, A., Ward-Griffin, C., & McWilliam, C. (2001). The evolving experience of simultaneous formal and informal caregiving. Presentation at the 15th Annual Research Conference, Building Nursing Knowledge: The Path to Excellence, London, Ontario.

Phillips, J. (Ed.). (1995). *Working carers: International perspectives on working and caring for older people.* Aldershot, UK: Avebury.

Phillips, J., Bernard, M., & Chittenden, M. (2002). *Juggling work and care: The experiences of older adults.* Bristol, UK: Policy.

Provincial Government of Ontario. (1991). Regulated Health Professions Act. Ottawa: Author.

Ross, M. M., Rideout, E. M., & Carson, M. M. (1996). Nurses' work: Balancing personal and professional caregiving careers. *Canadian Journal of Nursing Research, 26*(4), 43–59.

Rutman, D. (1996). Caregiving as women's work: Women's experiences of powerfulness and powerlessness as caregivers. *Qualitative Health Research, 6*(1), 90–111.

Stacey, M., & Davies, C. (1983). *Division of Labour in Child Health Care: Final report to the SSRC.* Warwick, UK: University of Warwick.

Twigg, J. (2004). The body, gender, and age: Feminist insights in social gerontology. *Journal of Aging Studies, 18*, 59–73.

Ungerson, C. (1990). The language of care: Crossing the boundaries. In C. Ungerson (Ed.), *Gender and caring: Work and welfare in Britain and Scandinavia* (pp. 8–33). New York: Harvester.

Walters, V., Lenton, R., French, S., Eyles, J., Mayr, J., & Newbold, B. (1996). Paid work, unpaid work and social support: A study of the health of male and female nurse. *Social Science and Medicine, 43*(11), 1627–1636.

Ward-Griffin, C. (2002, December). *Final report: Health professionals as family care givers of elderly relatives: Practice and policy implications* (submitted to Canadian Institutes of Health Research [CIHR] Institute of Gender and Health). Ottawa.

Ward-Griffin, C. (2004). Nurses as caregivers of elderly relatives: Negotiating personal and professional boundaries. *Canadian Journal of Nursing Research, 36*(1), 92–114.

Ward-Griffin, C., Brown, J. B., Vandervoort, A., McNair, S., & Dashnay, I. (2005). Double-duty caregiving: Women in the health professions. *Canadian Journal on Aging, 24*(4), 61–76.

Ward-Griffin, C., Keefe, J., Martin-Matthews, A., Kerr, M., & Brown, J. B. (2006). *Double-duty caregiving: Development and validation of the DDC Scale* (final report to Canadian Institutes of Health Research [CIHR] and Social Sciences and Humanities Research Council [SSHRC]; internal). Ottawa.

Wuest, J. (1998). Fraying connections of caring women: An exemplar of including difference in the development of explanatory frameworks. *Canadian Journal of Nursing Research, 29*(2), 99–116.

2

Dynamics of Carework

Boundary Management and Relationship Issues for Home Support Workers and Elderly Clients

Atiya Mahmood and Anne Martin-Matthews

Janice Simpson is a 48-year-old, divorced mother of three, employed for 6 years as a home support worker. She gets along well with the owner of the agency, although she reports her interaction with the owner's son (who frequently communicates work schedule information) as "strained." Although her work schedule can vary somewhat from week to week, Janice works full-time with three different clients: each weekday morning with Ruth Collins, a 79-year-old stroke victim; for 2 hours each afternoon with 82-year-old Clyde Weston, who has Alzheimer's disease; and for 2 hours each evening with Alice Carter, who has Parkinson's disease and severe arthritis. Janice has been assisting Mrs. Collins for almost 5 years and generally gets along well with her client and Mrs. Collins' co-resident daughter. Mrs. Collins' husband is also co-resident in the home, and although he is not officially a client of homecare services, he does benefit from Janice's care in terms of laundry, housekeeping, and meal preparation. She finds Mr. Collins helps her a lot in getting her work done, and is especially good at humoring his wife on her "bad days." However, his health has been failing recently, and this is changing the nature of Janice's work in the Collins household. Mrs. Collins' daughter, employed full-time outside the home, has given Janice many "tips" on the physical and personal care of her mother.

Janice has been assisting Mr. Weston for almost 2 years. As his co-resident son works outside the home in the day, she is usually alone with Mr. Weston when she is working there, and his unpredictable outbursts and agitation frighten her. She rarely complains to the agency about this, as she fears she will lose her job. Janice's third client, Ms. Carter, age 78, lives alone and receives assistance from other workers as well as Janice, although Janice has no interaction with these coworkers. Ms. Carter is verbally abusive and has a drinking problem. Although she is not afraid of Ms. Carter, Janice finds the home setting difficult, as the house is very cramped and untidy. If she moves any items so as to make her job easier, Ms. Carter accuses Janice of stealing. Janice has asked for a transfer from this client, but this has not happened as yet.

Introduction

Health care policy and economics in the late 20th century fueled a major movement of long-term health care services from centralized facilities like hospitals and institution-based care to home-based care in many countries (Alcock, Danbrook, Walker, & Hunt, 1998; Aronson & Neysmith, 1996, 1997; Cameron & Phillips, 2003; Royal Commission on the Future of Health Care in Canada, 2002; Sorochan, 1995). Much of the research and writing on home care is focused on broad issues of policy and on the juxtaposition of formal and informal care provision (e.g., Aronson & Neysmith, 1997; Cameron & Phillips; Hollander & Chappell, 2002; Jamieson, 1991). However, caught in the midst of these policy debates are homecare recipients (most of whom are older adults) and their family members and carers, often struggling to respond to immediate needs in the context of a homecare system that is in flux. Health care providers are added to this mix when they enter homecare settings as case managers, community health nurses, occupational or physical therapists, and, most typically, home support workers (Martin-Matthews, 2007).

An underlying assumption in the shift from hospital- to home-based care is that this type of health care provision is less disruptive for the person receiving care as it allows him or her to remain at home. However, when the practices and procedures, and rules and regulations, of homecare agencies (themselves informed by local, regional, and national policy debates) operating in the public sphere enter the private sphere of the home, they necessitate the negotiation of boundary management between *home* and *work*. Thus, an important and often overlooked part of the homecare experience is the experience of "home" as the site of carework. Rubinstein (1990) has stated that the *meaning of home* and the domestic order change when the family home becomes a setting for long-term care.

A limited number of studies (e.g., Angus, Kontos, Dyck, McKeever, & Poland, 2005; Dyck, Kontos, Angus, & McKeever, 2005; Tamm, 1999) have explored how the introduction of homecare activities in the home affects the routines and social interactions of the household members. Most homes are not equipped for any paid work related to long-term or chronic health care provision (however, family members engaged in paid work outside the home may sometimes bring work home). Tamm (1999) argued that "the meaning of home" as a place of autonomy and private territory, and as an existential center for the family, is often disrupted and changed with the incidence of chronic illness, functional impairment, and rehabilitation therapy in that location.

Homecare allows health care activities from the public sector to move into private residential space. The home is, then, not just a place of residence but also a work setting for staff engaged in the work of care. Can this combination of private home and public workplace function together? To address this issue, we explore the following questions in this chapter: How are the boundaries between "home" and "work" experienced, blurred, and managed in a homecare setting? How do these experiences and management of boundaries redefine or reinforce the *meaning of home* for health care recipients and the experience of homecare work for home support workers? Analysis of qualitative data from a Canadian study of homecare identifies issues related to boundary management and negotiation by homecare recipients and home support workers. We briefly review homecare and home support work in Canada and the relevant literature on boundary management strategies in relation to the concepts of *home* and *work*. Research themes relating to boundary negotiation are then examined from two perspectives: home support workers' perceptions of their work roles and expectations as they deal with agency guidelines and unmet client needs, and elderly homecare recipients' perspectives on the *meaning of home*, especially when it becomes the site of care. We then present a conceptual framework, to serve as a tool to guide future research.

Homecare and Home Support Work in Canada

Approximately 1 million people in Canada use homecare services annually (Shapiro, 2002). Homecare work involves a wide variety of workers (e.g., nurses, care managers, social workers, physiotherapists, occupational therapists, and home support workers) with different levels of training and qualifications. Most homecare workers provide home support, and are often defined as "nonprofessional services" in the form of personal assistance with daily activities, such as bathing, dressing, grooming, and light household tasks. They are variously known as *home support workers*, *personal care workers*, *community health workers*, *home helps*, *home aides*, or *homemakers* (Martin-Matthews & Phillips, 2003). In this chapter, we use the term *home support worker* to denote this type of employment in the provision of homecare.

In 2001, an estimated 32,000 home support workers provided between 70–80% of the homecare needs for Canadian homecare recipients. This includes both personal care (bathing, toileting, grooming) and work related to instrumental needs (food preparation, cleaning, laundry). In Canada (as in other countries discussed in this book), home support workers typically work 8 to 9 years in this sector, despite low pay, little or no job advancement, variability of workload, and often irregular or sporadic work hours (Home Care Sector Study Corporation, 2003).

Boundary Management Between "Home" and "Work"

> The topic of home-based [and homecare] work particularly illuminates the permeable quality of conceptual boundaries (of home and work, public and private). Located in the space of family, in the dwelling, such work brings wages into the place where "love," "duty," and "need" compel labor. (Prugl & Boris, 1996, p. 7)

As a by-product of change from the Industrial Revolution, throughout the late 19th and 20th centuries, *home* and *work* became increasingly distinct, mentally and physically, in many countries of the developed world (Kanter, 1977). Whereas *work* became the public realm of wage labor, taking place outside the residence, and was conceptualized as masculine, political, rational, and socially valued, *home* became identified as private territory, feminine and nonpolitical, and activities performed there contributed toward nurturing the paid worker. Themes of public and private, gender-based roles, and production and consumption became respectively ingrained with the concepts of *work* and *home* (Nippert-Eng, 1996).

Even if people may socially or mentally construct *home* and *work* as spatially and temporally separate domains, in reality, there are increasing instances of overlap. For instance, women who have to juggle both paid work and care-giving responsibility often do their paid work in the home. In the health care sector, paid homecare work takes place within the private sphere of clients' homes. However, it is more common for individuals who work outside the home to assume divided approaches to *home* and *work* than integrated ones where paid and unpaid work, including caregiving work, can spatially and temporally overlap. Hence it is common for these individuals to erect boundaries between the two spheres of home and work. The nature of these boundaries (spatial, temporal, or behavioral) and the ways in which boundaries are defined and controlled are critical in understanding how work and home life are interpreted and how activities and settings in these two realms are arranged (Mahmood, 2002a). The boundaries between these spheres of home and work may blur when one person's home becomes the site of another person's work, as happens in the delivery of homecare.

Space is not a neutral backdrop. Bounded spaces actively influence the behavior of people within them (Ardener, 1993). When multiple, divergent activities (e.g., domestic work, homecare work, and professional or paid work) occur in the same space, there is the potential for change in the structure of home environments, in the boundaries between public and private, and in living and work patterns to accommodate those activities (Ahrentzen, 1990). This chapter examines the boundary management issues experienced by home support workers and their elderly clients, and provides insights into carework situations.

Workers' Perspectives: Integration and Segmentation in Boundary Management

Nippert-Eng (1996) argued that people conceptualize and juxtapose *home* and *work* on a continuum of *integration* and *segmentation*: "Boundary work is the key process that reflects and helps determine how much we integrate/segment home and work" (p. 7). In a total integration scenario, *home* and *work* have no conceptual boundaries separating their content or meaning. All spaces and times are multipurpose. At the other end of the continuum, *home* and *work* are experienced as completely separate "segmented" worlds. Here the boundaries are clear, impregnable, and mutually exclusive, resulting in distinctive characteristics for each sphere. In reality, most conceptualization of *home* and *work* falls somewhere in between.

Though boundary placement (or removal) is a mental activity (Zerubavel, 1991), it is established and enhanced through a largely visible collection of essential, practical activities. We impose boundaries on everything, including our daily activities, settings for these activities, and the people with whom we pursue these activities. Through the negotiation of boundary management, structural properties are perpetuated and changed, and conceptualization of *public* and *private*, and *work* and *home*, are continued, modified, and restructured (Mahmood, 2002b).

In her conceptualization of boundary placement (segmentation) and boundary removal (integration), Nippert-Eng (1996) did not detail why and how some of these boundaries (as strategies of segmentation) are placed as they are, or how these boundaries are removed or made more permeable (through strategies of integration). In order to relate *segmentation* and *integration* to the experiences of home support workers and their clients, we draw upon another set of concepts developed by Felstead and Jewson (2000). These concepts refer to boundary management in home-based work situations, but are shown here to be relevant to homecare work situations. Felstead and Jewson's (2000) concepts of *technologies of self* help us to identify the issues that underlie boundary segregation and boundary integration.

Felstead and Jewson (2000) argued that the social construction of time and space, the policing of daily activities, and the management of the interface between household and paid work (in this case, formal homecare work) are typically achieved through the generation of a series of technologies of self. The term *technologies of self* "refers to ways in which people, more or less consciously and reflexively, mobilize and organize their attitudes, practices and feelings in the course of their everyday lives" (Felstead & Jewson, 2000, p. 116). Although our data do not permit us to examine the behaviors that home support workers and clients enact as part of boundary management, they do allow us to examine the issues identified by each in relation to boundaries. The "technologies of self" identified by Felstead and Jewson guide our interpretation of the verbatim accounts of the home support workers and elderly clients interviewed in our studies.

These include *isolation* (the social and geographic isolation of home support workers from coworkers), *variability* (the unpredictability of workloads across the boundaries of the homecare setting and the outside health care sector), *invisibility* (the lack of credibility and status of home support workers), and *switching* (movement between the realms of *home* and *work*—in this case, homecare work's time and space). From the perspective of the older adult client of homecare, a potentially relevant *technology of self* includes *encroachment* (the intrusion generated by the presence of home support workers in the home).

Elderly Clients' Perspectives: The Meaning of Home When Care Comes Home

Throughout their lives, people develop subtle connections to their homes (Marcus, 1995). The meaning of home is generated through interaction between people and the home environment in the context of their life experiences. At the most general level, it links people to their environments. For older adults, *meanings of home* include home as a representation of self-identity, independence, and safe haven, and home as a place of choice regarding lifestyle and activities (Marsden, 2001; Rubinstein, 1989). At the most basic level, homes provide shelter to people. Psychological, cultural, and social meanings are embedded in the home environment. Oswald and Wahl (2005) stated that different aspects of *meaning of home* are emphasized throughout the life span, with bonding and place attachment aspects of home emphasized in later life and old age. However, Oswald and Wahl argued that these *meanings of home* are associated with ambiguous feeling throughout people's lives. This is especially true for older adults. The home is simultaneously a comforting and familiar place and a burdensome and anxiety-producing place that is often unsafe, hard to maintain, and not barrier-free for people with mobility challenges.

Sixsmith (1986) reduced a broad range of *meaning of home* categories to three different modes of everyday home experience. *The physical home* mainly deals with the spatial features, style, affordances, and modern conveniences of the home environment. *The social home* portrays the relationships with others. Finally, *the personal home* encompasses issues of home as an extension of self, as haven and private space, as well as continuity. This linking of meaning of home to different modes of everyday home life experience is relevant to elderly recipients of homecare. Dyck et al. (2005) and Angus et al. (2005) highlighted the social, physical, as well as personal space– or body space–related experience of home and homecare in their study on the homecare experience of both care provider and caregiver. Thus a focus of our chapter is on the relevance of home as a social, physical, and personal space, discussed within the context of the homecare experience of elderly people.

In addressing these issues, we examine the responses of home support workers and elderly clients to a series of questions asked about the giving and receiving of in-home care. The verbatim accounts enable us to answer these questions:

- How are the boundaries between *home* and *work* experienced, blurred, and managed in a homecare setting?
- How do these experiences of, and the management of, boundaries redefine or reinforce the *meaning of home* for health care recipients and the *meaning of homecare work* for home support workers?

The Voices of the Workers and the Clients

We interviewed both workers and elderly clients at two points in time. In Phase I, 150 home support workers and 155 elderly clients were interviewed, and in Phase II (18–24 months later), 137 of the home support workers and 118 of the elderly clients from Phase I were interviewed again. In this chapter, the verbatim responses of the workers and clients in both phases of the study are used.

Clients were between the ages of 57 and 95, with an average age of 78 years: Most were women, and a majority was widowed and had lived in their current community an average of 35 years. They had been receiving home support services for periods that ranged from one month to 9 years.

The home support workers were all female (mostly Canadian-born) with an average age of 40 years. Sixty-seven percent were married or living with a partner, and over half had children living at home. Almost 47% of them had high school education, although some, a minority, had completed additional nursing or health care aide certification. In contrast to employment patterns among home support workers in the United Kingdom, 85% worked part-time in this job (Martin-Matthews & Phillips, 2003), with an average of 15 hours a week. Only 11% of the home support workers were employed for more than 30 hours per week.

Although the original panel study did not specifically ask about boundary management and the *meaning of home*, the open-ended nature of some interview questions permitted the generation of data relevant to the issues of the meaning of home and boundary management. The verbatim accounts of the workers and clients in response to these open-ended questions were content-analyzed through the lens of boundary management issues among home support workers and the negotiation of *meaning of home* among homecare clients. In the data from the home support workers, our analyses are based on responses to questions concerning circumstances in their lives that impact their job, the effect of their employment in homecare work on their home life, the effect of double-duty caregiving responsibilities (i.e., paid home support work and unpaid caregiving responsibilities in their own home), and, especially, questions as to what they like most or least about their jobs and on their relationships with their older adult clients.

In the data from the interviews with elderly homecare recipients, we examined responses to questions concerning the most and least liked aspects of receiving home support, the additional (unpaid) assistance provided by workers for clients, and the expectations of clients and family members as to the nature of homecare work.

Our interpretations of these data were informed by the literature that tells us that those who do paid work in the private setting of the home (e.g., home-based workers) are often subject to a range of limitations and restrictions from their employers (e.g., agency policy), their clients, and other household members (e.g., family norms). Further, "There is a potential for confrontation between two powerful sources of meaning and identity—home and work. There is a potential collision of values, ideas and roles" (Felstead & Jewson, 2000, p. 115). Although this statement was made in reference to home-based work, we examine here its applicability to homecare work. Home support workers, who bring the public domain of work into the private home of their clients, are often required to manage the interface—or interfaces—between expectations of home and paid work. Homecare agency policies typically prescribe strong boundaries between paid work and home life. In this context, then, what kinds of boundary management issues arise when home becomes the site of care?

Boundary Management Involved in Caregiving: Perspectives of Home Support Workers and Elderly Clients

Boundary Management: Home Support Workers

The boundary management issues identified by Felstead and Jewson (2000) in home-based work situations (e.g., isolation, invisibility, and variability) were well reflected in the verbatim accounts of the home support workers. They identified issues of boundary conflict involving their social and geographic isolation from their employers and coworkers. The following statements provide examples of experiences of *isolation*. One worker (age 50, home support worker for 17 months) stated, "I have no complaints—other than lack of support from one another due to isolation." Another worker (age 21, home support worker for 6 months) noted the lack of access to teamwork (that can be found in public health care settings): "Not a chance to talk to other homemakers, especially if working on some case—sort of case conference."

Issues of boundary conflict associated with the *invisibility* of the work were also noted by workers, especially in terms of the lack of credibility and status of home support workers in the delivery of health and social care. These were expressed in terms of the lack of communication, support, and recognition of services within home support agencies. One worker (age 36, home support worker for 52 months) stated, "Homemakers are supposed to be the 'ears and eyes' for Home Care but Home Care [agency] doesn't pay any attention to our recommendations." Another (age 49, home support worker for 4 months) voiced this in terms of inflexibility of scheduling: "I would also like the agency to make note of my preferences re: scheduling. They don't seem to pay any attention to what I request." Yet another (age 41, home support worker for 2 months) reflected on the issue of invisibility in terms of the lack of acknowledgment of the importance of their work: "I know that I do a good job but I never felt adequate at the agency because they didn't let me know I was doing a good job, i.e., no pats on the back."

Boundary conflict issues were also expressed in terms of *role ambiguity* and the *variability* of work. One home support worker (age 30, employed 11 months) expressed role ambiguity in terms of the work schedule: "[What I least like about my job is] not knowing [what] my schedule is going to be one week to next." For another (age 39, home support worker for 7 months), role ambiguity is reflected in the context of income: "Only thing is that you can't count on steady income." Another (age 19, home support worker for 13 months) identified the issue of the variability of work in terms of clientele: "[What I least like about my job is] getting different clients every day. I am constantly moving around from place to place." Some workers were concerned about the ambiguity of their work—what they could or could not do under the homecare agency guidelines. As one home support worker (age 36, employed for 4 ½ years) stated, "There are some real inconsistencies in what we are to do—especially regarding medications—sometimes we can give them and sometimes not. There doesn't seem to be any reasonable explanation."

The blurring of boundaries was also reflected in the experience of *switching* or movement between the realms of *home* and *work*: For home support workers, this boundary blurring occurred in the context of extra work and unpaid work. Providing extra assistance to an older client in time of need (even outside their paid work hours) is frequently associated with the development of a friendship with the client. One home support worker (age 59, employed for 3 years) described her experience as follows:

> In case of emergency, when I had a client who needed my help after hours I've been instructed just to leave them and let them handle their own problems. I think they [the agency] were more interested in the hours they had to pay me beyond my usual time. What is the use of having a homemaker? I felt like I had done the right thing (staying to help her).

This blurring of boundaries was frequently associated with the development of affective relationships between worker and client. In some cases, both worker and client defined the relationship as "like kin" and used the language of fictive kin in these descriptions. One worker (age 39, home support worker for 2 months) indicated, "[What I like most about my job is] just being with them—more like a family basis. You're not going in just to make the—you're there to help. The pay cheque's nice, but that's not why I took the job." Another (age 57, home support worker for 11 years) said, "A lot are like parents to me.

I've looked after my own parents until they died and I guess they are like substitutes." Yet another one (age 47, home support worker for over 4 years) saw this relationship as one between grandchildren and grandparents. She stated, "Sometimes I give them my phone number or bring over dinner. I have no grandparents left, maybe that's why I like it." Some elderly clients too described this crossing of the emotional boundary between worker and client, referring to a worker as "like my own daughter" (Martin-Matthews, 2007, p. 240).

For home support workers, boundary management issues were exacerbated by a lack of boundary negotiation with employers at their homecare agencies. The experiences of isolation, role ambiguity, variability of work, lack of recognition of work, or invisibility of work were often accompanied by miscommunication or lack of communication with the agency. The boundary between public and private was sometimes blurred when home support workers did extra work for their clients or developed an affective relationship with their clients. Some boundary-blurring strategies such as *switching* between public and private domains in the clients' residence (extra hours of unpaid work, developing a role as fictive kin) were also reported by these home support workers.

The verbatim accounts of these workers and clients describe situations requiring boundary management and reinforce the salience of these issues when home becomes the site of paid care. However, they do not allow us to consider practices or actions and strategies in response to the boundary issues. As noted, the nature of the data available to us made it difficult to explore the types of strategies that home support workers employ to reduce some of these conflicts. These will be examined in work currently under way (Nexus Home Care Research, n.d.). This research will tell us whether home support workers manage these interfaces through strategies of *segregation* or *integration* within the home. And if so, what form do they take? We expect strategies of segregation to involve strong internal boundaries between the times and places of paid work and home life. Strategies of integration will, we expect, be required when there are weak internal boundaries between paid work and home life. This may occur when the homecare worker becomes emotionally attached to an elderly client, considers the client to be a friend or fictive kin, and does additional work for the client even if not paid for that work.

Boundary Management: Homecare Recipients

The analyses of the verbatim accounts of the elderly recipients of home support services identified five issues relevant to the *meaning of home*. These are *home as continuity*; *home as refuge from the outside world*; *home as place of control, independence, and security*; *home as social space for relationships with family and friends*; and *home as an ordered and clean place*. These are illustrated and examined below, along with verbatim statements that illustrate boundary conflict or disruption of *meaning of home*.

Boundary maintenance and conflict: "Meaning of home" continued, redefined, and (re)established: The importance of aging in place and the meaning of home as continuity were recurring themes amongst the older adult clients. Most of these clients generally felt that homecare reinforced and supported this. One client (age 68, married, homecare client for 12 months) stated, "I couldn't stay in my own home [without homecare]. I would have to go to an institution—because I can't even manage with meals or anything, such as washing dishes or laundry." Another client (age 78, widowed, homecare client for 18 months) said, "I'm concerned that the service will be cancelled. I don't want to move. With my poor vision, it would take me too long to find my way around a new place." Similar sentiments are expressed by other elderly clients.

However, for a few older adult clients, there was disruption of "meaning of home as continuity" when they started to receive home support services. Home support work was perceived as an encroachment because of disruption of their (client's) daily routines. Changes in the home support worker's schedule or in the rotation of numerous different workers were problematic for clients. One client (age 73, widowed, homecare recipient for 12 months) stated, "My life is disrupted.... Also the constant training of new homemakers is difficult.... I would like somebody to be here long enough for me to get to know them and for them to know where things are."

The verbatim accounts of older adult clients also included statements related to positive aspects of the meaning of home as a safe haven and refuge mediated by the help and support from the home support worker. One client (age 80, widowed, homecare recipient for 7 years) reflected on this aspect of the meaning of home:

> The feeling that somebody cares and will be there on Tuesday. It gives you a feeling of security to know that someone is coming in. It is good to know the jobs will get done.... If I had a problem I know she would be here either on her time or mine.

On the other hand, some clients experienced a disruption of the meaning of home as a private space and refuge as a result of the presence of the home support worker in their house. One client (age 57, widowed, receiving homecare for 2 years) stated her concern in terms of privacy and security:

> Lack of privacy. I had two homemakers who eavesdropped every time the phone rang. I had another homemaker who kept tasting a cake batter, then put spatula back in the bowl. That turned my stomach. I also had a homemaker who stole from me, and didn't pay my bills when I asked her to—I was charged for late payments.

Another client (age 78, married, receiving homecare for one month) echoed similar sentiments: "There is an invasion of privacy. I had a homemaker for 2 full days while my husband was away. She was too efficient and capable. It is healthier for me to have to do a few things myself."

Some older adult clients experienced a disruption of meaning of home as a place of control, independence, and security, and experienced boundary management conflict in viewing the home support worker as an intrusion. They spoke of the roles and routines of home support workers as challenging the meaning of home as a place of control and independence for them. One client (age 75, married, receiving homecare for 2 years) stated, "I wouldn't want to be bothered with having somebody here all day or another day of the week. If I didn't keep doing some of the work myself I would degenerate." Another one (age 78, married, homecare client for 3 years) said, "Some homemakers should respect the home of the client; they should feel that it is your home and not theirs."

However, some elderly clients see the support provided by the home support worker as enhancing their meaning of home as a place of control and independence. The following statements reflect this viewpoint: "Overall it's a wonderful service. Before I got Home Care I was in and out of hospital over two to three years. Now I am feeling better and because of the help I haven't needed to go into hospital" (age 80, widowed, homecare client for 7 years).

Among some elderly clients, the patterns of interaction with home support workers contributed to the meaning of home as a social (interaction) space. One client (age 80, widowed, receiving homecare for 5 years) stated, "I appreciate somebody friendly coming in and offering to do my work. When you are alone it's nice to have somebody friendly come in—with a big smile and willing to chat a little." Another client (age 68, widowed, receiving homecare for 4 years) said, "It brings in a breath of fresh air and helps with depression.... Aside from my family the only friend I have is the [home support worker]."

The meaning of home as an ordered and clean place has also been identified in research by Dyck et al. (2005). It was also reflected in the comments of a minority of elderly clients who specifically acknowledged the maintenance of order as an issue for them. One client (age 81, widowed, receiving homecare for 5 years) said, "It is important that she is ... getting my work done. Getting my house in order." Another (age 62, married, homecare client for 48 months) observed, "I can keep my house fairly clean—it doesn't become run down. That would bother me."

These responses of the older adult recipients of home support services highlight how the "meaning of home" is reconstructed and reinterpreted in terms of their current health status and receipt of home support work. For some older adults, the receipt of care "at home" is a positive experience that reinforces important meanings of home, whereas for others it is disruptive and a hindrance to their privacy, thus detracting from the meanings they associate with their homes.

Conclusion and Suggested Framework for Future Research

How do the findings of the previous section extend our understanding of boundary management issues among home support workers and elderly homecare recipients? For answers, we revisit the findings to develop a conceptual framework to guide future research on boundary management in caregiving. An important component in the caregiving experience is the presence of the informal, family caregiver(s). Although in a minority of caregiving situations, informal caregivers are not available or present and thus care is provided solely by formal paid caregivers, most elderly people in need of care receive assistance from both informal and formal carers.

Although this chapter has focused on the interaction between paid workers and elderly clients, it does not provide information on the informal caregiver(s) whose presence is implied but not explicitly addressed in these analyses. However, previous research by Martin-Matthews (2007) as well as research discussed in other chapters of this volume (Ward-Griffin, chapter 1) and elsewhere (Ward-Griffin, Brown, Vandervoort, McNair, & Dashnay, 2005) highlight the need to examine the caregiving triad—the elderly care receiver, a formal (paid) caregiver, and informal (typically family) caregiver(s). In the conceptual framework that we have developed in response to these findings, we include the caregiver triad to provide a comprehensive picture of boundary management issues in the homecare experience.

According to Felstead and Jewson (2000), even when the *home* and *work* realms are not geographically distinct, they still reflect the norms presumed by social and cultural models to give rise to practices that encourage segmentation between these two realms. These structural expectations combine with personal realities as we create our own unique images of these categories. Thus, we suggest that the home support workers, their homecare clients, and informal caregivers maintain, reinterpret, or blur the boundaries between *work* and *home* as a form of adaptation and accommodation to caregiving work in home settings. Our argument is that the manifestation of boundaries between *home* and *work* is tied to the social, spatial, and temporal context within which homecare work is embedded. Under certain circumstances, home support workers, their homecare clients, and informal caregivers will utilize strategies of segmentation as mechanisms to achieve boundary management. These may include the enforcing of strict temporal routines in the home in order to maintain the residential characteristics of the home, or not allowing health workers to alter the homelike décor and furnishing to avoid converting the private home into a public hospital-like setting. However, in other circumstances they will utilize integrative strategies, such as when formal and informal caregivers work together to accomplish a task, or overlap each other in their caregiving responsibilities. In such cases, members of the caregiver triad may perceive other members of the triad as "like" kin.

Our findings suggest that home support workers, elderly homecare recipients, and informal caregivers create an "intermediate domain" between the spheres of *home/private* and *work/public* where carework practices, roles, and relationships exist along a continuum of integration and segmentation. This concept of an "intermediate domain" is similar to that discussed by Ward-Griffin elsewhere in this volume (chapter 1) and in Ward-Griffin et al. (2005). In this intermediate domain, the homecare clients, informal caregivers, and home support workers employ strategies of segregation between the public health care work domain and the private residential domain by reenacting or reinterpreting some of the boundaries between *home* and *work* that enable them to preserve certain traditional *meanings of home*, such as home as a source of *continuity* and *control*. At other times, they engage in integrative boundary removal strategies, such as defining the home support worker as *fictive kin* of the client, or having home support workers perform tasks beyond their paid work duties.

However, some of the policies and procedures related to health care work that are developed mainly for work in public health care settings (such as hospitals and long-term care facilities) are not congruent with caregiving needs and roles in the home setting. This results in role ambiguity and frustration on the part of the home support worker. When societal boundaries between *public* and *private* are strong, paid work like homecare work in private settings often becomes "invisible" or lacks the credibility of work in public settings, resulting in the isolation of home support workers. The concept of "intermediate domain" as described by Ward-Griffin is relevant here, as these workers find themselves in an intermediate position, doing public work in the private domain of the household. Our findings address these aspects of homecare work through the themes of *isolation*, *role ambiguity and variability*, and *invisibility* of home support work (e.g., lack of communication, support, and recognition of home support workers' services within home support agencies).

This chapter provides some preliminary evidence that, amongst home support workers and their elderly clients, boundary management strategies do indeed exist along a continuum of integration and segmentation of *work* and *home* practices. However, further research is required on these strategies.

All players in the homecare triad often have to reformulate or redirect their boundary management strategies to accommodate homecare work in residential settings. Boundary management is a dynamic process. Current segregating practices between the *home* and *work* realms may become more integrative when homecare work or care recipients' household compositions change, if the client's conditions require modification in the nature of the work, or when perceptions of *work* and *home* start changing in society at large.

In this chapter, the empirical data are derived from settings within the private spheres of clients' residences. However, homecare work, like any other activity, is embedded within larger socioeconomic, cultural, and political contexts. Thus, the rules and resources of the larger sociospatial environment also influence the types of activities that can take place within these homecare environments, as illustrated in the work of Giddens (1984) and others (Mahmood, 2002a). The members of the homecare triad interpret (and interact with) the rules and resources of the sociospatial and temporal contexts of their homecare environments. These environments help to generate ongoing behavior (activity) and routines that help them to accommodate health care work within their residences.

The intent of this chapter was to ground the findings in the open-ended data and, in the spirit of conceptual model generation rather than model testing, to formulate a conceptual framework for future research in homecare. Based on the data analysis and interpretation, we propose the following model for future research on boundary management in homecare settings. The participants in the client, formal caregiver, and informal caregiver triad negotiate the boundaries between private home and public health care work in the intermediate domain, and this boundary negotiation is mediated by the structures of the social, spatial, and temporal environment of the private residential setting; the organizational environment of the homecare agency; and the public health care system. The following figure (Figure 2.1) is a diagrammatic representation of this conceptualization. Although the testing of this model is beyond the capacity of our data and the scope of this chapter, our findings provide substantial support for the potential of this conceptual model to advance knowledge and understanding of boundary management and relationship issues for home support workers and homecare recipients.

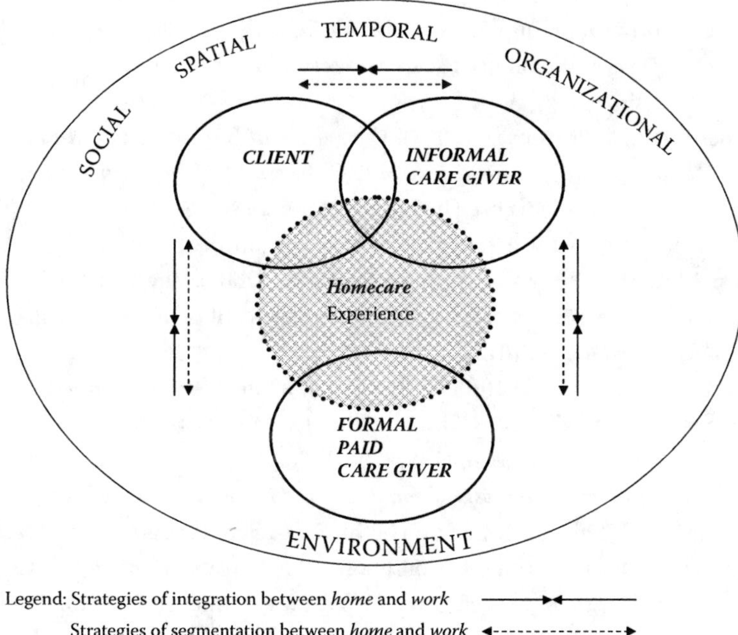

Figure 2.1 Conceptualization of the homecare experience for the caregiver–care recipient triad as embedded within the social, spatial and temporal, and organizational environments of *work* and *home*.

References

Ahrentzen, S. B. (1990). Managing conflict by managing boundaries: How professional homeworkers cope with multiple roles at home. *Environment and Behavior, 22*, 723–752.

Alcock, M., Danbrook, C., Walker, D., & Hunt, C. (1998). Home care clients, provider and costs. *Canadian Journal of Public Health, 89*(5), 297–300.

Angus, J., Kontos, P., Dyck, I., McKeever, P., & Poland, B. (2005). The personal significance of home: Habitus and the experience of receiving long-term home care. *Sociology of Health & Illness, 27*(2), 161–187.

Ardener, S. (1993). Ground rules and social maps for women: An introduction. In S. Ardener (Ed.), *Women and space: Ground rules and social maps*. New York: St Martin's.

Aronson, J., & Neysmith, S. (1996). The work of visiting homemakers in the context of cost cutting in long term care. *Canadian Journal of Public Health, 87*(6), 422–425.

Aronson, J., & Neysmith, S. (1997). The retreat of the state and long-term care provisions implications for frail elderly people, unpaid family caregivers and paid home care workers. *Studies in Political Economy, 53*, 37–66.

Cameron, C., & Phillips, J. (2003). *Care work in Europe: Current understandings and future directions: Case study of care work in residential and home care* (UK Report). Retrieved September 4, 2007, from http://www.ioe.ac.uk/tcru/carework.htm

Dyck, I., Kontos, P., Angus, J., & McKeever, P. (2005). The home as a site for long-term care: Meanings and management of bodies and space. *Health & Place, 11*, 173–185.

Felstead, A., & Jewson, N. (2000). *In work, at home*. London: Routledge.

Giddens, A. (1984). *The constitution of society*. Cambridge: Polity.

Hollander, M. J., & Chappell, N. L. (2002). *Final report of the study on the comparative cost analysis of home care and residential care services*. Victoria, BC: National Evaluation of the Cost-Effectiveness of Home Care.

Home Care Sector Study Corporation. (2003). *Canadian Home Care Resources Study: Synthesis report*. Ottawa: Home Care Sector Study Corporation.

Jamieson, A. (1991). Trends in home-care policies. In A. Jamieson (Ed.), *Home care for older people in Europe: A comparison of policies and practices* (pp. 273–295). Oxford: Oxford University Press.

Kanter, R. M. (1977). *Work and family in the United States: A critical review and agenda for research and policy*. New York: Russell Sage Foundation.

Mahmood, A. (2002a, Fall). Managing blurring of boundaries: A conceptual framework for social, spatial and temporal analysis of live-work settings. *Seniors' Housing Update, 11*(2), 1–3.

Mahmood, A. (2002b). Work and home boundaries: Sociospatial analysis of women's live-work environments. Unpublished doctoral dissertation, University of Wisconsin–Milwaukee.

Marcus, C. C. (1995). *House as a mirror of self*. Berkeley, CA: Conari.

Marsden, J. (2001). A framework for understanding homelike character in the context of assisted living housing. *Journal of Housing for the Elderly, 15*(1/2), 79–96.

Martin-Matthews, A. (2007). Situating "home" at the nexus of the public and private spheres: Ageing, gender and home support work in Canada. In S. Arber, L. Andersson, & A. Hoff (Eds.), *Gender, ageing and power: Changing dynamics in western societies* (*Current Sociology* Monograph Series, Vol. 1). *Current Sociology, 55*(2), 229–249.

Martin-Matthews, A., & Phillips, J. (2003, November). Home care work in Canada and England: Comparative perspectives of home care workers on relationship issues in the provision of home-based services to elderly persons. Paper presented at the annual conference of the Gerontological Society of America, San Diego, CA.

Nexus Home Care Research. (N.d.). *Home care in Canada: Working at the nexus of the public and private spheres.* Retrieved September 3, 2007, from http://nexushomecare.arts.ubc.ca

Nippert-Eng, C. (1996). *Home and work: Negotiating boundaries through everyday life.* Chicago: University of Chicago Press.

Oswald, F., & Wahl, H. (2005). Dimensions of the meaning of home in later life. In G. Rowles & H. Chaudhury (Eds.), *Home and identity in late life: International perspectives.* New York: Springer.

Prugl, E., & Boris, E. (1996). Introduction. In E. Boris & E. Prugl (Eds.), *Homeworkers in global perspective: Invisible no more* (pp. 3–17). New York: Routledge.

Royal Commission on the Future of Health Care in Canada. (2002). *Building on values: The future of health care in Canada.* Ottawa: Author.

Rubinstein, R. L. (1989). The home environment of older people: A description of the psychosocial processes linking person to place. *Journal of Gerontology, 44,* S45–S53.

Rubinstein, R. L. (1990). Culture and disorder in the home care experience: The home as sickroom. In J. F. Gubrium & A. Sankar (Eds.), *The home care experience: Ethnography and policy* (pp. 37–57). Newbury Park, CA: Sage.

Shapiro, E. (2002). *The health care transition fund: Synthesis series: Home care* (Cat. J13-6/2002-2). Ottawa: Minister of Public Works and Government Services Canada. Retrieved September 3, 2007, from http://www.hc-sc.gc.ca/hcs-sss/pubs/home-domicile/2002-htf-fass-home-domicile/index_e.html

Sixsmith, J. A. (1986). The meaning of home: An exploratory study in environmental experience. *Journal of Environmental Psychology, 6,* 281–298.

Sorochan, M. (1995). Homecare in Canada. *Caring, 14*(1), 12–19.

Tamm, M. (1999). What does a home mean and when does it cease to be a home? Home as a setting for rehabilitation and care. *Disability and Rehabilitation, 21*(2), 49–55.

Ward-Griffin, C., Brown, J. B., Vandervoort, A., McNair, S., & Dashnay, I. (2005). Double-duty caregiving: Women in the health professions. *Canadian Journal on Aging, 24*(4), 379–394.

Zerubavel, E. (1991). *The fine line.* New York: Free Press.

3

Visible and Blurred Boundaries in Familial Care

The Dynamics of Multigenerational Care in Singapore

Kalyani K. Mehta and Leng Leng Thang

Introduction

Three successive phases of generational relations are known to characterize generational relations between parents and their children (Morioka, 1996). In the first phase, parents support the younger generation by providing care and financial support; then parents support the younger generation in the care of grandchildren; and in the final phase, the direction of assistance is from the younger generation to parents. This cycle of care permeates multigenerational family care, with the roles of caregivers and care recipients evolving and changing over the life span of the family.

Although the notion of a cycle of care recognizes the older generation as both the provider and recipient of care, the mention of intergenerational family care commonly evokes images of older persons receiving care by family members, usually a daughter or daughter-in-law. Such an image reflects the reality of the increasing need in the care of old and frail people in the context of an aging society. However, this image fails to portray the complex web of family care that not only consists of the immediate family but also often includes other players, such as a foreign domestic worker or maid. In addressing the interplay between the caregivers and care recipients in the context of Singapore, this chapter includes in the equation paid foreign domestic maids in the family setting. This chapter also echoes some of the points made by Mahmood and Martin-Matthews in their study of homecare helpers in Canada (see chapter 2). What is the impact of the presence of a paid worker on the family dynamics? To what extent has their presence contributed to the blurring of the boundaries of care between the private and public, between the professional and personal, and between home and work? However, the homecare helpers in Canada do not reside within the family household, whereas foreign domestic maids in Singapore co-reside with the care recipient. Besides eldercare, the chapter will also consider care in the reverse direction: that of older persons providing care to the grandchildren in the family milieu. In examining multigenerational family care from a life course perspective, we portray older persons as both providing care as well as being recipients of care.

In order to provide international readers with a context for understanding these issues, we first provide some background information about Singapore, including the changing demographic profile, family care policy, and norms. This is followed with an overview of the conceptual focus and data. We will then discuss several emerging themes that impact on the blurring of the boundaries in intergenerational and multigenerational care in an aging society.

The Changing Demographic Profile of Singapore

In the context of the Asia Pacific region, Singapore represents a unique case of a rapidly aging, geographically small nation of only 4 million people living in 659 square kilometers and characterized by a multiethnic and multilingual population composed primarily of Chinese, Malays, and Indian people. Singapore is one of the fastest aging countries in the Asia Pacific region, even by the standards of a contemporary Asia noted for the speed of demographic aging. The pace of population aging that developed countries experienced over a period of 80 to 115 years is being experienced in less than half the time in a number of Asian countries such as Japan and Singapore (Mehta, 1999, p. 57; Population Aging in Asia and the Pacific, 1996, p. 9). The proportion of older persons above 65 years is projected to increase from 8% of the total population in 2000 to 19% in 2030.

However, the older cohort (75 years and above) is more likely than the younger cohort to be living with children only (i.e., divorcees, widows, and/or widowers) or not living with a spouse or children (i.e., living alone or living with nonfamily members) (Singapore Department of Statistics, 2000). As people age, their chances of entering widowhood, a normative life transition, are higher. In terms of gender, higher percentages of males (74%) are living with spouses than females (32%), again reflecting the likelihood of older males having spousal carers as compared to older females. Societal norms prescribe males to marry females younger than themselves, thus leading to a greater likelihood of widowhood among women. Census data (Singapore Department of Statistics) also indicate that Singapore society is characterized by relatively high percentages of Singaporean elders living with their children only, or with spouses and children. In total, 87% of the elders above 65 years are living with family members. Against the backdrop of these national trends in living arrangements, we now address the most common kind of eldercare practiced in Singapore: multigenerational family care.

Mosaic of Family Care

The most typical family care arrangement in Singapore consists of multiple generations within one household or living in separate households that are within close proximity (commonly defined as within a 2-kilometer range). Socioeconomic changes such as the proliferation of the dual-income family, a dramatic increase in women's labor force participation rate, and increasing inflation explain the need for intergenerational interdependence across households. Cultural norms and expectations in Asian families buttress the expectations for intergenerational interdependence over the life course (Mehta & Thang, 2006). Housing in Singapore is primarily dense and high-rise due to land constraints. Given the associated space constraints within Singaporean households, especially in government-built flats, family members who share filial responsibilities may not be living under the same roof. Intersecting this space constraint is economic constraint. Middle-class and lower-class families have to juggle responsibilities for the care of older generations as well as younger generations within these two types of constraints. Coping strategies for meeting the needs of the family are therefore constrained within the parameters mentioned above and by the pressures created by women's employment.

The pervasiveness in Asian countries of family as the most important source of care to older people has been well documented. Ofstedal, Knodel, and Chayovan (1999) compared Taiwan, Thailand, the Philippines, and Singapore on the topic of filial support. In Singapore, 70% of older persons 59 years and above receive financial support from their children (Chan, 1997). This proportion remains consistent with increasing age, suggesting a continuation of "filial support" from children at least for current cohorts of older persons. The familial realm of care is at once desired by the family and similarly encouraged by the state, which regards family as the first line of defense in care of older people.

Measures and policies relating to intergenerational support include tax relief, such as that given to adult children and grandchildren for maintaining their parents and grandparents. An employed woman can also claim tax relief for child(ren) being looked after by the grandparents. There are also housing schemes that encourage co-residence or living in proximity with older generations. Lastly, the Maintenance of Parents Act seems a preventive policy to ensure that adult children provide financial support to their aged parents (for more details, see Thang, Teo, Mehta, & Chan, 2003).[1]

By encouraging living in close proximity through priority housing schemes and housing grants, multigenerational care is promoted beyond the multigenerational household setting. This reflects the state's effort to cope with the concerns for the possibility of reduced (elder) care in the family in future, acknowledging the trend toward declining multigenerational co-residence and the norm for women's participation in the workforce.[2]

A policy of promoting multigenerational care is also reflected in a report of Singapore's Inter-Ministerial Committee on the Ageing Population (IMC). In the IMC workgroup on cohesion and conflict in an aging society, which aims to "propose policy measures to strengthen our social fabric and intergenerational cohesion" (IMC, 1999, p. 172), policy recommendations center on suggestions to promote extended family ties and reciprocity. These include the following: "[T]he teaching of family values in school textbooks should also include illustrations of grandparents as an integral part of the family structure," giving family-based concessions based on extended family status at government-controlled recreational facilities, and giving additional incentives to public housing applicants who choose to stay in close proximity to their grandparents (as well as parents). The final point under "promoting extended family ties" in the report reiterates the objective that the measures will not "merely enhance intergenerational interaction or lessen intergenerational conflict. It will also help to reinforce the role of the family in supporting senior citizens and expand the resource base of the family to do so. This will help families support their older members and lessen the conflict between the rich and the poor" (IMC, 1999, pp. 177–178).

However, in Singapore, one landmark government policy has been especially important in the relationship between employment and care for elderly relatives. The Foreign Maid Scheme was introduced in 1978 with the main aim of facilitating women's continued employment. "Today, the transnational domestic worker has become an ubiquitous feature of the average double income middle and upper-class Singaporean household" (Rahman, Yeoh, & Huang, 2005, p. 233). In contrast to the home support workers described by Mahmood and Martin-Matthews (chapter 2) and by Mears and Watson (chapter 8), the domestic worker lives in the same household as her employer and carries out tasks that range from household chores and child minding to caring for the frail elder members. Here there is a blurring of the boundaries between one care recipient and another, from the viewpoint of the foreign maid. Both types of care recipients fall within her domain of care delivery. Thus, despite being an employed worker, the foreign maid assumes roles and functions typical of a caregiver such as the wife, daughter, or daughter-in-law, thereby blurring the boundaries between family and nonfamily roles.

The implications of the inclusion of a foreign stranger in the family fold have been explored by others, especially from the gendered perspective (Wong, 1996; Yeoh & Huang, 1999, 2000; Yeoh, Huang, & Devasahayam, 2004). In this chapter, we consider the position of the foreign maid from a family care perspective, focusing on the position of this "partner" who is both a paid worker and a quasi-family member in the provision of family care. The following quote summarizes the ambiguity of the transnational domestic worker:

> While the employer-transnational domestic worker relationship runs the gamut from those akin to master-slave relationships to businesslike relationships where the employer treats the transnational domestic worker as worker while maintaining a comfortable distance, the transnational domestic worker's ambiguous position as neither "family" nor complete

> "outsider" may result in a tension-ridden relationship. (Rahman et al., 2005, p. 244)

On one hand, we have observed families where the foreign maid is so intimate with the family members that she learns the language spoken and is trusted with information to which only a family member would be privy. On the other hand, some families train their foreign maids to address the male employer as "sir" and his female counterpart as "ma'am." In either situation, the functions she is expected to perform, as laid down in the employment contract, are care for young and/or old depending on the family composition and needs.

Through its policies, Singapore government has paved the way for an "extra pair of hands" to be available to the typical family carers to juggle their family care responsibilities while simultaneously holding a formal job. However, the state requires the employers to pay a monthly levy for employing a foreign maid. Tax relief in the form of the foreign maid levy waiver is available for married women only.[3] To keep the employment of maids only for families who have care needs, the state provides concessionary levy fees of S$200 (instead of the normal levy of S$295) if the family has children or grandchildren younger than 12 years old or older persons above 65 years old. However, with the combined salary and levy of at least S$520+/–, not including the fees payable to the employment agency and the travel cost for sending the foreign maid to her homeland every 2 years (one contract normally lasts for 2 years), such a care arrangement is not readily available to families with limited financial resources.

Understanding Multigenerational Family Care in Singapore

The Singaporean multigenerational family care system has complexities that must be considered within the national ideological framework, multicultural context, and fluid global environment. There are two main pillars of the national Singapore policy that are directly relevant to the focus of this book. First, Singapore is not a "welfare state" such as the United Kingdom, Canada, or Australia. The individual citizen is constantly reminded to be self-reliant and to save for his or her old age. The "Many Helping Hands" policy is endorsed by the government, meaning that the family, community, and finally government should be responsible for those who require help. The family is, as mentioned above, identified as the first line of defense (IMC, 1999, p. 13), whereas community-based services provide help for those who have no family support.

The majority of Singaporeans are Asians, and as such they share a common value base, despite differences in religious orientation, language, or country of origin. A common shared value is the care for older generations within the family, often referred to as *filial piety*. In the context of rapid demographic aging in Singapore, care for older people is becoming a great challenge to the adult generation. How do Singaporean families cope with family, work, and parenting pressures? Where does the foreign maid feature in the family care web? What are the contributions of the different generations toward keeping the family on an even keel, in terms of the emotional, economic, and psychological aspects of family life? Another value shared by most Singaporeans is a negative attitude toward residential care or the institutionalization of elders. For senior Singaporeans, a strong stigma is attached to institutionalization, because it symbolizes abandonment by the family. This is inculcated in adult children through socialization; hence, they are also aware of the elders' perceptions.

Antonucci and Jackson (1989) identified three main types of reciprocity: immediate, deferred (over time), and generalized (over the life course). In the context of this chapter, deferred and generalized reciprocity are applicable. However, although the concept of filial piety may have underlined the need for and provision of care, behaviors that reflect filial piety are not without tensions and ambivalence in Singaporean society. Bengtson, Giarrusso, Mabry, and Silverstein (2002) have discussed the relevance of the concept of "ambivalence" in advancing our understanding of the competing and contradictory nature of intergenerational relationships. In this chapter, we examine multigenerational family care in terms of both reciprocity and ambivalence. In doing so, we focus on older families who need care as well as older persons who provide care. Although the cultural ideology for filial support and economic factors for dual-earner families support continued intergenerational reciprocal care, the practical constraints such as health and competing commitments (e.g., employment responsibilities and conjugal ties) introduce the element of ambivalence. The entry of the foreign maid further creates a new dimension in the family equation and contributes to the blurring of the boundaries of care networks.

The empirical data for the chapter are derived from several sources that we have collected on aging families, older Singaporeans, the adult generation of family carers, and service providers in the eldercare industry. The qualitative data in this chapter are primarily derived from focus-group discussions and in-depth interviews from sections of data relating to caregiving.[4]

Emergent Themes in Multigenerational Care

In the literature on caring in the Singapore context, reciprocity—expressed sometimes as filial piety (Mehta, 1999; Mehta & Ko, 2004; Thang, 2000)—and ambivalence (Teo, Graham, Yeoh, & Levy, 2003) are two concepts relevant to family care. In this chapter we focus on multigenerational care from an intergenerational perspective, including both the care for the old by younger generations and care for the young by the older generation, that is, the grandparents. The examination of care with an intergenerational lens leads to better understanding of the interplay of reciprocity and ambivalence in the Asian context.

1. Multigenerational Households and Mutual Help

Older persons staying in multigenerational households usually indicate that they have provided or are providing care to their grandchildren living in the same household. When asked whether one has taken care of a grandchild when he or she was younger, elderly people in multigenerational households typically responded, "Yes, I did, because we stayed together in the same house."

Caring for the young seems to define the role of the grandparents in multigenerational households, reflecting the closeness to this relationship. A grandfather describes how he and his wife cared for their grandson when he was young:

> Yes I am close, close [to my grandchildren]. For example, with my grandson here, when he was still young, my wife and I took care of him. We sent him to school, picked him up from school. My wife would prepare his meals. Because his mother was working, so I took care of his well-being. I also took care of another grandson when he was very young. My wife took care of him and of his meals. His mother was working too: sometimes going in the morning and coming back at night, going in the

> afternoon and coming back at night. My wife and I took care of him, so that we will always have strong relationships with our grandchildren and children. (L1, GPP)

For many families, the sense of gratitude and reciprocity is in turn reflected among adult children in the middle generation. "Repaying back" as a result of a sense of indebtedness to one's parents exemplifies reciprocity and sentiments of gratitude (Huang, 2002). As an adult child in the same household as the grandfather quoted above asserted,

> Well, of course ... taking care of the grandparent also, of course I want to give the best I can give to them.... [I]f you can survive until now, now is the time for us to repay back on what they have done for us. And its time for us to ... and we know that life is ... very short ... so I want to give the fullest attention to them. (N2, GPP)

When asked if the adult child would want to take care of her grandchildren when they become grandparents in the future, this daughter responds positively and expresses disapproval of the norm of engaging maids as caregivers, as grandparents would certainly play the role better.

This multigenerational household represents the ideal of containing family care within the domestic domain, where help is received and given in a reciprocal manner in a multigenerational cycle of care. Multigenerational living also makes it easier for intergenerational reciprocity. A Chinese grandmother from Malaysia who now lives with her daughter's family in Singapore perceives her current state as desirable, both for herself and for her daughter's family. She emphasizes the importance of her presence to her granddaughter, suggesting that grandparents are the most appropriate child minders for grandchildren when compared with the option of having a maid at home. By perceiving the maid as less adequate, she has explicitly drawn a visible boundary between familial care and nonfamilial care, delegating the maid to the latter.

> "People bring you up, you bring others up too." So it's a natural process. You can't say the child is my daughter's responsibility and you don't have to care anymore. I still feel that I can help, unless I'm told I'm a nuisance, then I know, I stay away, pack up and go back to Malaysia. But I feel that they like me to be around, to be with the child, and that is like a bonus in my life.... I feel that I am able to contribute to my children's upbringing of their children. (N1, GPP)
>
> Living apart is practical if the distance is not a gap.... But ... by living apart, the child may come back [home], and then you find that the home

> is empty, except for four walls. The child feels that she's very confident that there's always somebody at home when she gets home. That's why we are very close, and we will always make fun, poke at each other, and because of that, although she's a single child, she's not a selfish child. She has that warmth, of course that cheekiness is there, and she always feels very confident of herself, because she knows she's coming back to somebody. (N1, GPP)

Grandparents reap the benefits of reciprocity from their grandchildren as well. As an Indian grandfather shares with pride and expectation,

> I tell you when sometimes I go to the therapist for backache, both of them [grandchildren] helping me now. Now I got leg ache now, this also, neck here pain, can you just help me.... We give them a lot, we must expect a lot from them too. (E1, GPP)

Likewise, when multigenerational families do not co-reside, there is also less expectation for grandparents to take care of the grandchildren. A mother, when asked if the grandmother helps take care of the grandchildren, replied,

> No, because we didn't stay together. If we stayed together, then the differences will be obvious.... It's difficult when they don't stay together. It's like a cat that you look after since young, it will stay with you. (D2, GPP)

For grandparents, co-residing in multigenerational households heightens the expectations of caring for their grandchildren. But even for those who live apart, caring for their grandchildren is increasingly a conscious decision that they have to make, especially now with the norm of dual-worker couples in Singaporean families. In our studies, older persons express ambivalence about this. This ambivalence reflects their reluctance to be full-time carers of their grandchildren, combined with their lack of options due to the pressing needs for childcare in dual-worker households with financial constraints. However, where sufficient financial resources permit, maids "allow grandparents to assume their nurturing role to their grandchildren, without taxing their physical stamina" (Teo, Mehta, Thang, & Chan, 2006, p. 128).

2. *Dilemma in Family Care*

These issues create dilemmas in family care. Feelings of ambivalence expressed by the older generation because they felt worn down by the commitment of childcare do progress to feeling upset about the insensitivity of the parent generation in understanding their needs (Teo et al., 2003). Family members who have primary responsibility for the care of elders also report being emotionally and mentally drained and in need of some respite.

> I need a break I tell them [her siblings]. I will have a nervous breakdown, I tell them, when I am very stressed up. I tell them, 'please give me some space.' (FCP)

Health concerns arise both for middle generations providing eldercare and for older generations providing (grand)childcare. As one Chinese grandmother living with her son's family noted when asked if she will take care of a great-grandchild soon to be born into the family,

> I will be helping out but I'm afraid that I'm old and my legs are too weak, it's ok when I'm seated but it's different when I'm standing or moving around. Now when the child is small I may still be able to take care, but when the baby grows up and I have to carry it around, it's not going to be easy for me. My legs are weak and I'm afraid that accidents might happen. I myself don't matter but the baby is important. For a decade I have not been helping baby to bath[e] and I'm afraid I can't even hold them properly. (GPP)

Expectations of multigenerational care "down" the generations to include (grand)childcare are further questioned by grandparents who do not perceive caring for grandchildren as their responsibility:

> Because this grandchild is not my responsibility, it is my children's responsibility.... Because if you look after someone, you have a responsibility. It wears down one's [*sic*] physically. You want to relax. Once you take on such a responsibility, you cannot relax. (FG2, n7; TFP)

Among those older persons who are relatively healthy, multigenerational caregiving responsibility is considered to be in conflict with their desire for a relaxing life and freedom in retirement. This is an emerging group of older persons who symbolize a departure from the earlier generations of self-sacrificial grandparents who willingly assumed childcare responsibilities, seeing them as their duty for the family. Modern grandparents, in contrast, stress and protect their own freedom and space ("What Grandmas Are Saying No To," 2004). However, they do not draw the boundary strictly but step in to help when necessary. One grandmother who counted herself fortunate for being free of childcare responsibilities said,

> I am as free as a bird. Other people my age, I have quite a number of friends, who have to look after grandchildren, and sometimes the Grandpa goes out, Grandma stays at home. They take turns to go out, you know, to enjoy life, and that's part and parcel of life. If you are in that situation, if you have to do it, got to do it! [If] you are free, then you are lucky, that's all! (TFP)

Another elderly couple had the philosophy that "we should never feel that our life has been stifled because of having a family and children," and asserted that they made their position on grandparenting clear to their children:

> Grandmother: I don't want to have that responsibility. I am done raising five, so that grandchildren, I should have the luxury of [enjoying them], you know?
> Grandfather: Having said that, all our children know that if there's an emergency, we are available. (G1, GPP)

The emergency situation arose when their eldest daughter was without a domestic maid for 4 to 5 months. In the meantime, she needed to work as a teacher while taking care of three sons.

> So I said "ok, let's make an arrangement where the children come to our place."... So I give them lunch and see that they do their homework. And when she finished her work, she'll come and pick them up. I also said "look, when I cook for lunch, I make extra and pack it up for you. So you take it home and just make the rice and you'll have your meals." Because she won't have time to cook and all that. But again I was the one who said that this is from Mondays to Fridays, on Saturdays and Sundays I shouldn't see them. Then sometimes over the weekend she phones and says "would you like to come over and we'll do something?" I'll say "no cannot ... Saturdays and Sundays I shouldn't see you." (G1, GPP)

Drawing a boundary around interaction and to frame expectations is one strategy to deal with the demands for childcare. To cope with caring needs, some couples resort to a system of having two sets of grandparents rotating to care for the grandchildren, for example, one set of grandparents to take care during the odd days of the week and the other grandparents doing so during the even days of the week. This relieves grandparents from the burden of full-time care.

The more common strategy, however, is to include the foreign maids in the care equation. Increasingly, grandparents assume the presence of the foreign maid when they are asked to help in caring for their grandchildren.

> Yeah, we would help. I think most of my friends, we all help out, but, there is a maid to look after. We do not do all the difficult work in the house, sort of thing. I mean looking after children is not easy ... a lot of things running around and that sort of thing! Haha. So if they have a maid, yes, the grandparents can go there, supervise and all that sort of thing you know? But if there is no help, you can't. You can't expect grandparents.... And on top of that, you are very old.... You don't have the energy.... Don't play a fool. Children are very rough, they are very active. (TFP)

However, this positioning of the foreign maid in an intermediate role between adult children, grandchildren, and grandparents can lead to conflicts between young parents and their older parents. As a letter by a 31-year-old young parent to the forum of Singapore's *Straits Times* ("Grandparents, Please Help Out," 2004) showed, not only does the younger generation take for granted that grandparents, especially those who are healthy, should provide care for grandchildren, but also grandparents take for granted that they will do so only if the children employ a maid for them, that is, putting them as "supervisors" over the maids.

3. Impact of the Foreign Maids in Family Dynamics

In general, both the grandparent and parent generations have come to expect that the maid is a natural addition, especially in middle- or upper-income families. For a family with young children (and older persons needing care), it is fairly common to have a maid at home.

> It was a hard time looking after the child because I never had a maid at all. So through birth till the time my daughter grew up it was actually interchanging from my mother, mother in law and myself. My mother took on the night role. (GPP)

Nonetheless, the entrance of an outsider, especially someone from a different culture and set of customs, into the family is not always readily accepted. Grandparents who view themselves as the guardians and transmitters of values worry about the inability of maids to perform the important role.

> When people talk about playing with the children, and they have maids, I am always trying to make this point—that the maid input to the children's mind, is one of the worst things that can happen. So your job, or your thing, when we go and see them, is to quickly sort that out. Because they will soon pick up the stand which their maid has. I mean, I'm sure you realize it. (FG4, n1; TFP)

A grandfather emphasized the importance of grandchildren to justify his disapproval for maids as caregivers of his grandchildren,

> Well they are very important.... "They are very precious."... [T]hese children I never let the maids touch, even my children I never let ... my grandchildren I don't let. They're like precious diamonds.... If you have a diamond, surely you will wear it, you don't want the maid to wear it for you. They are like diamonds, I will hold, I will guide them. They are my children, my grandchildren, like diamonds. I never have maids to look after the children, I look after. The maids do housework. (H1, GPP)

To the dedicated mothers who are concerned with providing the best possible childcare for their children, maids cannot be trusted to care for very young children (Graham, Teo, Yeoh, & Levy, 2003). Moreover, the close relationships developed between the children and the maid as a result of intimate contact—for example, the maid sleeping with the children—could be a source of discomfort or envy.

Within the context of eldercare within the family, the issues of providing quality care may be less of a concern, as maids are perceived as relieving the physical demands of caring for dependent elderly persons. However, some adult children are equally concerned with not giving the best to their parents by relegating the responsibilities to a maid. One care recipient reaffirms such a difference:

> They [parents] still need you around. Even with the maid, the maid is still a maid. To them ... the maid ... is not your relative. (Daughter, FCP)

> It feels different when your own child looks after you and other people.... It's different, when [they] bathe me, wipe me.... [The maid] would be in a hurry to do it. [My daughter] will take her time to do it. [She] does a more thorough job. (Elder Parent, FCP)

More often, the issues of eldercare concern elder neglect. There is general adult concern that children who leave their parents solely to the care of maids may neglect dependent elders with high physical care needs. In some families, the elder parent lives alone with a maid paid for jointly by a few children.

The case of H (Huang, 2002) illustrates a typical problem faced by older persons who are taken care of primarily by a maid. In this case, although the aging mother did not wish to disclose her sense of disappointment with her son, the interviewer detected her unhappiness with the total caregiving responsibility her son had thrust on the maid. To her son, a child's responsibility is fulfilled when he provides his mother with three meals and "a safe environment." He also admitted that he "won't really communicate" with his mother. In this case, as for other families, the expectation for the maid to fulfill all the needs in caring for older parents at home does not necessarily equate with quality care. Our studies indicate that this can lead to frustration for both the elderly, who seek emotional care also, and for the maid if she is overworked. Many of the current cohort of Singaporean elders also face communication barriers due to the lack of a common language (such as English) with the foreign maids. The overreliance on the maid may give rise to occasions of elder abuse, especially if there is little or no respite provided for the employed foreign maid.

It is a paradox that the hiring of a maid facilitates the continuity of filial responsibility on the part of the adult children, yet it could blur the boundaries between direct filial care from adult children and purchased care delivered in the family home, even when paid for by the adult children. In the eyes of the society, as long as the elder person is kept within the family fold, his or her co-resident adult child is perceived as filial, even though most of the physical (and even emotional) care is being provided by a nonfamily member such as the foreign maid.

4. The "Cost and Benefits" of Hiring a Maid

Cost The cost of hiring a maid is often the main concern of less well-to-do families. "If you employ a maid, you also need money. If you don't have money, how do you employ a maid?" (FG 1, 6; TFP). Some families have to give up other luxuries or travel holidays in order to meet the cost of a foreign maid.

A letter to the forum of a local newspaper describes the situation of an unmarried son who must employ two maids to take care of his bedridden mother. He lamented spending two-thirds of his monthly income of S$2,100 on caring for his mother and raised the issue that if 40% of families in Singapore are earning a household income of only S$2,059 or less (as shown in the census; Singapore Department of Statistics, 2000), these families will fall into difficulty if they have a bedridden older person to care for ("More Help for Those Who Look After Aged Parents," 2006). The concern about the cost for taking care of older persons often includes the cost of hiring a maid as the essential caregiver.

Managing Conflict

Those family members with primary responsibility for care of elders recognize how having a maid at home largely relieves the stress of the family caregiver and improves relationships between the elderly and the caregiver.

> I have to work, then she pass urine, vomit ... fall ill.... I'm unable to do all these myself. Sometimes I'll feel burnt out, I'll lose temper.... With a maid [I] will be more relieved, not so pressurized and stressful. (Daughter, FCP)

Maids also enable the primary caregivers to maintain a desirable "space" with the elderly:

> She will now do things herself [with the help of the maid], and won't control here control there.... She won't bother me, I won't bother her. (Daughter-in-law, FCP)

The maid is helpful in promoting a more manageable family relationship by reducing the incidence of conflicts in both close and strained relationships:

> When you stay together for a long time, there will definitely be conflicts. Now that there's a maid, it's better ... for our relationship. If you're always together with somebody you know very well, it's easier to get angry.... [My mother] ... has stroke, it'll be very dangerous if she gets angry. The maid is an outsider, so we won't anyhow throw our temper.

In addition, the extra help also gives the primary caregivers more freedom:

> Now that there's a maid, it's better. I still can do my own things.... This is better for our relationship. (Daughter, FCP)

Managing Communication The maid sometimes becomes the link and helps manage family communication. Huang (2002) noted the emergence of a "triangular" communication pattern between the primary care dyads (the main caregiver and care recipient) and their maids in her study of the presence of maids in Singaporean families. Maids facilitate communication in various ways: by becoming "go-between when the elder parent and adult children have strained relationships," by becoming the confidant of the elder parent, and by informing the adult child of the concerns of the aging parent. However, family members also report instances where maids may become the source of arguments between family members, as when one person dislikes a particular maid and wants to dismiss her but another family member wishes to continue employing her.

It is not uncommon to hear of conflicts between maids and the grandparents at home, with the blurring of lines of authority thus leading to a state of ambiguity. As one family member noted,

> If you happen to have a grandparent together with a maid at home, then that's a different scenario altogether, because sometimes communication is very bad between the grandparent and the maid and the owner of the house. Grandparent also feels that they have the right to discipline the maid. That's very complicated. (TFP)

The foreign maid, as an employed worker in the family setting, plays an ambiguous role in the family care setting. Although some employers choose to set visible boundaries and regard the maid as an outsider, comparatively more families accept the outsider into the family fold and engage with the maid as a careworker in a trust relationship.

> It's either I worry about the person all the time, or I let go a little. It's like even now when I'm out of the house and I know my [maid] caregiver is completely, totally reliable. My dad trusts her. I think that trust is a very important thing. (Huang, 2002)

In the situation above, the adult son and maid caregiver share the caregiving responsibilities, making the process much easier to manage. However, for the adult child–maid caregiving formula to work, the trust of the elder parent in the maid was essential. However, situations such as this remain precarious as the contract with the maid was for 2 years; overdependence on the maid could leave the family in the lurch if she decided to terminate after the 2 years.

Throughout this chapter, we have shown how reciprocity and ambivalence overlap and underscore the complexity of intergenerational and multigenerational care. The presence of the maid adds an important element to the family dynamics of care. Ultimately, the role and functions of the foreign maid in the family vary according to the family's needs. The "match" of the personality of the maid with those of the care recipient as well as the other family members is also a crucial factor to consider in the equation. Although government policies encourage family care for the aging population, and the Foreign Maid Scheme has facilitated the hiring of an "additional pair of hands" to support the working couples, there are economic costs and other social factors to consider.

Conclusion

As other chapters in this book note, the provision of providing eldercare within the family is often accompanied by stress and tension, due to moral values of filial piety and gratitude, pressure of time constraints, competing commitments, and sacrifices called for. It is also undeniable that carers feel a sense of satisfaction and fulfillment in the long run. In the Singapore context, national policies have provided family caregivers another option—the foreign maid—to assist in providing care to aging parents and young children. On the one hand, the foreign maid can be an indispensable care assistant; on the other hand, she is costly and impacts on the family dynamics in that she is also seen as a temporary aid. A competent and loyal maid can blur the boundary between filial and hired care, between formal and informal care, and between direct and indirect care. For the adult children who have to juggle different responsibilities (spanning work and home, different generations, personal, and civic), the reliable foreign maid can be a boon, allowing them to pursue their careers and leisure without compromising the societal expectation of filial behavior.

In the context of the "Many Helping Hands" policy of the Singapore government, the foreign maid is also one of the "helping hands," increasingly a critical one in the face of the graying population and lack of caregivers in the family. In this way, the government also plays a role in blurring the boundary between familial and nonfamilial care roles with policies facilitating the employment of maids in the homes.

As long as the stigma attached to institutionalization continues, the foreign maid as an eldercare assistant will be a viable and desired option for Singaporean families that can afford to have one. However, for the Foreign Maid Scheme to improve and serve the needs of the family better, the government should increase support beyond levy concessions. In recent years, nongovernmental organizations and civil society groups have been formed to promote better living conditions for foreign maids in Singapore (Rahman et al., 2005). They have recommended utilization of the revenue collected from the foreign maid levy for programs and services to improve the livelihoods of foreign maids.

Situated at the intersection of familial and nonfamilial care, foreign maids should receive many of the same benefits and services as family caregivers. Hence, the state should make available respite services and other programs for caregivers to include these maids, who are quasi-family caregivers as well. As quasi–family members, maids may experience conflicts with employers and others in the family and require support in the form of counseling and other psychological and emotional guidance. As the direct caregiver for both young children as well as dependent elderly, the maid is present in every phase of the cycle of care. As the outsider to the family, her presence is ironically highly significant in ensuring care within the familial realm, although not necessarily without tensions and conflicts. Within the Singapore context, norms of filial piety are prevalent, therefore the "extra pair of hands" provided by the foreign maid helps working adult children to live up to societal expectations. In the family microcosm, the complexity of roles, functions, and caregiving arrangements highlights the visibility of boundaries in some situations while blurring the boundaries between familial and nonfamilial care in other situations.

Notes

1. The law mandates only financial support. It is optional for parents whether to activate this financial assistance. Sometimes parents may not wish to "shame" their children by activating the law.
2. Singapore's relevant legislation is as follows:

Aged Dependent Income Tax Relief is given to children or grandchildren for the maintenance of their parents or grandparents.

Grandparent Caregiver Tax Relief is where working mothers whose child is being cared for by his or her grandparents will get a Grandparent Caregiver Tax Relief of S$3,000.

The **Maintenance of Parents Act** (passed in 1995) is a preventive policy to ensure that children provide financial support for their aged parents.

The **Multi-Tier Family Housing Scheme** encourages co-residence by giving priority allocation for public housing to extended-family applications.

The **Joint Selection Scheme** encourages close-proximity living of the generations by allowing parents and married children to have priority in selecting separate public flats in the same estate.

The **Central Provident Fund (CPF) Housing Grant** is available to married first-time applicants; they will be eligible for a housing grant if they buy a resale flat from the open market near their parents' house.

3. A married woman may claim twice the amount of foreign maid levy paid for one maid against the earned income taxable. Women who are separated from their husbands, divorced, or widowed and have co-residents who are children eligible for child relief may benefit from the relief of the foreign maid levy. However, the relief does not apply to single taxpayers and male taxpayers (Singapore Government, 2004).
4. The three sources of primary data are as follows: (1) The Tan Foundation research project (TFP) focused on the needs of Singaporean seniors and their views of the government's social policies. Six focus-group discussions (FGDs) were conducted among a variety of seniors ranging from professionals to homemakers, and in-depth interviews were conducted with 10 social care agencies to gain insight into their opinions of the needs of their senior clientele. (2) The Grandparenting Project (GPP), with a qualitative component, consisted of in-depth interviews with 15 three-generational families. The latter included an interview with a member of each generation, totaling 45 interviews. In both projects questions related to the challenges of caregiving, coping strategies applied, and mix of formal and informal sources of care. (3) The Family Caregiving Project (FCP) has completed eight focus group interviews with caregivers. One of its foci is the experiences of adult children and children-in-law in relation to caring for parents and parents-in-law. These family caregivers have identified the role played by the foreign maid in the web of family-based care. In all these empirical sources of data, *care* or *caregiving* was defined gen-

erally as physical, emotional, financial, and social care. The authors attempted to draw out the "lived experiences" of the family members, ranging from the elders to the grandchildren.

Acknowledgments

The authors would like to express their gratitude to the Tan Foundation and the National University of Singapore (R-134-000-040-112; R-134-000-050-112) for providing funds to carry out the research projects.

References

Antonucci, T. C., & Jackson, A. S. (1989). Understanding adults' social relationships. In K. Kreppner and R. Lerner (Eds.), *Family systems and life-span development* (pp. 303–317). Hillsdale, NJ: Erlbaum.

Bengtson, V., Giarrusso, R., Mabry, J. B., & Silverstein, M. (2002). Solidarity, conflict, and ambivalence: Complementary or competing perspectives on intergenerational relationships? *Journal of Marriage and Family, 64*, 568–576.

Chan, A. (1997). An overview of the living arrangements and social support exchanges of older Singaporeans. *Asia-Pacific Population Journal, 12*(4), 51–68.

Graham, E., Teo, P., Yeoh, B., & Levy, S. (2003). Intergenerational relationships, fertility and the family in Singapore. Unpublished report of summary of research findings, National University of Singapore.

Grandparents, please help out. (2004, May 23). *Straits Times.*

Huang, J. R. (2002). Foreign maid as caregiver: Impact on primary caregiver-elderly relationship. Unpublished honours thesis, National University of Singapore.

Inter-Ministerial Committee on the Ageing Population. (1999). *Inter-Ministerial Committee report of the ageing population*. Singapore: Ministry of Community Development and Sports.

Mehta, K. (1999). Intergenerational exchanges: Qualitative evidence from Singapore. *Southeast Asian Journal of Social Sciences, 27*(2), 111–122.

Mehta, K., & Ko, H. (2004). Filial piety revisited in the context of modernizing Asian societies. *Geriatrics and Gerontology International, 4*, S77–S78.

Mehta, K., & Thang, L. L. (2006). Interdependence in Asian families: The Singapore case. *Journal of Intergenerational Relationships, 4*(1), 117–125.

More help for those who look after aged parents. (2006, May 15). *Straits Times.*

Morioka, K. (1996). Generational relations and their changes as they affect the status of older people in Japan. In T. K. Haraven (Ed.), *Aging and generational relations: Life-course and cross-cultural perspectives.* New York: Aldine de Gruyter.

Ofstedal, M. B., Knodel, J., & Chayovan, N. (1999). Intergenerational support and gender: A comparison of four Asian countries. *Southeast Asian Journal of Social Science, 27*(2), 21–42.

Population Aging in Asia and the Pacific. (1996). *Economic Commission for Asia and the Pacific (ESCAP) and Japanese Organization for International Co-Operation in Family Planning.* New York: United Nations.

Rahman, N. A., Yeoh, B. S. A., & Huang, S. (2005). "Dignity overdue": Transnational overseas workers in Singapore. In S. Huang, B. S. A. Yeoh, & N. A. Rahman (Eds.), *Asian women as transnational domestic workers.* Singapore: Marshall Cavendish.

Singapore Department of Statistics, Ministry of Trade and Industry. (2000). *Singapore census of population.* Singapore: Author.

Singapore Government. (2004). *Individual income tax: Relief for foreign maid levy.* Retrieved September 3, 2007, from http://www.iras.gov.sg/ESVPortal/iit/iit-se-a1.1.6.9+foreign+maid+levy.asp

Teo, P., Graham, E., Yeoh, B., & Levy, S. (2003). Values, change and intergenerational ties between two generations of women in Singapore. *Ageing and Society, 23,* 327–347.

Teo, P., Mehta, K., Thang, L. L., & Chan, A. (2006). *Ageing in Singapore: Service needs and the state.* London: Routledge.

Thang, L. L. (2000). Aging in the East: Comparative and historical reflection. In T. R, Cole, R. Kastenbaum, & R. E. Ray (Eds.), *Handbook of humanities and aging* (2nd ed.). New York: Springer.

Thang, L. L., Teo, P., Mehta, K., & Chan, A. (2003). A study of older adults in Singapore. Unpublished report, Tan Foundation, Singapore.

What Grandmas are saying no to. (2004, August 8). *Straits Times.*

Wong, D. (1996). Foreign women domestic workers in Singapore. In G. Battistella & A. Paganoni (Eds.), *Asian women in migration* (pp. 87–107). Quezon City, the Philippines: Scalabrini Migration Centre.

Yeoh, B. S. A., & Huang, S. (1999). Singapore women and foreign domestic workers: Negotiating domestic work and motherhood. In J. H. Momsen, *Gender, migration and domestic service* (pp. 277–300). London: Routledge.

Yeoh, B. S. A., & Huang, S. (2000). Home and away: Foreign domestic workers and the development of civil society in Singapore. *Women's Studies International Forum, 23*(4), 413–429.

Yeoh, B. S. A., Huang, S., & Devasahayam, T. (2004). Diasporic subjects in the nation: Foreign domestic workers, the research of the law and civil society in Singapore. *Asian Studies Review, 28*(1), 7–23.

4

Family Caregiving and Helping at the Intersection of Gender and Kinship

Social Dynamics in the Provision of Care to Older Adults in Canada

Joanie Sims-Gould, Anne Martin-Matthews, and Carolyn J. Rosenthal

> Rita is a married bank clerk, with one 21-year-old child and one grandchild. Rita provides approximately 5 hours of care per week to her 71-year-old sister-in-law, Aggie. Aggie is in fair physical and poor mental health and lives in her own home. Rita provides personal care, general care, and household care for Aggie. Rita also provides emotional support once a week and financial support two to three times a week. In addition to the care provided to Aggie, Rita also provides care to her 76-year-old mother, Edith. Edith also lives at home and is in good physical health and poor mental health. Rita helps Edith with financial support every 6 months. Andrea, Rita's sister, provides daily personal assistance to Edith, as does Mike (Rita's husband). Andrea also provides help several times a week with general care and household care, as well as daily help with emotional support. Mike helps Edith with general care every one to two months as well as household care two or three times a week. Betty, a longtime and close friend of Edith, assists with daily emotional support and weekly financial support. Rita receives help from several sources that assist her in her caregiving. She receives assistance with household chores, home and yard maintenance, moral support, and transportation from Andrea, Mike, and Edith's good friend Betty.

This vignette outlines the caregiving contributions of a primary caregiver, Rita, and the activities of other family members and friends in the care of two older relatives, Aggie and Edith. In contrast to most caregiving research that focuses on one caregiver and one care receiver, this vignette depicts the weblike structure and dynamic nature of family caregiving. It highlights multiple contributions in caregiving, both to the older person receiving care and to those involved in care provision. By providing reference to the different types of contributions and the multiple players involved in caring for older relatives, this vignette illustrates the complexity within family caregiving. It reflects the boundaries and intersections between caregiving and helping, and the competing care demands when there are multiple care recipients.

Using quantitative and verbatim data from 250 individuals with significant caregiving responsibilities, this chapter explores the complexity of family caregiving as demonstrated in the opening vignette. Through the focus on boundaries, relationships, contributions, and intersections, we consider the "network" of individuals providing assistance to an older relative(s) and extend our analysis beyond the typical focus on the caregiving dyad. We examine the relationship between the unpaid "caregiver" and other identified "helpers" in the provision of care. As well, we examine the role of gender in the networks. Our analysis is guided by three research questions: Who helps the caregiver, how do helpers help, and how do gender and kinship influence helping networks of employed caregivers?

Helpers, Caregivers, and the Influence of Gender and Kinship

Care of older adults, also described in the literature as *family caregiving, informal caregiving, informal support, eldercare,* and simply *caregiving,* is an increasingly salient component of supporting an aging population (Guberman & Maheu, 2002; Keating, Fast, Frederick, Cranswick, & Perrier, 1999; Perry, 2004). Guberman & Maheu (2002, p. 28) stated that "homecare [of older adults], as it is conceptualized in current [Canadian] social policy, would be seriously compromised without the contribution of family caregivers." It is estimated that 75–90% of care to older adults living in the community is provided by unpaid family caregivers, with the bulk of this care being provided by women (Abel & Nelson, 1990; Guberman & Maheu; Keating et al., 1999; Li, 2004; Stone, 2001).

Despite *significant* advances in family caregiving research over the past 25 years, there remain knowledge gaps (Boaz & Hu, 1997; Fast, Keating, Otfinowski, & Derksen, 2004; Keating, Otfinowski, Wenger,

Fast, & Derksen, 2003; Marshall, Matthews, & Rosenthal, 1993; Peek & Zsembik, 1997). To date, family caregiving research has largely focused on studies of the "primary" caregiver, and has emphasized the motivation and costs associated with caring for an older family member. The intent of this research "has been to describe commonalities in the caregiving process … the result has been a homogeneous portrait of caregiving provided by highly committed female individuals who are motivated by attachment and norms of filial obligation" (Pyke & Bengtson, 1996, p. 380). This focus has generated a body of research on individual caregiver stress and burden, but has done little to advance knowledge and understanding of the roles, responsibilities, and relationship dynamics when multiple family members contribute to the care of elderly kin. In contrast to the dominant research focus on the primary caregiver, little research has been conducted on the contributions of other caregivers or helpers within the family caregiving network, or how families, rather than just individual caregivers, organize to provide care to an older person.

In addition to a scarcity of material on the presence and contributions of multiple individuals in caregiving, very little is known about the intersection of gender and kinship when multiple individuals are involved in the provision of care to an older person. Gerontological research on family caregiving has highlighted many of the gender differences associated with the provision of care tasks (i.e., Aronson, 1992; Campbell & Martin-Matthews, 2003; Crocker Houde, 2002; Hequembourg & Brallier, 2005; Stoller, 1994; Walker, 2001), the balance of caregiving and paid employment (i.e., Gignac, Kelloway, & Gottlieb, 1996; Sarkisian & Gerstel, 2004), and the differential experience of stress, burden, and physical ailments associated with caregiving among men and women caregivers (i.e., Navaie-Waliser, Spriggs, & Feldman, 2002). Research has shown that women, particularly wives and adult daughters, provide assistance with more household tasks than do their male counterparts, and that men seldom provide personal care.

Caregiving and gender studies have been instrumental in creating an awareness of the extent of care provided by women, but there remains a dearth of knowledge around the different types of care and circumstances that both men and women experience (Hequembourg & Brallier, 2005; Opie, 1994; Romoren, 2003). Similarly, researchers have noted that very little is known about the collaboration of adult kin, particularly siblings, in the context of providing care to an aging parent (Connidis, 2001; Ingersoll-Dayton, Neal, Ha, & Hammer, 2003; Matthews, 2002; Matthews & Rosner, 1988). Matthews (2002, p. 5) contended that "there is very little [research] that focuses on the ways in which the family labor of meeting parents' needs is divided." As a consequence, the support that these adult children extend to one another in the context of providing care is not well understood (Connidis, Rosenthal, & McMullin, 1996).

Understanding the Multiple Contributions

Kahn and Antonucci (1981) and Cantor (1991) provided a conceptual framework to advance our understanding of multiple contributions within the context of family caregiving. Kahn and Antonucci's (1981) convoys of social support and Cantor's (1991) social care model both reject the idea of a single caregiver, suggesting that care is provided by a "convoy" or network of individuals. The models depict caregiving as a care system, comprised of multiple individuals (Antonucci, 1990; Antonucci & Akiyama, 1995; Cantor, 1991). The convoy model, with attention to social ties and social relations, conceptualizes caregiving based on contributions and relationships. It provides a framework for understanding who is involved in the provision of care and what they contribute. Although Kahn and Antonucci's convoy model and Cantor's social care model extend understandings of family caregiving beyond the caregiver–care recipient dyad, they do not include a mechanism for examining how multiple individuals assist *one another* in their work as caregivers (as in the vignette of Rita and her family).

To improve our understanding of caregiving, we extended previous social care models to *include different types of contributions.* Figure 4.1 shows the distinction between two types of contributions not previously identified in gerontological research, direct help and assistive help.

Direct help is help given to the older person by helpers (those individuals who are not the primary caregiver) and is represented by the solid black arrow. The dashed arrow highlights *assistive help* extended from helpers to the caregiver. The dotted arrow in Figure 4.1 highlights the relationship most commonly discussed in caregiving research—the care given by a primary caregiver to the older person receiving the most care, most often called *caregiving.*

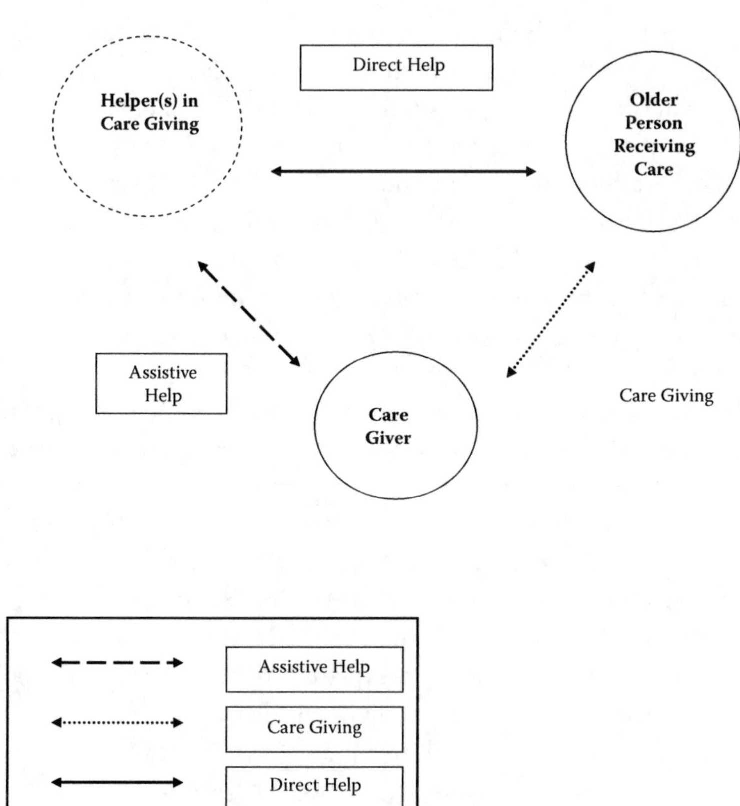

Figure 4.1 A conceptual diagram of help in caregiving.

We use the term *caregiver* to refer to individuals who helped one or more older individuals with at least one Activity of Daily Living (ADL) or two Instrumental Activities of Daily Living (IADLs) (Katz, Ford, Moskowitz, Jackson, & Jaffee, 1963). ADLs include feeding, bathing, dressing, toileting, and help with medication; and IADLs include transportation, shopping, and doing errands, laundry, household chores, meal preparation, home maintenance, and yard work.

In our model, specific attention is paid to contributions from "helpers," those individuals who provided assistance ("help") to the caregiver (assistive help) and/or directly to the older person receiving care (direct help). This extends previous work on caregiving in that it includes helpers and assistive and direct help in caregiving and provides visual representation of the relationships and contributions discussed within the context of this chapter. Drawing on the vignette in the introduction, caregiving would be conceptualized as care given to Aggie or Edith by Rita. Direct help would be the assistance provided to Edith by Andrea, Mike, and Betty, whereas assistive help would be the assistance provided to Rita by Andrea, Mike, and Betty. Most research on caregiving, in contrast, would focus solely on the performance of caregiving tasks by Rita in the care of Aggie or Edith.

In addition to examining multiple contributions in caregiving, our model also provides a mechanism for examining how gender and genealogy influence who helps whom in the context of family caregiving. Gender and kinship help explain how individuals get locked into making commitments or can be "excused" from participating in others (Finch & Mason, 1993). For example, in their study of male caregivers, Campbell and Martin-Matthews (2003) used the concept of legitimate excuses to explain how men have traditionally been "excused" from participating in family caregiving. Examining the influence of gender and kinship on contributions in caregiving contributes to an understanding of who helps whom, how they help, and whether there are gender differences in the provision of care.

Another important dimension in understanding helping and caregiving contributions by multiple individuals within a family is whether certain helping relationships take primacy over others. Cantor (1979, 1991) and Penning (1990) described a hierarchical compensatory model of social support whereby the care provided by some caregivers is preferred over others. For example, spouses and adult children (especially daughters) are more highly "ranked" in terms of their position in the social support hierarchy and are more likely to be identified as active contributors to caregiving. This premise is similar to that reported in Finch and Mason's work (1993), which also suggests that certain attributes like gender or kinship status might influence who contributes. The model shown in Figure 4.1 also allows us to examine whether certain relationships take primacy over one another in helping and caregiving.

Men and Women, Helping, and Caregiving: Who Helps and How?

Data for this research were derived from the Canadian Aging Research Network (CARNET) Work and Eldercare Study of 250 people, a follow-up study to the CARNET Work and Family Study that surveyed 5,496 employees. The Work and Eldercare Study was conducted to examine the patterns of formal service use and the frequency, type, and duration of help provided by caregivers and those who they identified as providing "help" in caring for the older adult receiving care; 250 individuals (108 men and 142 women) completed the survey questionnaire. The individuals reported on various aspects of care provision for up to three older adults; they also provided information on caregiving contributions for up to three "helpers." To determine the type and frequency of help provided by helpers, respondents were asked five different questions. In a successive series of questions, individuals were asked,

> Within the past six months, how often *has this person* (helper one, helper two, helper three) helped your older relative/friend with feeding, bathing, dressing, toileting, or taking medication (personal care)?; second, by providing transportation, doing shopping and/or errands (general care)?; third, with laundry, household chores, meal preparation, home maintenance or yard work (household care)?; fourth, with moral or emotional support (emotional support)?; and fifth, with money management, or negotiating on behalf of their older relative (financial support)?

Individuals were asked to check the appropriate response category for each question, in relation to each helper, to indicate frequency of helping with that particular type of activity (i.e., daily, several times a week, once a week, 2–3 times a month, once every 1 or 2 months, once or twice in the last 6 months, and never). To examine patterns of assistive help (the help provided to the respondent caregiver who then in turn provides help to the older relative), respondents answered the question, "In the last six months has anyone assisted *you* in helping your elderly relatives/friend in any of the following ways: household chores, childcare, financial assistance, home/yard maintenance or repair, moral/emotional support or other?" Responses were dichotomous with a "check–no check" response format; respondents were asked to check each item where they received help (household chores, childcare, financial assistance, home/yard maintenance or repair, moral/emotional support, and other).

As will be described below, the vast majority of older adults receiving care (98%) were family members. Similarly, almost all caregivers and helpers were family members. Therefore, in the analysis and discussion that follow, we use the terms *family, family caregiving*, and related terminology, rather than the more general terms *informal care, older adults*, and so on. It is also important to note that the CARNET Work and Eldercare Study focused on individuals currently employed. As such, respondent caregivers had an average age of 43 years. This average age dictates that the sample consists predominantly of adult children caregivers and not spousal caregivers. The focus of this chapter is therefore on adult children's caregiving, not on spousal caregiving, with the majority of respondents caring for a mother, mother-in-law, or father.

Table 4.1 shows select sample characteristics of respondents in the CARNET Work and Eldercare Study. As shown in Table 4.1, of the 250 individuals surveyed in the Work and Eldercare Study, 54% responded "yes" when asked if they were the person who provided the most care to their older relative or friend. These individuals were identified as primary caregivers, whereas those who responded "no" were considered to be nonprimary caregivers. A substantially higher proportion of women (59%) than men (48%) identified themselves as primary caregivers, whereas a higher proportion of men (52%) than women (41%) identified themselves as nonprimary caregivers. This emphasizes the gendered nature of family caregiving, where women are most often primary caregivers. Among this group of employees, if women are not the primary caregiver, they are identified as being the number one nonprimary caregiver. At the same time, however, it is important to note that close to half the men were, in fact, primary caregivers. Marital status also differed slightly between caregiver groups. Nonprimary caregivers and men in particular were more likely to report being married than were primary caregivers.

The frequency distribution of reporting one helper, two helpers, or three helpers differed between primary caregivers and nonprimary caregivers for both men and women. Male primary caregivers reported having only one helper with greater frequency (64%) than female primary caregivers (48%), whereas female primary caregivers reported a higher frequency of having two or more helpers than male primary caregivers. The distribution of helpers for nonprimary caregivers was similar for men and women.

TABLE 4.1 Sample Characteristics of Respondents

	Respondent Caregiver Is the Primary Caregiver (N = 135)				Respondent Caregiver Is Not the Primary Caregiver (N = 114)			
	Men (N = 51)		Women (N = 84)		Men (N = 56)		Women (N = 58)	
Average age	43	43	44	42				
	N	%	*N*	%	*N*	%	*N*	%
Marital Status								
Married	40	78	67	80	51	91	46	80
Common-law	5	10	4	5	2	4	1	2
Separated	3	6	1	1	2	4	2	3
Divorced	1	2	7	8	0	0	3	5
Widowed	0	0	0	0	0	0	2	3
Single and never married	2	4	4	5	1	2	4	7
Only Person Providing Help								
No	39	83	64	81	50	100	53	100
Yes	8	17	15	19	0	0	0	0
Number of Helpers								
One	26	63	30	48	15	33	14	27
Two	7	17	20	32	14	31	17	33
Three	8	19	13	21	16	36	20	39

Consistent with gender differences in the frequency of identifying helpers, there are also gender differences in the identification of those helpers. For example, women who identify themselves as the primary caregiver are more likely to report a sister as their number one direct helper, whereas male primary caregivers identify their spouse. This finding takes the gendered division of caring work one step further than previous research in that it reflects the predominance of groups of women in the provision of care. Not only do women form the bulk of caregivers, even when a spouse is present, but also the bulk of their support comes from their sisters.

Although women identify sisters as their "number one helper" with greater frequency than do male respondents, adult siblings figure heavily as helpers for both men and women. Indeed, the helping network almost always consists of a spouse, sibling(s), and/or sibling(s)-in-law. Both male and female caregivers indicate receiving substantial help from siblings and/or siblings-in-law.

Assistive help did not follow the same pattern. Spouses were most frequently identified as assistive helpers for women and men, with women identifying sisters with similar frequency to spouses. Daughters, sons, sisters, brothers, and other family were all listed as assistive helpers. Women (both primary and nonprimary caregivers) identified friends as assistive helpers more frequently than men.

As highlighted early on in this chapter, help can be provided both indirectly, to the primary caregiver (we refer to this as *assistive help*), and directly, to the older person. In terms of assistive support, respondents were asked if they received help that assisted them in their caregiving responsibilities. Types of assistive help included childcare, general care, household chores, home and yard maintenance, and moral support. Both men and women identified moral support as the type of support received most often. Female caregivers indicated receiving help most often with moral support, followed by household chores and home and yard maintenance. This is very similar to the type of help received by male caregivers, who indicated receiving help most often with moral support and household chores.

The types of direct help included personal care, general care, household care, emotional support, and financial support. With respect to direct help, female caregivers indicated that they provided general care and emotional support to the older person with greatest frequency. Male caregivers were most likely to report that they provided emotional support and household care with greatest frequency. The provision of personal care by a helper was the least frequent type of care identified by both male and female respondents.

As important as it is to understand what people contribute individually in caregiving by way of the performance of certain helping and caregiving tasks, a critical piece of understanding caregiving comes from examining the composition profile of family caregiving networks. In this study, most networks (35%) consist of two individuals; however, there is almost an equal distribution of networks comprising one, three, and four individuals. The vast majority of networks (87%) are composed of kin, and in most cases, one or two of these individuals are consanguineous kin (related by blood rather than marriage).

The average helping family network in this study is small, 2.4 for men and 2.5 for female respondent caregivers. However, although

TABLE 4.2 Proportion of Women in Helping Network

	Proportion of Women (%)						
Network Size	00	25	33	50	66	75	100
1.0	26 (52%)						24 (48%)
2.0	8 (9%)		1 (2%)	55 (63%)	1 (2%)		22 (25%)
3.0	1 (2%)	1 (2%)	20 (36%)		24 (43%)		10 (18%)
4.0		6 (10%)	1 (2%)	24 (42%)		22 (39%)	4 (7%)
Total	35 (14%)	7 (3%)	22 (9%)	79 (32%)	25 (10%)	22 (9%)	60 (24%)

the average size is small, 45% of the helping networks include three or four individuals.

Table 4.2 shows the size of helping and caregiving networks cross-tabulated with the proportion of women in the network. Although our findings on the identification of helpers would suggest that helping and caregiving networks are predominantly female, that is not entirely the case when network size is cross-tabulated with the proportion of women in the network. Over half the caregiving networks either are predominantly male in composition or have an equal number of male and female members. As Table 4.2 shows, close to one third (32%) of the caregiving networks have an equal number of men and women. One quarter of the networks (26%) are predominantly male (including 14% that are all male). Forty-three percent are mostly female, including 24% that are all female. The most common configuration (63%) of helping or caregiving networks is two individuals, with one woman and one man providing help.

Discussion

This chapter contributes to an overall picture of helpers and caregivers and the intersection of gender, kinship, and family composition in the organization of family care. The chapter disentangles some dimensions of helping and caregiving such as the distinction between direct and assistive help and caregiving. *Direct help* is defined as the help given by caregivers and helpers to an older person. *Assistive help* is the help given to a caregiver or helper. Consistent with research on caregiving that stresses gender differences in the provision of care to older relatives and friends (Abel & Nelson, 1990; Cicerelli, 2003; Globerman, 1994; Miller, 1996; Perry, 2004; Phillips, 2000), our findings highlight that there are gender differences in patterns of assistance among those we have called *helpers*.

In this study, the structure of caregiving networks differed by gender. Female primary caregivers have more helpers than do male primary caregivers. This may indicate that female primary caregivers are members of more highly organized care networks than are male primary caregivers. The finding that female primary caregivers most commonly named a sister as their first helper, whereas males named their spouse, reflects both the strong family bonds between women in the North American kinship system (Connidis, 2001, pp. 125, 210) and the enduring assumption of caring roles by women. The strong ties between sisters might facilitate more frequent communication or enable women to organize their own efforts and those of others in the caregiving network. Not only do women form the bulk of caregivers, even when a spouse is present, but also the bulk of their support comes from their sisters. Women also report that their daughters and sisters-in-law are assistive helpers more frequently than men. Women tend to rely on other women for assistance, whereas men rely on their spouses for help.

The results on direct help corroborate and extend Cantor's (1979) theory of hierarchical compensatory support. Cantor's (1979) theory postulates that there is a hierarchy in terms of who is preferred as a primary caregiver, secondary caregiver, and so on, and that family takes primacy over paid care. Results of our study show a similar pattern in the identification of helpers, with one additional component. The identification of helpers has a gendered dimension. Women identify sisters as direct helpers, whereas men most often identify spouses as helpers. Although gender plays a role in the selection of helpers, it is not known if there are other factors like those identified by Finch and Mason (1993) including geographical proximity, employment commitments, and family life stage that also influence the identification of helpers. The CARNET Work and Eldercare Study did not ask about the geographical proximity, employment status, or family life stage of helpers. Questions in the CARNET study focused on the identification and contributions of helpers, not on the characteristics of those helpers. The inclusion of variables outlined by Finch and Mason would further advance understanding of the nature and role of helpers in caregiving and the application of Cantor's hierarchical compensatory theory.

As stated, women identify sisters as their number one helper with greater frequency than do male caregivers; however, both women and men identify adult siblings as helpers. Both men and women indicate receiving substantial help from siblings and siblings-in-law. This finding highlights the importance of adult sibling ties in later life (Connidis, 2001; Eriksen & Gerstel, 2002; Ingersoll-Dayton et al., 2003; Matthews, 2002) and also begins to underscore some of the similarities in the provision of help for men and women. Although research on the sibling tie has predominantly focused on the socio-emotional aspects of the relationship, adult sibling ties clearly have an instrumental component. Both male and female caregivers receive instrumental help such as household help and home maintenance from siblings in the context of caregiving for an older relative. The sibling relationship, within the present examination of helpers, is clearly more complex than has been depicted in gerontological research literature. According to Ingersoll-Dayton et al. (2003, p. 52), "[M]ost research on sibling caregiving to date has emphasized the conflict that occurs among siblings … considerably less attention has been devoted to sibling cooperation." In this study, siblings play an important role in helping in the context of family caregiving through their contributions to one another and to the older person receiving care.

Although there are differences in the helping networks of women and men, there are also similarities. Both men and women receive help from helpers for a variety of tasks. Similarly, male and female respondent caregivers report comparable patterns in the frequency and type of direct help to their older relative. Acknowledging similarities between women and men, as in this study of helpers, is important as it helps to avoid the flattening of women and men "into a single dimension, ignoring their heterogeneity and seeing them as of significance only in contrast to the other gender" (Lopata, 1995, p. 116). There are similarities in both assistive and direct help reported by women and men.

Although there are similar response patterns regarding help provided and more similarities than differences in the help received by women and men, these findings must be interpreted cautiously. In her work on gender differences in caregiving, Miller (1996, p. 195) found that women and men ascribe different meanings to their caregiving contributions related to the gender role stereotypes that individuals ascribe to their contributions; this is likely also true of help. Women and men may define help differently and, as such, identify helpers and helping using these differential meanings. For example, household help or general care may mean something very different to women than men. Research has shown that women are often bound by strong norms of nurturing, whereas men have more of a managerial approach (Miller, 1996; Raschick & Ingersoll-Dayton, 2004). According to Raschick and Ingersoll-Dayton (2004, p. 321), women operate from "an internalized model of caregiving," whereas men, according to Russell (2001, p. 355), have "greater perceived control ... the ability to choose to act or not act."

Consistent with research on the size of caregiving networks, the average helping network in this study is small, 2.4 for men and 2.5 for women (Aartsen, van Tilburg, Smits, & Knipscheer, 2004; Fast et al., 2004; Piercy, 1998). However, although the average size is small, some 45% of the helping networks include three or four individuals. This average masks an important finding, with almost half of helping networks consisting of three to four individuals who are making contributions to either the caregiver or the older person.

As shown in the results, 24% of the networks are all female, whereas 14% are all male. All-male networks contain up to three individuals, whereas all-female networks contain up to four. This finding emphasizes the involvement of men in helping and contrasts with conceptions of female-dominated care. Although men may not be primary caregivers as often as their female counterparts, they are identified as helpers. Men's identification as helpers also shows that groups of men organize together to provide help and care, an activity more often attributed to groups of women. This finding emphasizes the presence of both men and women in helping.

Our data and analysis focused on the structure of caregiving networks and on the provision of direct and indirect care and help. We did not—and could not—examine the ways in which family members negotiate the division of caring labor. It will be an important task of future research to seek to understand the dynamics within caregiving networks. Neysmith and MacAdam (1999, p. 12) contended that "a person does not operate outside of relationships; nor does she or he exercise rational choice based on a calculation of self-interest … decisions are made within a web of social relations." The members of caregiving networks in our study may well be part of such a web of social relations. We may also infer that families juggle responsibilities by providing assistance to one another and through the provision of support directly to the older person. This picture of caregiving contrasts with previous conceptualizations of family caregiving, where there has been one caregiver acting alone in her caregiving. Emerging research, grounded in feminist, life course perspectives and social structural approaches, suggests that a focus on individual roles and stresses is too simplistic (Phillips, 2000); we have drawn the boundary around care too tightly, thus focusing on one primary caregiver. Clearly, this is the case with respect to caregiving research. In many cases there are multiple individuals beyond the primary caregiver involved in caregiving. Including both direct and assistive help in our analysis allows for better understanding of the complexity of family caregiving and the demands placed on multiple individuals within a family. Examining assistive and direct help also contributes, at least by inference, to a sense of the coordination and juggling involved in the provision of care to an aging family member and the multiple boundaries that exist within caregiving. These are important considerations, particularly for the development of suitable policy and programs to support family caregiving. It is not always the primary caregiver who needs support and flexibility, but also many others who are involved in supporting the primary caregiver and the older person receiving care.

Conclusions

The findings from this chapter illustrate some specific elements of helping and caregiving in the context of family caregiving. Men and women, kin and nonkin, and consanguineous and affinal relatives organize in concert to provide care to an older person in the context of family caregiving. To fully understand family caregiving, the contributions and relationships of the multiple "players" must be included beyond the caregiver–care receiver dyad.

This chapter stresses the relational nature of family caregiving. Whereas the gerontological caregiving literature tends to focus on individuals who provide direct care to an older adult, our study views caregiving as a group effort. The findings show that the "group" consists primarily of family members who organize in such a way as to provide the care that an older family member requires. In this conceptualization of care work, it is not really important whether the help goes directly to the older person or to another helper or caregiver, if all these efforts are viewed as having the common, ultimate goal of meeting the needs of the older family member.

This chapter identifies intersections and overlaps between and within helping and caregiving. The findings demonstrate the importance of not only the number of individuals involved in family caregiving or how they contribute to the care of their older relative, but also the ways in which they care for one another. Individuals contribute both directly to the older person(s) requiring care and also in an assistive manner to other helpers and caregivers. The findings in this study show that the boundaries between caregivers and helpers and between direct and assistive help are more blurred than typically portrayed in the literature. Both caregivers and helpers give direct care to the care recipient, and both receive help from other caregivers or helpers. Further, although our study focused on the receipt of assistive help by caregivers, it seems reasonable to assume that caregivers also provide assistive help, at least from time to time.

In conclusion, caregiving is a concept that includes caregiving and helping, and caregivers and helpers. As such, family caregiving is better conceptualized as a web or matrix of contributions as opposed to a single linear relationship between one caregiver and one care recipient. Elsewhere in this volume, Mahmood and Martin-Matthews (chapter 2) and also Ward-Griffin (chapter 1) emphasize family caregiving as consisting of multiple relationships and contributions. Those chapters demonstrate the relevance of issues of boundary negotiation, management, and maintenance. Future studies on caregiving and helping should examine the negotiation, management, and maintenance of relationships and contributions among multiple caregivers and helpers. The roles, contributions, and influences of the care recipient(s) must also be explored.

References

Aartsen, M. J., van Tilburg, T., Smits, C. H. M., & Knipscheer, K. C. P. M. (2004). A longitudinal study of the impact of physical and cognitive decline on the personal network in old age. *Journal of Social and Personal Relationships, 21*(2), 249–266.

Abel, E. K., & Nelson, M. K. (1990). Circle of care: An introductory essay. In E. K. Abel & M. K. Nelson (Eds.), *Circles of care: Work and identity in women's lives* (pp. 4–34). New York: State University of New York Press.

Antonucci, T. C. (1990). Social supports and social relationships. In R. H. Binstock & L. K. George (Eds.), *Handbook of aging and the social sciences* (3rd ed., pp. 205–227). San Diego, CA: Academic.

Antonucci T. C., & Akiyama, H. (1995). Convoys of social relations: Family and friendships within a life span context. In R. Bleiszner & V. H. Bedford (Eds.), *Handbook of aging and the family* (pp. 355–371). Westport, CT: Greenwood.

Aronson, J. (1992). Are we really listening? Beyond the official discourse on needs of old people. *Canadian Social Work Review, 9*(1), 73–87.

Boaz, R. F., & Hu, J. (1997). Determining the amount of help used by disabled elderly persons at home: The role of coping resources. *Journal of Gerontology: Social Sciences, 52B*(6), S317–S324.

Campbell, L. D., & Martin-Matthews, A. (2003). The gendered nature of men's filial care. *Journal of Gerontology: Social Sciences, 58B*(6), S350–S358.

Cantor, M. H. (1979). Neighbors and friends: An overlooked resource in the informal support system. *Research on Aging, 1*(4), 434–463.

Cantor, M. H. (1991). Family and community: Changing roles in an aging society. *The Gerontologist, 31*(3), 337–346.

Cicerelli, V. G. (2003). Mothers' and daughters' paternalism beliefs and caregiving decision making. *Research on Aging, 25*(1), 3–21.

Connidis, I. A. (2001). *Family ties & aging.* Thousand Oaks, CA: Sage.

Connidis, I. A., Rosenthal, C. J., & McMullin, J. A. (1996). The impact of family composition on providing help to older parents. *Research on Aging, 18*(4), 402–429.

Crocker Houde, S. (2002). Methodological issues in male caregiver research: An integrative review of the literature. *Journal of Advanced Nursing, 40*(6), 626–640.

Eriksen, S., & Gerstel, N. (2002). A labor of love or labor itself: Care work among adult brothers and sisters. *Journal of Family Issues, 23*(7), 836–856.

Fast, J., Keating, N., Otfinowski, P., & Derksen, L. (2004). Characteristics of family/friend care networks of frail seniors. *Canadian Journal on Aging, 23*(1), 5–19.

Finch, J., & Mason, J. (1993). *Negotiating family responsibilities.* London: Tavistock/Routledge.

Gignac, M., Kelloway, K. E., & Gottlieb, B. H. (1996). The impact of caregiving on employment: A mediational model of work-family conflict. *Canadian Journal on Aging, 15*(4), 525–542.

Globerman, J. (1994). Balancing tensions in families with Alzheimer's disease: The self and the family. *Journal of Aging Studies, 8*, 211–232.

Guberman, N., & Maheu, P. (2002). Conceptions of family caregivers: Implications for professional practice. *Canadian Journal on Aging, 21*(1), 27–37.

Hequembourg, A., & Brallier, S. (2005). Gendered stories of parental caregiving among siblings. *Journal of Aging Studies, 19*, 53–71.

Ingersoll-Dayton, B., Neal, M. B., Ha, J., & Hammer, L. B. (2003). Collaboration among siblings providing care for older parents. *Journal of Gerontological Social Work, 40*(3), 51–66.

Kahn, R. L., & Antonucci, T. C. (1981). Convoys of social support: A life-course approach. In J. G. March, S. B. Kiesler, J. N. Morgan, & V. K. Oppenheimer (Eds.), *Aging: Social change* (pp. 383–405). New York: Academic.

Katz, S., Ford, A. B., Moskowitz, R. W., Jackson, B. A., & Jaffee, M. W. (1963). Studies of illness in the aged. The index of ADL: A standardized measure of biological and psychological function. *Journal of the American Medical Association, 185*, 914–919.

Keating, N. C., Fast, J. E., Frederick, J., Cranswick, K., & Perrier, C. (1999). *Eldercare in Canada: Context, content, and consequences*. Ottawa: Minister of Industry, Statistics Canada.

Keating, N. C., Otfinowski, P., Wenger, C., Fast, J. E., & Derksen, L. (2003). Understanding the caring capacity of informal networks of frail seniors: A case for care networks. *Ageing & Society, 23*, 115–127.

Li, L. W. (2004). Caregiving network compositions and use of supportive services by community-dwelling dependent elders. *Journal of Gerontological Social Work, 43*(2/3), 147–164.

Lopata, H. Z. (1995). Feminist perspectives on social gerontology. In R. Blieszner & V. H. Bedford (Eds.), *Handbook of aging and the family*. Westport, CT: Greenwood.

Marshall, V. W., Matthews, S. H., & Rosenthal, C. J. (1993). Elusiveness of family life: A challenge for the sociology of aging. In G. L. Maddox & M. Powell Lawton (Eds.), *Annual review of gerontology and geriatrics: Focus on kinship, aging, and social change* (pp. 39–72). New York: Springer.

Matthews, S. (2002). *Sisters and brothers/daughters and sons: Meeting the needs of old parents*. Bloomington, IN: Unlimited Publishing.

Matthews, S., & Rosner, T. T. (1988). Shared filial responsibility: The family as the primary caregiver. *Journal of Marriage and the Family, 50*, 185–195.

Miller, B. (1996). Beyond gender stereotypes: Spouse caregivers of persons with dementia. *Journal of Aging Studies, 10*(3), 189–205.

Navaie-Waliser, M., Spriggs, A., & Feldman, P. H. (2002). Informal caregiving: Differential experiences by gender. *Medical Care, 40*(12), 1249–1259.

Neysmith, S. M., & MacAdam, M. (1999). Controversial concepts. In S. M. Neysmith (Ed.), *Critical issues for future social work practice with aging persons* (pp. 1–26). New York: Columbia University Press.

Opie, A. (1994). The instability of the caring body: Gender and caregivers of confused older people. *Qualitative Health Research, 4*(1), 31–51.

Peek, C. W., & Zsembik, B. A. (1997). The changing caregiving networks of older adults. *Research on Aging, 19*(3), 333–362.

Penning, M. J. (1990). Receipt of assistance by elderly people: Hierarchical selection and task specificity. *The Gerontologist, 30*(2), 220–228.

Perry, J. (2004). Daughters giving care to mothers who have dementia: Mastering the 3 R's of (re)calling, (re)learning, and (re)adjusting. *Journal of Family Nursing, 10*(1), 50–70.

Phillips, J. (2000). Working carers: Caring workers. In M. Bernard, J. Phillips, L. Machin, & V. Harding Davies (Eds.), *Women ageing: Changing identities, challenging myths* (pp. 40–57). London: Routledge.

Piercy, K. W. (1998). Theorizing about family caregiving: The role of responsibility. *Journal of Marriage & Family, 60,* 109–118.

Pyke, K. D., & Bengtson, V. L. (1996). Caring more or less: Individualistic and collectivist systems. *Journal of Marriage & Family, 58*(2), 379–383.

Raschick, M., & Ingersoll-Dayton, B. (2004). The costs and rewards of caregiving among spouses and adult children. *Family Relations, 53*(3), 317–325.

Romoren, T. I. (2003). The carer careers of son and daughter primary carers of their very old parents in Norway. *Ageing & Society, 23,* 471–485.

Russell, R. (2001). In sickness and in health: A qualitative study of elderly men who care for wives with dementia. *Journal of Aging Studies, 15*(4), 351–367.

Sarkisian, N., & Gerstel, N. (2004). Explaining the gap in help to parents: The importance of employment. *Journal of Marriage and Family, 66*(2), 431–451.

Stoller, E. P. (1994). Teaching about gender: The experience of family care of frail elderly relatives. *Educational Gerontology, 20*(7), 679–697.

Stone, R. I. (2001). Home and community based care: Toward a caring paradigm. In L. E. Cluff & R. H. Binstock (Eds.), *The lost art of caring: A challenge for health professionals, families, communities, and society* (pp. 155–176). Baltimore: Johns Hopkins University Press.

Walker, A. (2001). Conceptual perspectives on gender and family caregiving. In J. W. Dwyer & R. T. Coward (Eds.), *Gender, families and elder care* (pp. 34–48). Thousand Oaks, CA: Sage.

5

Work and Care

Blurring the Boundaries of Space, Place, Time, and Distance

Judith E. Phillips and Miriam Bernard

Brenda Clark is in her late thirties and works full-time as a clinical psychologist. She moved to her current post because it offered the prospect of promotion, and she has been with her present employer for about 2 years. At the time of this interview, she was still on maternity leave after the birth of her first child and was hoping to go back part-time.

Brenda lives with her husband in a small village in a remote rural area, traveling for over an hour each way to get to work. Since her mother died 5 years ago, she has been caring for her father, who lives on his own, another hour's drive away in the opposite direction: "It is quite hard to do the drive [home from work] and then drive up to [Dad]." However, despite the multiple demands on her time and energy, she visits him weekly, and is in daily telephone contact. Her older brother lives near her father and does a lot of the care, including a weekly shop, being the one "on call," and showering him; Brenda comments, "I have got the sort of easiest job I suppose—my brother has got most of the job."

After her mother's death, her father suffered a heart attack and was very ill: "[H]e was given months to live then, but he is still here." Talking about this time, she says, "I had a strong feeling that I wanted to go and live [there,] but my husband said it was a bit silly: We couldn't give up our lives to look after my dad." This means that the nature of what Brenda does for him has changed: Originally, it was a lot of emotional and psychological support—"that's being part of a professional breed." More recently, it has involved consulting with other professionals to organize various services, including a rota of carers ("it's a big part of his social life[,] the home helps"); getting him Disability Living Allowance, a pendant alarm, a scooter, and a wheelchair; and moving him into a new flat. She feels that being on maternity leave has in fact made the practicalities of visiting regularly easier. She and her husband also take him away on holiday.

At her former place of work, her manager was very understanding and supportive when her mother died: "[H]e looked after me totally.... I just sort of came to a full stop, so he took over, which was very caring of him." However, in her current post she says this about workload pressures and the organizational culture:

> I didn't tell my boss for a year that my dad was as ill as he was.... I got more close to my colleagues than my boss. It is more of a judgment telling your boss. I also wanted a promotion, so I didn't want to look as if I'd overloaded myself in other directions and wouldn't be there. I even got the promotion before I told her I was pregnant.

Brenda sees herself maintaining the caring role she has for her father, and her advice for other carers would be as follows: "It's a bit like with a baby: Never turn anybody down who wants to help ... include them and work as a team.... I think everybody is better off that way."

Introduction

The "spatial contexts" in which care is provided have become an important topic of concern for the many families juggling work with caring responsibilities. The growing body of caregiving literature has traditionally either focused on co-resident care or looked at proximity of caregiver and receiver based on home location (Hoff, 2006; Lewis & Meredith, 1988; Townsend, 1957). Yet, as more families juggle work and care, and often have to commute in different directions to do so, the spatial dimensions of caregiving and work locations are increasingly complex issues to be considered. Moreover, the influence of modern telecommunications challenges the extent to which geographical proximity remains important in relation to contact, caregiving, and care receiving. Nowadays, it could be argued that political, cultural, and social boundaries can all be transcended to provide care. However, what is also evident from the literature is that the spatial nature of caregiving has been underconceptualized (Milligan, 2003). Boundaries have conventionally been drawn between private-domestic and informal spaces inhabited primarily by women, and public-market and formal spatial domains. However, a blurring of the boundaries between these dichotomous spaces (as illustrated in chapter 2 by Mahmood and Martin-Matthews) has increasingly occurred, challenging in its wake our conceptualizations of care.

Our central argument in this chapter is that despite global trends and technological advancements, geography remains important: Distance, space, and time still exert boundaries on what people both can and are able to do—often leading to distinctive forms of caring being provided at particular distances from home and work. However, we go on to show that in the daily realities of working and caring, boundaries are, more often than not, considerably blurred. This further suggests to us that we perhaps need to develop a rather more nuanced understanding, both conceptually and empirically, of how distance, space, and time are experienced by working carers in the context of the changing global and local geographies of the 21st century.

In order to make this argument, we draw on two distinct but overlapping bodies of knowledge: one from geography, and the other from sociology. The chapter addresses boundaries—blurred or otherwise—in terms of those key geographical concepts of space, place, distance, proximity, and time. We consider how these terms are defined in the geographical literature and how they have been operationalized in empirical work. This is followed by an examination of existing research on working and caring in which we specifically focus on distance considerations. In this examination, we draw on one of the first empirical British studies to specifically explore the experiences of working carers of older adults (Phillips et al., 2002), relating our findings to those from other studies. As we will show below, distance (and its associated concepts of space, place, proximity, and time) is still a key consideration for many working carers whether it is experienced and accommodated literally, emotionally, or both.

Juggling Work and Care: The Experiences of Working Carers of Older Adults

The study we draw upon was a mixed-method, five-phase study that took place in England over a 2-year period between 2000 and 2002. It was conducted in two public sector organizations: a Social Services Department (SSD) and a National Health Service (NHS) Trust. These organizations were selected because we were particularly interested in looking at the experiences of carers who were caring in a professional, as well as an informal, capacity. Both the NHS Trust and SSD serve a mixed urban and rural population, and although not coterminous, they share some geographical areas.

Both organizations had approximately 5,000 employees each, ranging from highly paid professionals, such as consultants, to poorly paid cleaners. Women outnumbered men in both organizations by 4:1, with men often taking on more of the managerial and senior positions. With 55% of staff over the age of 40 in the NHS Trust and 64% in this age group in the SSD, there was clearly the "structural potential" (Martin-Matthews & Rosenthal, 1993) for eldercare to be a concern for both employers and employees. Both organizations also had a predominantly white workforce (at least 97% white).

In order to define and identify carers, the 2001 UK Census question was used as one element of a screening questionnaire sent to all employees. The question is framed in this way:

> Do you look after or give any help or support to family members, friends, neighbours or others because of long-term physical or mental-ill health or disability, or problems related to old age?

Workers were requested not to count anything they did as part of their paid employment, and were asked to specify how many hours a week they spent caring (3 or less, 4–9 hours, 10–19 hours, 20–49 hours, or 50 or more hours). Following on from this, more extensive quantitative data were obtained from those workers who identified themselves as carers of older adults (60 or more years old) and who completed a lengthier questionnaire (n = 204). This questionnaire drew extensively on the previous work of colleagues in North America, notably the Canadian Ageing Research Network (CARNET) study (Martin-Matthews & Rosenthal, 1993) and Neal, Chapman, Ingersoll-Dayton, and Emlen (1993), and asked about the nature of the care they give, the work they do, and the juggling that ensues. In addition, we selected 48 of these carers to be interviewed, chosen to ensure a spread of gender, job type, and hours, as well as the distance they lived from their care recipient. All carers who lived at least 60 minutes away from the person they were caring for were selected to be interviewed, as were a number of former carers (for further details on method and analysis, see Phillips, Bernard, & Chittenden, 2002). However, before considering the findings of this study and how they relate to other social scientific literature on working and caring, we turn first to a consideration of what the geographical literature says about the concepts of space, place, time, and distance.

Space, Place, Time, and Distance: Boundaried or Blurred?

In conventional geographical definitions, *spaces* are usually organized into *places* and are often thought of as bounded settings (for example, bounded by topography, state, or political boundaries) in which social relations and identities are constituted (Massey, 1994; Tuan, 1977). Place therefore is significant in terms of social interactions, in forming social relationships, in shaping behaviors, and because of the meanings attached to them in caring, as in many other contexts. Related notions of distance and proximity have also been fundamental to the extent to which social relationships can play out in such geographically bounded places. During the latter half of the 20th century, considerable work was undertaken looking at aspects of space and place, in particular at sense of and attachment to place (Scharf, Phillipson, Smith, & Kingston, 2002); at meanings, identities, and memories associated with places and spaces (Peace, Holland, & Kellaher, 2006; Rowles, 1978); and at placelessness (Augé, 1995).

Historically speaking, the 1970s was also a period when space and place began to be linked with *time* in the geographical literature. "Space-time geography" was articulated most clearly in the writings of Torstein Hagerstrand (1967), who conceived of space as locational (i.e., space that can be surveyed and measured) and "external" (to the individual). He depicted individual biographies as paths in space and time. In Hagerstrand's conceptualization, transactions required, for the most part, nearness in space, and movement was allowed to take only a limited amount of time. Time, as well as space, therefore imposed boundaries on human behavior. A key critique of this work was that although it rendered space transparent, unproblematic, and fully knowable, it was, almost inevitably, environmentally deterministic (Agnew, Livingstone, & Rogers, 1996; Gregory & Urry, 1985). Human agency, and the possibilities of its interaction with structures, was missing from this conceptualization.

By way of contrast, Gould and White (1986) and Graham Rowles (1978) both developed work on mental maps. In these conceptualizations, space was considered to be experiential and "inside." More recent work from feminist and postmodern geographers (Harvey,

1990; Massey, 1994) again combines space and time, regards them both as experiential and locational, and requires us to conceive of them in more flexible and relational ways.

Thus, our understanding of the importance of these concepts has moved from thinking of them as "fixed" geographical entities to seeing them as more flexible networks of social relations and, by implication, to understanding the notion of space and place as flexible locales for care. Places can be sites where complex social relationships are played out in relation to care, work, home, and wider social relationships.

Globalization has further challenged the significance of place and, by implication, *distance.* Time–space distanciation, meaning the stretching of social systems across time and space, has resulted in interaction with people who are in fact absent in time or space (Giddens, 1990). Moreover, with the introduction of mobile technology, geographical proximity may no longer be the overriding factor in contact and support (Ley & Waters, 2004). It can be argued that globalization in this sense has compressed space and time, along with distance (Massey, 1995), and challenged and dissolved "old boundaries" (Denis & Sev'er, 2003).

Measuring Distance

If space, place, and time are fluid and changing concepts, then one of the associated and perennial difficulties we still face is the question of how to measure and boundary distance—in travel time or spatial proximity? Perceptions of time and space, along with mode of transport, will influence distance, and our perceptions of distance also change as our lifestyles change and, for example, we commute longer distances to work (Green, Hogarth, & Shackleton, 1999). In terms of our concern here with working and caring, what Rosenmayr and Kockeis (1963) tellingly termed "intimacy at a distance" is also highly relevant, as is Mason's (1999) notion of "distance thinkers": people who reason that it is possible to conduct kin relations at a distance. People who see geographical distance as compatible with the development of meaningful relationships blur both literal and emotional distance. Such blurring may, however, be challenged if caring for parents at a distance becomes necessary. A further factor that is also of significance is the extent to which the caregiver is familiar with the community surrounding the care recipient: If it is the parental home where the caregiver grew up, then he or she may still know and have established contacts. Even if there are great distances involved in the care-giving relationship, then the actual place may be perceived by the caregiver as "emotionally near."

The difficulty of operationalizing distance is exacerbated by the fact that distance measurements and thresholds differ between research studies. Some studies take "travel time" as the measurement (De Jong, Wilmoth, Angel, & Cornwell, 1995; Joseph & Hallman, 1996; Wagner, 2003), whereas others look at distance in terms of spatial measurements—miles or kilometers (Szinovacz & Davey, 2001). For example, Mercier, Paulson, and Morris (1989) defined *proximate children* as those living within 60 miles. In another study, Parker, Call, and Kosberg (2001) found that distance has a substantial negative impact on personal contact with parents, particularly for distances greater than 100 miles. Living in a different country also imposes different constraints on, and expectations for, care and contact. Although this will undoubtedly affect "hands-on" support, modern technology now permits us, should we wish, to be in regular contact through long-distance phone calls, webcams, and the like.

Like space and place, then, distance need no longer be considered as simply a boundaried and linear function determining access or not to people we care for or who care for us. Distance becomes blurred with, and affected by, other related characteristics such as the location of the destinations, personal time budgets for travel, travel velocities of particular transport systems, and so on. As the geographer Derek Gregory argued,

> [S]ocial life does possess a geometry but we have to go beyond looking at the straight lines of distance across flat plains between point A and B, and consider distance more in terms of it being "along difficult and hilly tracks." (Quoted in Crang & Thrift, 2000, p. 227)

Not surprisingly, this has made the task of operationalizing distance in empirical studies notoriously difficult and inconsistent, as we show below.

Geographies of Caring and Working

We turn now to a more detailed examination of the existing literature on working and caring, but an examination in which we specifically focus on distance considerations. It is important to preface this by observing that considerable work that has been done to date has implicitly, rather than explicitly, addressed the geographical dimensions with which we are concerned here. Although there are some studies that have been conducted from a geographical perspective (Joseph & Hallman, 1996; Wagner, 2003), the bulk of research on working and caring has come from a predominantly sociological and/or social policy standpoint.

In order to structure this discussion, we look first at changing notions of distance as reflected in ideas about proximity and the distances at which people now live, including long distances and international distances. Second, we consider distance in terms of distance thresholds and distance decay, looking at what people do and do not do at varying distances, and how distinctions between literal and emotional distance are evident. Third, we highlight how new understandings of distance are being constructed and reconstructed through the use of modern technologies and what impacts this has on carers. Finally, we discuss how distance considerations are accommodated and interwoven into the lives of working carers, showing something of the complex negotiations and dilemmas that go into making these difficult decisions.

Proximity and Distance: Toward a Blurring of Boundaries?

In considering the literature on caring, we would argue that notions of distance and proximity have always provided connections between spaces and places, even where there was no overt geographical perspective. For example, early studies on caregiving in the context of family life focused on contact and care, and looked at residential proximity in terms of children living with older parent(s) or at those who could provide daily care because of living in close proximity. The classic British studies on the family life of older people (Sheldon, 1948; Townsend, 1957; Young & Willmott, 1957) showed how proximity played a vital part in the provision of care, both emotionally and practically. Households containing older people were often complex and often multigenerational. Intergenerational reciprocity of care occurred on a daily basis, and older people were surrounded by others with whom they had close and supportive relationships—both within and beyond their own households. They lived essentially within what Frankenburg (1966) termed "an environment of kin," and the more intimate the care, the more bounded were the places and spaces in which that care was transacted. These studies also showed that the heaviest care fell to those who were co-resident or living nearby.

With greater geographical dispersion being more of a feature of family life, children (as well as other relatives) are now much more likely to maintain separate households than they did 40 years or more ago. Indeed, our study (Phillipson, Bernard, Phillips, & Ogg, 2001) of the family life of older people conducted in the same geographical areas as those of Townsend (1957), Young and Willmott (1957), and Sheldon (1948) found that older people today have, at most, only one child close by (within 4 miles). Moreover, caring at a distance has become an important issue for many geographically mobile families, for whom cross-national and international migration is commonplace. However, as we show below, longer distances of necessity tend to change the kind of care that can be offered. In one sense, then, distance very much imposes boundaries on care—at least on the practical and intimate tasks that might need to be performed. On the other hand, distance has become blurred and compressed by the advent of modern technologies that enable emotional, if not practical, support to be given in ways not accessible to previous generations of carers.

Distance and the Doing of Care

The provision of "hands-on" care clearly remains a task constrained by distance, and research has consistently found that distance thresholds operate (see chapter 5 by Neal, Wagner, Bonn, and Niles-Yokum). In our study, we examined distance decay effects using four travel time categories: 1 to 30 minutes, 31 to 60 minutes; 61 to 120 minutes, and over 120 minutes. As in other research, a distance decay effect operated, with far fewer carers providing care at distances over 30 minutes of traveling time away. Indeed, only 28 people (15%) in our sample provide care over 30 minutes of traveling time away.

These findings might be somewhat surprising to an international readership, but what has to be borne in mind here is that, unlike in Canadian and U.S. work (Keating, in press; Wolf & Longino, 2005), small distances were perceived somewhat differently by our British respondents. What might seem to be relatively "close" locations (e.g., 20 miles or less) were often viewed as a long way, even if traveling by car. The nature of the environments in which our respondents lived and worked also meant that it might often take a fairly long time to travel even short distances. Thus, the first two time categories translate into fairly short geographic distances and typically reflect trips that may be undertaken frequently and are often fitted around work. However, there is no clear link at the "shorter" time thresholds between distance and the nature of the tasks undertaken.

Euan Freeman, for example, is 58 years old, spent most of his working life as a social worker, and, at the time of the interview, had been working half-time for the previous 2 years. He is closely involved in the care of his parents-in-law, who live within walking distance. They are both in their eighties, and they both suffer with arthritis and memory problems. Euan finds that working part-time means he is able to schedule taking his in-laws to hospital appointments when he has his days off, and he also helps them with gardening and DIY activities. In the interview, Euan described undertaking predominantly practical rather than intimate tasks, and this was common amongst our sample of working carers, irrespective of distance: They were far more likely to assist with instrumental activities such as meal preparation, shopping, and gardening than with personal care such as bathing.

The third time category in our study (61 to 120 minutes) involves longer trips, some of which may be taken daily, or on certain days or over a weekend. Here, Cheryl Davidson, a full-time manager of a social services daycare unit for older people, describes how the time taken to undertake the daily care of her 81-year-old mother-in-law adds up:

> I need to be in work at 8 in a morning and I finish about 5. I was going from [home] to [my mother-in-law's] in a morning to get her washed and changed.... I was going back after work ... it is an hour's journey from here [work] to her house and then another hour back home. So, it was adding another six hours on to my working day.

The final time category in our study encompasses long-distance trips that were not usually possible in a day and that meant that carers like Brian Cawthorne were living lives almost completely circumscribed by distance and time:

> Once every 4 weeks I was going down to spend a weekend or a long weekend. While I was working [based 3–4 hours away from home and 40 minutes away from his mother,] it was very difficult to manage.... So 3 nights a week and every other weekend I would go down to the South Coast; because the other weekend I'd come up here to my wife. I took on an awful lot then. I was working all the time and then also trying to go down and spend time with Mum and it got me down.

Other research shows that there is no simple association between long distances and the amount of care that is available. Warnes (1992), for example, demonstrated that living over a particular threshold (150 kilometers) does not in fact mean that there will be greater provision of support than is provided by those living 1,500 kilometers away. However, what other research does show is that as distance increases, substitution of contact types occurs, and family is increasingly substituted for friends at longer distances (Dewit, Wister, & Burch, 1988; Keeling, 2001). Moreover, where longer distances are involved, Ley and Waters (2004) have argued that what they describe as "spatial stickiness" operates. In other words, a distance decay function comes into play—the longer the distance, the less likely people are to provide care. They use as illustration what they term "astronaut" families. These are family members who relocate their families to Vancouver, Canada, yet conduct their business from Taiwan and commute across the Pacific Ocean. This in turn has fundamental implications for family relationships, as older members transported to Canada may be left isolated and away from their "home." Ley and Waters suggested that there is a geographical imperative continuing to reward spatial proximity over separation when it comes to family care and the sustainability of relationships.

There is now substantial evidence that distance from the care recipient influences the decision about who becomes the primary carer (Phillipson et al., 2001). In our study, too, proximity also played a part in that some carers had simply been the geographically nearest person at the time informal care was required. However, what also came through was how difficult it is, in many instances, to be categorical about who is, or is not, the "main" carer. For some people, this was patently clear—particularly if they were "the *only* daughter or son"—but for others, the distinction between "main" carer and others is, more often than not, very hazy. Indeed, our data indicate that only in 44% of care situations did carers identify themselves as the primary carer.

Distance, then, affects the "doing of care" in different ways and is in turn linked with, and itself affected by, a whole host of other factors such as whether one is working full- or part-time, whether one has siblings or not, and what one's family and work situations are like. Distance not only has literal connotations involving physical journeys by car and airplane, but also has emotional aspects that add further layers and meanings to our understanding of distance and its effects on work and care.

New Understandings of Distance

Although, as we noted at the start of this chapter, many aspects of our daily lives have undergone rapid change, studies still show that older people remain crucial to family life and that children tend to maintain regular contact (weekly or more; Phillipson et al., 2001). However, this is principally through the automobile and the telephone rather than through daily, face-to-face encounters. In our study, too, these were of prime importance for those who were trying hard to juggle the demands of both working and caring. The provision of emotional support and monitoring can, to some extent, be conducted over the telephone and differs markedly from the provision of physical instrumental care (Parker et al., 2001). Having access to a telephone at work to keep in touch with the person being cared for has been shown in earlier studies of working and caring to be very helpful for carers (Baldock, 2000; Phillips, 1995; Watson & Mears, 1999). This was reiterated in our study, too, but, with the current widespread use of mobile phones, it did not assume the importance it has in previous research.

Telephones were used by our carers in a variety of ways, from making simple practical arrangements with relatives who were close by, to transcending long distances and providing emotional support if face-to-face contact was difficult. Cheryl Davidson clearly illustrates the former use when she tells us, "We shop for her [mother-in-law]; she rings every week with her shopping list." By contrast, Ursula Vine describes how she uses the phone to provide emotional support at a distance:

> We talked on the phone. We talked on the phone quite a bit ... and probably that was harder than anything else: the constant distressing telephone

> calls when she was unwell. And we'd just listen, encourage and she'd cry. So that was quite tough, and there'd be at least one a week, at least.

Although the advent of the mobile phone (and other advances like e-mail and webcams) is an obvious boon in many instances, there is another side to this story that highlights what we term the *tyranny of the telephone*, and where it is clearly a major instrument in blurring the boundaries of care and what can or cannot legitimately be expected of working carers. Patricia Quinn, a full-time social worker caring, with her husband, for her alcoholic mother-in-law, vividly describes how problematic being accessible by phone can be when one is trying to juggle work with caring:

> I have lots of calls from her [mother-in-law] … if she can't get hold of her son, she's ringing me and she'll leave me a message every five minutes … bad days for her mean bad days for me. You end up switching the [mobile] phone off because I haven't given her my work's number because that would put extra pressure on [me].… She might ring me up to give me abuse because she's not happy because I haven't done something she wanted straight away. And another minute she'll ring me up and tell me how wonderful I am.

Although an inability to visit regularly may itself create conflict and guilt for some carers (Baldock, 2000), others like Patricia Quinn find that the current facility for being in almost constant contact via the telephone (and other technologies) may generate new and different kinds of anxieties and stress for working carers.

If caring, and the distances one has to travel to undertake it, undoubtedly generates anxiety and stress, then adding the additional dimension of paid employment away from home complicates the picture further. Crucially, distance has been shown to be predictive of difficulties in balancing work and care (Wagner, 2003). The impacts this has on people's lives have been clearly shown in Joseph and Hallman's research (1996), which investigated the spatial arrangement between the employed caregiver's home, his or her workplace, and the care recipient's home. They termed this spatial arrangement the "locational triangle" and found that it impacted in different ways. For instance, travel time to work impinged largely on the work side of work–family balance, whereas travel time to the older person impinged more on the family side. In other words, leisure time spent with immediate household members was sacrificed rather than work time to attend to older relatives. Family interference with employment was also greater for those with dual responsibilities (children and parents who needed care), and, in terms of adjustments that needed to be made, it was the home–eldercare axis, rather than the home–work axis, which was most amenable to change. In its most extreme cases, living at a distance from the care recipient, especially if very distant, can have severe impacts on work as days, and even weeks (for international travel), may have to be taken from work.

The implication here is that distance (and long distances in particular) has largely negative connotations when it comes to considerations of care and support: It is an undesired barrier to care. Yet, distance may in fact provide what Finch and Mason (1993) and others (Campbell & Martin-Matthews, 2000) called a "legitimate excuse" not to provide care, and, in this sense, long distance could be framed in a more positive light. By contrast, another interesting aspect of distance in our study is where proximity "allows" other family members to effectively devolve responsibility for care and support to the nearest family member. As we know from other studies, the nearest person is, more often than not, a daughter, and this is borne out in the present study too.

Karen Lamont, for instance, is a part-time district nurse, and has looked after her 72-year-old mother since her dad died of cancer some 5 years previously. Although she is the second oldest of four sisters, she is the one who lives nearest (a 10-minute drive away) and who sees her mother at least twice a week. Two of her sisters live in East Anglia and Yorkshire (over 200 miles away), whereas her youngest sister is about 10 miles away. Karen sees her mother at least twice a week, and although she describes her mum as "an active lady," Karen does a lot of "the heavy things," such as major shopping, hedge cutting, and lawn mowing. She also takes her mum to her hospital appointments, where they monitor her angina. However, even though her sisters live away, Karen was adamant "that if anything happened, they'd be there like a shot." Her situation clearly illustrates how distance can also create a certain amount of ambivalence in relationships (Connidis & McMullin, 2002). On the one hand, there was a willingness to help her mother, but on the other hand, she felt some resentment that she was the only one available to care. She also felt she was caught between the demands of employment and caregiving. Just as Ward-Griffin described in chapter 1, many of our study participants were "professionals" as well as informal carers, and this sometimes meant that other family members would absolve themselves of any responsibility because there was someone in the family whose "job" it was. Interestingly, such expertise might even override distance considerations, as in the case of Patricia Quinn. Patricia was a full-time residential social worker, and spoke passionately about the attitudes of her family and the care she provides for her own parents, who live nearby, and especially for her mother-in-law, who lives a very long distance away near Bristol (at least a 3-hour drive):

> I've got a mother-in-law that's 87.... She's from a big family, there's six of them [but] we do the caring.... Have I got brothers and sisters? Yes. Has my husband? Yes. Do we share the caring responsibilities with anyone else? No.... They [her sister-in-law and husband] took my mother and father-in-law ... to [near Bristol] because she lives round the corner, to care for them, but they don't ... she's not a carer. I mean, she does what she can but ... I've got one brother and he actually lives at home. I think he would do a lot more but like most men you have to ask and, like most people, my parents are very proud and they won't ask.... I would love for one of the people in the family to take responsibility. It would be lovely not to have to do it, but it doesn't happen.

Adjusting to Distance

One further and essential element in contemporary understandings of distance as it affects working and caring is that families have a history, as well as a geography, over time. Different periods in the life course may require relocation depending on the individual's circumstances, and caring necessarily alters in response to certain events such as the birth of a child or declining health of an older person. For an older individual in need of care and support, the physical environment may increasingly become inappropriate and may require a change in place and a readjustment of space (Lawton, 1980). However, this does not usually happen in isolation, and it is important in our considerations of working and caring that we look at the family care-giving trajectory and at the adjustments that are made to accommodate different members over time (Wagner, 2003; Warnes, 1992). All such considerations are affected by both history and geography or what McKie, Gregory, and Bowlby (2002) evocatively described as *caringscapes*: the time–space frameworks in which care is carried out through the life course.

In caring for older people, carers often have to make difficult and complex distance-related decisions. In the United Kingdom, Green and Canny (2003), for example, found that job relocation would often impact significantly, and negatively, on care for older adults. Our carers too were deciding between, for example, whether to have a longer commute to work or a longer-distance commute to care; whether to relocate to be nearer the parent or older person, or whether to relocate a parent or older person to one's own home; whether to move the parent or older person to residential care nearer one's own home or that of a sibling; or whether to rely on other, more proximate family members to provide support (Phillips et al., 2002). Brenda Clark (our case study at the start of this chapter) told us that although she is currently able to manage the distance and traveling to care for her father, she and her husband anticipate that either their own, or her father's, circumstances might change in the future, and that long distance may then become more of a problem. Other carers in our study were investigating long-term care and urging a friend or relative in need of care to move nearer to them. However, this did not always translate into practice, as Brian Cawthorne recalls:

> At one point I did try and get her [his mother, who lived on the South Coast] to move up to Stone near us … and she just didn't want to because she's got the church, she's got her friends, the family, her brothers … she said no emphatically: she won't move.

We can set these longer-term considerations against other more immediate ways in which some of the carers in our study tried to accommodate distance. One notable feature of our study was the number of carers who opted to use holiday time to fulfill their caring duties, even when other options were available like carer's leave. Here, too, there were distance decay effects operating in that, with longer distances and increased travel time, more people were likely to make use of holiday time. This is yet another example of how accommodations to the distances involved in working and caring are made on the home–eldercare axis, not on the work–home or work–eldercare axes (Martin-Matthews & Keefe, 1995).

Finally, women in particular seemed to deny distance, and were prepared to travel extensively in order to meet the care needs of older adult relatives (see also Lee, Dwyer, & Coward, 1990). The experience of Naomi Ormrod reflects this. She is a part-time community care worker who vividly recalls the time when her mother, who lived over 2 hours away in North Wales, was taken ill:

> At the time … I was based [in the south of the county], I lived [10 miles away] then with my husband, and I used to go to work and finish work at

> about 10.30am, whiz off up there, look after her and come back about 9, 10 o'clock at night, go to work the next morning.... Get up about 5.30: uniform for school; one off to work; sandwiches for school; make sure that if it was football the kit was washed and ready; everybody's sandwiches; general wash up and tidy up before I went to work. If I knew she wanted anything I picked it up on my way. The car was always full of petrol, I just had a morbid fear of conking out somewhere in the middle of nowhere.... I don't even remember some of the journeys and that is frightening. I have sometimes turned up at that house, on the drive, not even thinking I've left ten minutes ago and that is frightening you know.

Naomi spoke about this period in her life, and particularly the last 6 weeks leading up to her mother's death, as just something she had to do: almost as if distance did not come into the equation.

Conclusion

This consideration of the spatial elements of working and caring leads us to conclude the following: First, the geographies of caring and working have become increasingly complex. However, although our notions of space, place, time, and distance have developed from clearly boundaried concepts to ones that more appropriately blur the boundaries, they fail, as yet, to adequately capture the nuances we see and experience. Second, in the context of working and caring, we argue that distance is not just a matter of geography and the separation of physical space: It is also a psychological separation that poses challenges and ambivalences that can be liberating as well as constraining for working carers. Indeed, juggling work and home life in both private and public spheres of home and workplace can be liberating and enable women to be mobile and have multiple identities as worker, mother, child, and so on. Blurring the boundaries in this context can be seen as positive. Third, globalization and technological advancements are rapidly changing the contexts in which we both work and care. They will go on doing so into the foreseeable future. Instead of negating the importance of geography, issues of space, place, time, and distance are if anything even more important and will continue to shape and fashion what people both can and are able to do. Fourth, if we are to develop a more nuanced conceptualization in a globalized context, we must not ignore the fact that both working and caring are life course activities: They have individual and family trajectories over time that will influence both family relationships and the nature and forms of care and support that can be provided with and for older people.

Yet, despite the flexibility of boundaries, some barriers still remain. In the workplace, for example, the introduction of flexible working patterns has still led to people setting aside their holiday time for caregiving. Topography also constrains movement, and access to services is still difficult in rural areas (Keating, in press). Space and time also constrain people (it is impossible to be in two places at once), creating boundaries as to what is possible in relation to care.

References

Agnew, J., Livingstone, D., & Rogers, A. (1996). *Human geography.* Oxford: Blackwell.

Augé, M. (1995). *Introduction to an anthropology of supermodernity.* London: Verso.

Baldock, C. V. (2000). Migrants and their parents: Caregiving from a distance. *Journal of Family Issues, 21*(2), 205–224.

Campbell, L., & Martin-Matthews, A. (2000). Caring sons: Exploring men's involvement in filial care. *Canadian Journal on Aging, 19*(1), 57–79.

Connidis, I. A., & McMullin, J. (2002). Sociological ambivalence and family ties: A critical perspective. *Journal of Marriage and the Family, 64,* 558–567.

Crang, M., & Thrift, N. (2000). *Thinking space.* London: Routledge.

De Jong, G. F., Wilmoth, J. M, Angel, J. L., & Cornwell, G. T. (1995). Motives and the geographic mobility of very old Americans. *Journal of Gerontology: Social Sciences, 50B,* S395–S404.

Denis, A., & Sev'er, A. (2003). Introduction. *Canadian Review of Sociology and Anthropology: Negotiating Boundaries in a Globalizing World, 40*(5, special issue), 497–501.

DeWit, D. J., Wister, A. V., & Burch, T. K. (1988). Physical distance and social contact between elders and their adult children. *Research on Aging, 10*(1), 56–80.

Finch, J., & Mason, J. (1993). *Negotiating family responsibilities.* London: Routledge.

Frankenburg, R. (1966). *Communities in Britain.* London: Penguin.

Giddens, A. (1990). *The consequences of modernity.* Cambridge: Polity.

Gould, P., & White, R. (1986). *Mental maps* (2nd ed.). London: Penguin.

Green, A., & Canny, A. (2003). *Geographical mobility: Family impacts.* Bristol, UK: Policy.

Green, A., Hogarth, T., & Shackleton, R. (1999). *Long distance living: Dual location households.* Bristol, UK: Policy.

Gregory, D., & Urry, J. (Eds.). (1985). *Social relations and spatial structure.* Basingstoke, UK: Palgrave.

Hagerstrand, T. (1967). *Innovation diffusion as a spatial process.* Chicago: University of Chicago Press.

Harvey, D. (1990). *The condition of postmodernity: An enquiry into the origins of cultural change.* Cambridge, MA: Blackwell.

Hoff, A. (2006). Geographical proximity and contact frequency between older parents and their adult children in Germany: Cross cohort and longitudinal perspectives. *Generations Review, 16*(2), 16–23.

Joseph, A., & Hallman, B. (1996). Caught in the triangle: The influence of home, work and elder location on work-family balance. *Canadian Journal of Aging, 15,* 393–413.

Joseph Rowntree Foundation. (2003, May). The effects on families of job relocations. *Findings, 533.* Retrieved September 3, 2007, from http://www.jrf.org.uk/knowledge/findings/socialpolicy/533.asp

Keating, N. (In press). *A good place to grow old? Critical perspectives on rural ageing.* Bristol, UK: Policy.

Keeling, S. (2001). Relative distance: Ageing in rural New Zealand. *Ageing and Society, 21,* 605–619.

Lawton, M. P. (1980). *Environment and aging.* Belmont, CA: Brooks/Cole.

Lee, G. R., Dwyer, J. W., & Coward, R. T. (1990). Residential location and proximity to children among impaired elderly parents. *Rural Sociology, 55,* 579–589.

Lewis, J., & Meredith, B. (1988). *Daughters who care: Daughters caring for mothers at home.* London: Routledge.

Ley, D., & Waters, J. (2004). Transnational migration and the geographical imperative. In P. Jackson (Ed.), *Transnational spaces* (pp. 104–121). London: Routledge.

Martin-Matthews, A., & Keefe, J. (1995). Work and care of elderly people: A Canadian perspective. In J. Phillips (Ed.), *Working carers* (pp. 116–138). Aldershot, UK: Ashgate.

Martin-Matthews, A., & Rosenthal, C. (1993). Balancing work and family in an aging society: The Canadian experience. In G. Maddox & M. Lawton (Eds.), *Annual review of gerontology and geriatrics: Focus on kinship, ageing and social change* (pp. 96–119). New York: Springer.

Mason, J. (1999). Living away from relatives: Kinship and geographical reasoning. In S. McRae (Ed.), *Changing Britain: Families and households in the 1990s* (pp. 156–176). Oxford: Oxford University Press.

Massey, D. (1994). *Space, place and gender.* Cambridge: Polity.

Massey, D. (1995). *For space.* London: Sage.

McKie, L., Gregory, S., & Bowlby, S. (2002). Shadow times: The temporal and spatial frameworks and experiences of caring and working. *Sociology, 36*, 897–924.

Mercier, J., Paulson, L., & Morris, E. (1989). Proximity as a mediating influence on the perceived aging parent-adult child relationship. *The Gerontologist, 29*(6), 785–791.

Milligan, C. (2003). Location or dislocation? Towards a conceptualisation of people and place in the care-giving experience. *Social and Cultural Geography, 4*(4), 455–470.

Neal, M., Chapman, N., Ingersoll-Dayton, B., & Emlen, A. (1993). *Balancing work and caregiving for children, adults and elders*. Newbury Park, CA: Sage.

Parker, M. W., Call, V. R., & Kosberg, J. (2001, July). Geographic separation and contact between adult children and their parents. Paper presented at the International Association of Gerontology 17th World Congress, Vancouver, Canada.

Peace, S., Holland, C., & Kellaher, L. (2006). *Environment and identity in later life*. Buckingham, UK: Open University Press.

Phillips, J. (1995). Balancing work and care in Britain. In J. Phillips (Ed.), *Working carers* (pp. 42–57). Aldershot, UK: Avebury.

Phillips, J., Bernard, M., & Chittenden, M. (2002). *Juggling work and care* (Joseph Rowntree Foundation Report). Bristol, UK: Joseph Rowntree Foundation with Policy Press.

Phillipson, C., Bernard, M., Phillips, J., & Ogg, J. (2001). *The family and community life of older people*. London: Routledge.

Rosenmayr, L., & Kockeis, E. (1963). Propositions for a sociological theory of ageing and the family. *International Social Science Journal, 15*, 410–426.

Rowles, G. (1978). *Prisoners of space*. Boulder, CO: Westview.

Scharf, T., Phillipson, C., Smith, A. E., & Kingston, P. (2002). *Growing older in socially deprived areas: Social exclusion in later life*. London: Help the Aged.

Sheldon, J. H. (1948). *The social medicine of old age*. Oxford: Oxford University Press.

Szinovacz, M., & Davey, A. (2001). Retirement effects on parent-adult child contacts. *The Gerontologist, 41*, 191–200.

Townsend, P. (1957). *The family life of older people*. London: Routledge and Kegan Paul.

Tuan, Y-F. (1977). *Space and place: The perspective of experience*. London: Arnold.

Wagner, D. (2003, November). Research on long-distance care givers: What we (don't) know (presentation for the symposium "Caregiving From Afar: Does Geographic Distance Matter?" at the conference of the Gerontological Society of America, San Diego, CA).

Warnes, A. (1992). Migration and the lifecourse. In A. Champion & A. Fielding (Eds.), *Migration processes and patterns: Volume 1. Research progress and prospects* (pp. 175–187). London: Belhaven.

Watson, E., & Mears, J. (1999). *Women, work and care of the elderly.* Aldershot, UK: Ashgate.

Wolf, D., & Longino, C. (2005). Our "increasingly mobile society"? The curious persistence of a false belief. *The Gerontologist, 45,* 5–11.

Young, M., & Willmott, P. (1957). *Family and kinship in East London.* London: Routledge and Kegan Paul.

6

Caring from a Distance

Contemporary Care Issues

Margaret B. Neal, Donna L. Wagner, Kathleen J. B. Bonn, and Kelly Niles-Yokum

Doris Blake is a 50-year-old account executive with a large international corporation headquartered in Chicago. As a part of her work, she travels frequently between the United States and various European countries. She also travels between the West and East coasts of the United States to visit and supervise team members located in other cities. The work-related travel places a strain on her marriage of 20 years. However, it is her other travel that creates the most unrest and stress for Doris and her husband, Evan. Doris is a long-distance caregiver for her mother, who lives in a small town in North Carolina.

Doris has been supervising the care of her mother for 4 years, because a fall led to a precipitous decline in her mother's overall health. After the fall occurred, Doris tried unsuccessfully to convince her mother to relocate to Chicago and live with her and her husband. Since that time, Doris, sometimes along with Evan, has made monthly trips to North Carolina to visit and oversee her mother's care. Fortunately, ongoing help is available at present. One of her mother's neighbors, a lifelong friend of the family, checks on her daily, does her shopping, and takes her to the doctor. Paid home health aides provide assistance in bathing and personal care. Doris feels, however, that the equilibrium of the support system for her mother is precarious, especially given that the neighbor is experiencing some health problems of her own. Thus, Doris lives in a constant state of anticipation that things will begin to unravel. Until that happens, though, Doris is respecting her mother's wish to remain in her home and is grateful to her husband for his ongoing support and help with the long-distance care.

Still, Doris worries about her marriage. Between her work-related travel and her care responsibilities, Doris recognizes that it is often her husband who bears the burden of her complicated situation. The idea of a job change has crossed her mind; although Doris loves her work, she realizes she is becoming less able to manage everything and still have some emotional energy to invest in her relationship with her husband.

The above fictitious situation demonstrates only a few of the dilemmas faced by contemporary long-distance caregivers as the boundaries of their many life roles become blurred. These caregivers often lead complicated lives. Like Doris, they attempt to incorporate managing care from afar, often including travel to their loved one's place of residence, into their already busy work and home lives. In this chapter we explore the intersecting worlds of family and work through the lens of geographic distance. In chapter 6, Phillips and Bernard introduce the reader to concepts that are central to understanding the role played by geographic distance in the "blurring of boundaries" between work and family. Here we address several issues specific to long-distance care. As American scholars, we rely primarily upon findings based on studies conducted in the United States, but we draw on research conducted in other countries as well.

In this chapter, we begin with a discussion of why distance matters and an exploration of the prevalence of caring at a distance. We then examine the factors that influence decisions leading to the spatial separation of family members. We explore the differences and commonalities between family caregivers who live near and those who live at a distance from the person for whom they are caring. We consider the type of care provided and the effects of care on work and family well-being. We also describe strategies used by those who are engaged in both paid work and long-distance care to minimize the negative effects of caregiving on their work and home lives. We also examine gender and social class differences with respect to these issues. Throughout this chapter we use the terms *caregiver* and *carer* synonymously. We note, however, that both terms are "problematic," as they assume not only that the care is provided at no cost to the recipient but also that caregivers are voluntarily providing care at no cost to themselves (Meyer, Herd, & Michel, 2000).

Why Does Distance Matter?

A key reason that distance is important to consider in discussions of caregiving is that geographic distance plays a role in determining who within a family will become the caregiver or caregivers, regardless of any competing obligations related to paid work (Stern, 1996). Typically, whoever lives closest is the person most likely to become the caregiver.

However, a paradox exists with respect to family relations and proximity (Baldock, 2000). Although proximity is not necessary for close family bonding to exist, the support of an adult child is assumed to be dependent upon close proximity. This paradox and the preoccupation with geographic proximity in the caregiving literature have contributed to the paucity of research on long-distance caregiving (Baldock). Consequently, relations between aging parents and adult children who live at a distance "remain invisible" (Baldock, p. 207).

Nonetheless, we do know that kin contacts are affected by time constraints and geographic distance (Smith, 1998; Szinovacz & Davey, 2001), which, in turn, may result in restrictions in the types and levels of informal care provided. Although close family bonds may not be affected by distance, geographic separation between older people and their adult children can reduce the availability of necessary informal services and may increase the necessity for paid services. Thus, the nature and amount of care provided by long-distance caregivers are likely to be influenced by the very distance that separates the caregiver from the care recipient. Also, those who are providing care at a distance encounter some different care challenges than do those caring for an elder who lives nearby.

For example, if geographic separation limits the caregiver's ability to provide the informal care needed by the elder, financial costs may be incurred in order to purchase formal care services. Furthermore, even if an elder is using formal services in the absence of a proximate adult child, the long-distance carer often may experience a shift in boundaries between work and family as he or she makes time to manage care from a distance, leaves work for a trip to see the elder, and/or takes on additional work assignments in order to be able to afford to pay for needed services for the elder.

Also, long-distance caregivers experience greater stress (e.g., Joseph & Hallman, 1996; Kolb, 2002), such as the added emotional distress felt by long-distance caregivers due to guilt and worry about not being near the elder who requires assistance (Baldock, 2000; Parker, Call, Dunkle, & Vaitkus, 2002; Wagner, 1997). Similarly, we know that carers who live at a distance of one hour or more and carers who co-reside with the care recipient experience the greatest emotional distress, as compared to other caregivers who live nearby but not with the care recipient (National Alliance for Caregiving & American Association of Retired Persons [NAC & AARP], 2004; Neal, Hammer, Bonn, & Lottes, 2003).

Geographic separation is an important factor to consider because in some cases it can be an indicator of poor family relationships and thus affect the care provided. For example, an adult child may have moved some distance away from his or her aging parent specifically as the result of relational difficulties with the parent. Older parents who are divorced and living at a distance from one another, as well as from their adult children, present an additional challenge, particularly if care is needed by both parents.

In sum, distance matters because of the possibility of reduced availability of informal care for elders and the physical, emotional, and financial toll placed on family caregivers who must travel to the elder or elders for whom they are providing care. The challenges can be particularly great for carers who have had difficult relationships with their care recipient, or those who have multiple caregiving responsibilities, such as those caring for both children and aging parents (Joseph & Hallman, 1996; Neal & Hammer, 2007); these caregivers may experience overlapping and/or conflicting family care-related boundaries. For carers who are engaged in paid work, greater role conflict and a need for workplace-based accommodations, such as work schedule flexibility or time off from work, can result. We examine the intersection of employment and long-distance care in a later section of this chapter.

What Is "Long Distance"?

At present, there is no clear consensus regarding what constitutes "long-distance" caregiving. Researchers to date have employed three basic approaches to conceptualizing long-distance care. These include temporal definitions (i.e., the amount of time it takes the caregiver to travel to the home of the care recipient), spatial definitions (i.e., the amount of physical distance, such as in miles or kilometers, between the caregiver's and care recipient's residences), or some combination of travel time and geographic distance.

Temporal definitions include those describing distance in terms of the time required to reach the elder. For example, Joseph and

Hallman (1996) divided respondents into four groups: those cohabitating with the elder, those living up to 30 minutes apart, those living 31 to 120 minutes apart, and those living more than 120 minutes, or 2 hours, away. Lee, Dwyer, and Coward (1990) defined *long-distance carers* as those living more than 30 minutes from the elder. More common has been the criterion of 60 minutes (e.g., De Jong, Wilmoth, Angel, & Cornwell, 1995; Silverstein, 1995), which was the operational definition preferred by caregivers who participated in focus groups convened, in part, to discuss this issue (Wagner, 1997). A much longer time, one day's travel, has also been used (DeWit, Wister, & Burch, 1988).

Spatial criteria, such as the number of miles or kilometers separating the caregiver from the care recipient, have also been used to differentiate long-distance from proximate caregivers. These definitions use varying criterion distances, from more than 10 miles (e.g., Glaser & Tomassini, 2000; Szinovacz & Davey, 2001) to 50 or 60 miles (e.g., Greenwell & Bengtson, 1997; Mercier, Paulson, & Morris, 1989; Schoonover, Brody, Hoffman, & Kleban, 1988). Greenwell and Bengtson (1997), for example, preferred the 50-mile definition, arguing that this represented a distance at which "frequent visits are possible without requiring an overnight stay" (p. S17).

Finally, a few researchers have used a combination of these or other types of criteria. For example, Frankel and DeWit (1989) used the criterion "beyond which frequent contact begins to become prohibitively costly." This definition could be spatially and/or time based, and is obviously entirely dependent on the perceptions of each respondent. Such a definition illustrates the way in which financial cost may act with geography to impose a boundary on how far someone can go to provide care. Alternatively, Baldock (2000) used a political definition, operationalizing *long distance* as living in another country. Technically, a caregiver and a care recipient living in different countries could be separated by only a few miles or a few minutes of travel time, although in most cases the geographic or temporal distance would be much greater. Caring for someone in another country illustrates the political and cultural boundaries that may affect the provision of care. Such boundaries can exist even within a country, however, such as when the carer and the care recipient live in different states or even counties in the United States, or in different provinces in Canada (Martin-Matthews, 1999), because the types of formal services available and eligibility requirements typically vary across such geopolitical lines.

How Common Is Caring From Afar?

In the United States, caregiving for an older family member is a normative experience (Brody, 1985). Among the many families who are providing care are caregivers who are living at a distance from their older care recipient. In 1987 in the United States, family and friends were estimated to provide 80% of the long-term care services received by older adults (Select Committee on Aging, 1987). A recent analysis (Spillman & Black, 2005) found that the use of formal services actually declined between 1994 and 1999, indicating the increased importance of informal care for the well-being of older persons. Because the United States has no national health insurance, individuals and families bear the burden of cost for care. The United States is unique among the 30 member nations of the Organisation for Economic Co-Operation and Development (OECD) in its lack of national health insurance (OECD, 2002). In fact, the United States is the only industrialized nation in the world without universal health insurance; it used to share this distinction with South Africa, but no longer is that the case (Vladek, 2003). For those elders whose incomes and assets are above the limits set for government-funded health and social services, most of the cost of long-term care services, too, is paid by the older person or his or her family members (Chen, 2003). But how many caregivers are providing, overseeing, and/or paying for care for older adults at a distance?

The first attempt to establish the prevalence of long-distance caring in the United States was made by the National Council on the Aging (NCOA; Wagner, 1997). In a telephone survey of people aged 18 and over, approximately 13% reported providing assistance to an adult aged 55 or over. Of those caregivers, 26% (3.5% of the entire sample) were caring for someone who lived one hour or more away. Using one hour's travel time, then, as the distance criterion, the study estimated that 6.7 million adults in the United States were engaged in long-distance caring.

Also in 1997, a national telephone survey was conducted in an effort to estimate the size of the caregiving population (NAC & AARP, 1997). That study found a smaller proportion of long-distance carers, with 10% of all family caregivers reporting they were caring for someone who lived an hour or more away. Thus, despite being conducted during the same year using the same criterion for "distance" and similar methodological approaches, these two studies arrived at very different estimates of the proportion of caregivers who provide care at a distance. The reason for the discrepancy is unclear.

In a more recent survey (NAC & AARP, 2004), an estimated 15% of caregivers were found to live an hour or more away from the person for whom they were caring. Similarly, a national study of 309 working couples caring for dependent children as well as aging parents found that 11% of both husbands and wives listed the parent they were helping most as living one or more hours away (Neal et al., 2003). The finding is noteworthy, because both members of these couples were employed (one full-time, the other at least half-time), they were caring for a dependent child, and not only were they caring for one or more aging parents, but also they were spending a minimum of 3 hours per week in parent care (see Neal & Hammer, 2007, for details about the larger study). Thus, these long-distance caregivers occupied multiple work and caregiving roles, experiencing many overlapping boundaries both between their work and family roles and within their different family roles.

Despite differences in study design, sampling techniques, data collection modes, and response rates, three of these four studies yielded fairly consistent estimates, indicating that from 11% to 15% of caregivers of adults or elders in the United States are helping older adults who live at a distance. Other caregiving studies, however, have yielded inconsistent results, most likely due to the variety of ways in which *long distance* has been defined. Although these definitional variations limit our ability to estimate precisely the size of the long-distance caregiving population, they do not preclude us from understanding the wide range of issues involved in long-distance care.

Who Are Long-Distance Carers?

Only a few studies in the United States have been conducted exclusively on long-distance caregivers. Several general studies of caregiving, however, have examined the variable of geographic distance.

The NAC & AARP study (2004) revealed that the average age of family caregivers to older adults in the United States was 46 years;

long-distance carers were concentrated in two age groups: 35–49 and 50–64. They also were more likely to be secondary caregivers, to be college educated, and to have higher incomes. Other studies, too, have found long-distance caregivers to be more highly educated (Lin & Rogerson, 1995; Wagner, 1997) and to have higher incomes (DeWit et al., 1988; Greenwell & Bengtson, 1997; Wagner, 1997). A greater percentage of long-distance carers also have been found to be employed (69%), compared to other caregivers (61%) (NAC & AARP, 2004). The findings of a more recent U.S. survey specifically of long-distance caregivers are similar: These carers' average age was 51, 70% reported having earned a college degree or graduate degree, and 62% worked full-time and 18% worked part-time (MetLife Mature Market Institute, 2004). The increased rates of employment, higher education, and greater incomes of these caregivers are important to highlight, as they reflect skills and resources that may enhance long-distance carers' abilities to negotiate the boundaries between work and home. However, there is also evidence that found long-distance carers have fewer resources in the form of fewer siblings (Lin & Rogerson; Smith, 1998) and are caring for parents who live in small cities and rural areas.

In an exploration of gender differences among long-distance carers, a national study of 309 dual-earner couples in the United States caring both for children and for aging parents found that just under 6% of both the husbands and wives in these couples reported living with the parent or parent-in-law they were helping most, whereas 11% (33 wives and 32 husbands) said they lived one hour or more away from the parent they were helping most (Neal et al., 2003). The remainder of both husbands and wives reported living less than 30 minutes away (75%), or living 30 to 59 minutes away (9%) (Neal et al., 2003). Thus, husbands and wives did not differ, on average, with respect to being long-distance carers. More husbands, however, reported that the parent they were helping the most was a parent-in-law (42%) than did wives (31%), which is consistent with the findings from Lee, Spitze, and Logan (2003). Among the 33 wives and 32 husbands who reported living one hour or more away from the parent or parent-in-law each was helping most, there were some other gender differences as well. The mean travel time to this parent for husbands was 4.3 hours, whereas that for wives was 3.1 hours (with travel time truncated at 12 hours); the average distance to the parent was 449 miles for husbands and 154 miles for wives (Neal et al., 2003).

We next turn our attention to some of the causes of spatial distance among family members.

Factors Associated with the Spatial Separation of Family Members

In the global economy of today's world, geographic mobility is often assumed. This is particularly the case in the United States, where family narratives typically include distance, beginning with the origins of ancestors before they came to the United States and continuing with the migration and dispersion of their offspring and their offspring's children across the country. Perceptions of the United States as a mobile society, however, may more accurately reflect historical rather than contemporary trends. In their recent article, "Our 'Increasingly' Mobile Society? The Curious Persistence of a False Belief," Wolf and Longino (2005) confronted this issue directly. They described a literature that is replete with concerns about our "increasingly mobile society" and the implications of this, for example, for reducing the amount of informal support available to older persons. Wolf and Longino demonstrated, however, that decreases, not increases, in mobility have actually occurred for many subgroups, with only one age group, 45 to 64 year olds, remaining relatively constant in its levels of mobility. They suggested that some of the mobility that does occur may be in response to, or at least supportive of, the informal care needs of family members.

The most commonly cited reasons for relocations of any distance in the United States have been housing related (51%), family related (26%), and work related (16%) (U.S. Census Bureau, 2004). However, among individuals who reported a "migration" (Wolf & Longino, 2005) or long-distance move, work was more often the cause, with 28% stating that work was the primary reason (U.S. Census Bureau). As Stern (1996) argued, the future needs of aging parents are rarely considered by young adults when they make a decision to move.

Retirement migration is another factor that contributes to the spatial separation of families (Wolf & Longino, 2005). Such migration can affect the patterns of caregiving, such as when aging parents make an amenity move that takes them further away from their adult children or when the adult children themselves make an amenity move. Moves in the reverse also occur, for example when chronic disabilities or widowhood create difficulties for maintaining independence and bring the elder(s) closer to their adult children.

Culture also appears to play a role in intergenerational distance and proximity between caregivers and care recipients. A study by Glaser and Tomassini (2000) compared the correlates of proximity to adult children among women aged 60–74 in Britain and in Italy. The findings revealed that parental characteristics such as health had more impact on parent–child proximity in Britain than in Italy. Glaser and Tomassini concluded that in Britain, proximity may arise more from the needs of the elder, whereas in Italy, there may be a cultural preference for closer proximity regardless of need, and/or that this greater proximity may arise from the needs of the child for financial support. Cultural norms, then, may affect geographic distance and the patterns of care, suggesting that in some societies, remaining proximate to an older parent "trumps" the professional work opportunities that might be available if the adult child were to move.

In sum, age is a factor associated with the spatial separation of family members, with the most mobility likely to occur within the very age group that provides the majority of care to older adults, those between 45 and 64 years old. This is also the age group within which the majority of long-distance carers fall. Work-related moves of adult children often result in long-distance caring, and retirement-related moves may too, although sometimes they are motivated, instead, by a desire to close the gap in distance.

Strategies Used for Managing Care at a Distance and Types of Help Provided by Long-Distance Carers

Given the diversity of the older population and aging families, there are numerous causes and effects of geographic dispersal. Similarly, a plethora of responses, or models, exist for managing this distance. Key strategies for carers managing care at a distance include enlisting support and assistance from a family member or friend who lives near the older adult, engaging formal services, and/or the caregiver him or herself making regular visits to provide services directly. These strategies allow working caregivers to engage in both family caregiving and paid work, and can result in blurred boundaries between carers' work and home lives. There are also many long-distance caregivers who ultimately choose to eliminate the boundaries associated with this distance by moving their parent closer, moving themselves closer to the parent, taking a leave of absence from work, or leaving their job entirely.

The NCOA survey of long-distance caregivers revealed a variety of care strategies, ranging from caregivers bearing sole responsibility for care to those acting as secondary caregivers only (Wagner, 1997). Approximately one half described their role as helping someone else provide care, and close to a third were sharing equally with someone else the responsibility for the care of an elder. Only 15% were the primary carer, and just 6% were the only caregiver.

The types of care provided by long-distance caregivers vary depending on the distance the carer is from the older adult. For example, three quarters of those living between 1 and 2 hours away from their older family member provided transportation assistance, compared with half of those who lived farther (3 or more hours) away (Wagner, 1997). Similarly, half of those living 1 to 2 hours from the care recipient provided help with meal preparation, compared to 43% of those living 3 or more hours away.

The nature of the help provided by long-distance carers is related to income as well as distance. For example, caregivers with household incomes of less than $50,000 are more likely than carers with higher incomes to perform direct personal care services, housekeeping, transportation, and meal preparation for their care recipients (Wagner, 1997). Nearly half of these long-distance carers (44%) paid for some or all of the costs of needed services for the person they were helping, at an average cost of $202 per month (Wagner, 1997). A more recent survey of long-distance caregivers revealed that average out-of-pocket expenses related to caregiving totaled $392 per month and included travel costs, long-distance telephone calls, and, for some, the purchase of goods or services for the care recipient (MetLife Mature Market Institute, 2004). Moreover, the amount of distance made a dramatic difference in the amounts expended: Long-distance carers living between 1 and 3 hours from care recipients spent an average of $386 a month, whereas those living more than 3 hours away reported average monthly costs of $674. For the relatively small group of respondents (10%) who paid for services to be provided by others, there were gender differences in expenditures: Women spent an average of $751 a month, compared to men who spent an average of $490 a month (MetLife Mature Market Institute, 2004).

Employment also affects the nature and amount of care provided. In addition to the income afforded by employment, employment sometimes provides opportunities for travel. For example, several of the emigrants in Baldock's (2000) study combined business trips with visits to elderly parents to offset both the time and monetary costs of travel to the home of the parent(s).

Thus, income and employment are factors that affect the provision of long-distance care. The financial costs of care represent a potential negative impact of long-distance caregiving on the carer and may act with geographic location to impose a boundary, or limit, on the amount and type of care provided. At the same time, the carer's employment may serve to provide the economic means to pay for services for the elder, or to travel to the elder, thereby eroding the boundaries between work and family.

Gender is another factor that may influence the types of strategies used to help manage work and family, as revealed above in the differences in expenditures for formal care on the part of female and male long-distance carers (MetLife Mature Market Institute, 2004). With respect to the use of formal and informal support mechanisms by employed carers, Niles (2002) found that of those carers who had some type of support program at work (13% of men and women), nearly 20% of men had used the program to assist them in their caregiving duties, compared to only 6% of women. Men were also more likely than women to have engaged the services of a geriatric care manager (4% versus 1%). Regardless of these gender differences, however, it is noteworthy that the majority of long-distance caregivers did not access the eldercare services provided by employers. These findings are consistent with other studies that have found low use of employer-provided supports by employed caregivers as a whole (Neal & Hammer, 2007; Wagner & Hunt, 1994). Nevertheless, they are somewhat surprising because we would expect such programs (e.g., information and assistance in locating services) to be of particular salience to carers who lived some distance away from their elder. Lack of knowledge of the existence of these programs is one cause. Another possibility is that the services as provided do not adequately address caregivers' needs, which include emotional needs resulting from guilt experienced at being far away from the elder (Parker et al., 2002; Wagner, 1997). Anecdotal evidence suggests that both of these factors play a role, as does a reluctance to use employer-provided services for a family-related matter (Wagner & Hunt, 1994).

Gender differences also have been found in the use of formal services available in the community (as opposed to employer-provided services). Specifically, Niles (2002) discovered that men were more likely to use formal services, whereas women tended to rely on family members for assistance. However, only 3% of men and women felt that the services provided by agencies in the community were helpful. Thus, although there were gender-specific patterns related to service use, the fact remains that programs and services for caregivers were underutilized and, when used, found to be unhelpful.

As noted earlier, another factor affecting the provision of care may be a history of interpersonal problems in the relationship between children and their parents. Such interpersonal difficulties actually may have caused, or contributed to, the geographic separation between parents and their adult children or other familial caregivers in the first place, and clearly can affect the amount, nature, and quality of care provided.

Finally, migration to another country is likely to complicate the provision of informal care, yet it is an aspect of long-distance caring that is not well researched (Baldock, 2000). How do those workers who leave their country of origin manage their filial obligations when parents are left behind and begin to require support and care? In an exploratory study of transnational migrants to Australia, Baldock (2000) found that these distant carers contributed to the care of parents who remained “back home” through letters, telephone calls, and return visits. She argued that this contribution has not been acknowledged in the literature on caregiving. It is likely that migrant groups vary in their response to the long-distance care needs of family members, depending, for example, on whether they are engaged in work that allows them to travel, as was the case with Baldock’s sample of university workers. Especially in the case of those whose aging parent lives on a different continent, distance is likely to play a key role in the types of arrangements made. Also, care at such a distance can be constrained by financial limitations, social implications (e.g., caregiving norms may differ culturally), and political concerns. For example, there may be worry that if the carer leaves the new country, he or she may not be allowed to reenter. This concern gives particular meaning to the issue of boundaries between caregiving and work. As Baldock pointed out, many questions remain regarding migration and caregiving: Under what circumstances do adult children who have emigrated return to their country of origin to provide care for their parents? Why do some aging parents volunteer to follow their child to the new country? How is caregiving responsibility negotiated among siblings when one of the siblings lives at a great distance? These questions illustrate how boundaries must be established, negotiated, and realigned concerning how and when to provide care versus meet one's work obligations.

Two Case Examples

The actual situations of two employed caregivers, described below (their names have been changed), illustrate two different approaches used by long-distance carers to manage their care responsibilities. These employees participated in a recent study examining the efficacy of one company's workplace eldercare programs, which included a standard resource and referral program and a geriatric care management program (Wagner, Hunt, Mathews, & Niles, 2005).

> Mr. Anderson's parents live in another state more than 800 miles away. Both parents are frail, and Mr. Anderson's father had recently been diagnosed with Alzheimer's disease. Mr. Anderson contacted the geriatric care management program offered through his employer for information and ended up using the service to conduct an assessment of his parents' needs. Following the assessment, the geriatric care manager identified several appropriate assisted living facilities, took the parents on a tour of these facilities, helped them make a selection, and managed their entire move. Mr. Anderson is pleased and grateful that there is someone to take on this responsibility and that his parents were able to continue living near their friends. He believes that having a professional manage things allowed him and his parents to continue to have a strong relationship without any conflict about decision making concerning the parents' care-related needs and where they should live.
>
> Ms. Brown had been caring for her mother-in-law, Ms. Norton, who lived in the same state as Ms. Brown and her husband but still 500 miles away. The situation finally became too much for the Browns to manage due to frequent disturbing reports from Ms. Norton's neighbors and a recommendation from the physician that more oversight was needed in order to protect Ms. Norton's well-being. Thus, the Browns worked out a solution to their long-distance care dilemma: They decided to move Ms. Norton into their home. Ms. Brown reports that she knows about the geriatric care management program offered by her employer, and that she is sure that if she "really needs it," she will

use it. Ms. Norton is relieved to have care that involves her family and not formal service providers.

Research conducted with employed caregivers suggests that those who have implemented the strategy used by the Browns—that is, the location-based coping strategy of relocating an aging parent into their home (Joseph & Hallman, 1996)—may be trading one set of problems for another. Although the boundaries imposed by distance are addressed by eliminating this spatial limitation entirely, often similar negative boundary outcomes result. For example, there is evidence that both co-resident and long-distance carers are at high risk of adverse work-related outcomes, such as needing to take a leave of absence from work (Gottlieb, Kelloway, & Fraboni, 1994; Neal et al., 2003) and higher levels of emotional stress (NAC & AARP, 2004; Neal et al., 2003).

The Effects of Caring From a Distance on Work and Well-Being

All employed family caregivers experience some degree of role conflict as they attempt to manage their work responsibilities, their nuclear family and home duties, and their eldercare responsibilities. For the approximately 60% of family caregivers who are employed (NAC & AARP, 2004), the need to make some accommodations at work in order to manage caregiving responsibilities is common. For example, more than half of employed caregivers had to go to work late or leave early in order to manage their care responsibilities (NAC & AARP, 2004). Long-distance carers, however, are more likely to miss a full day of work and less likely to come in late or leave early because of their caregiving duties (MetLife Mature Market Institute, 2003). Living at a greater distance from the care recipient is positively associated with difficulties balancing work and family for both men and women carers, and for men, being a long-distance carer is associated with considering a job change (MetLife Mature Market Institute, 2003). Geographic distance clearly contributes to difficulties in maintaining the boundaries between work and family.

To further explore possible differences in outcomes of caring for long-distance versus proximal caregivers for the purposes of this chapter, we used data from the Neal and Hammer (2007) study of working couples caring for both children and aging parents. We compared carers of a parent or parent-in-law who lived one hour or more away with those whose parent lived nearer. We also compared the patterns separately for husbands and for wives. These analyses, exploratory in nature given the small number of long-distance carers, nonetheless revealed some interesting differences. Among husbands, those caring at a distance had higher levels of family-to-work conflict, gave lower ratings of their overall performance as a caregiver, and gave somewhat lower ratings of their overall performance at work than did husbands who lived less than an hour away from the parent or parent-in-law whom they were helping most. Among wives, long-distance carers had somewhat higher levels of childcare stress, had somewhat lower levels of parent-care rewards and of family satisfaction, and reported poorer performance as a spouse and as a caregiver than did wives who lived nearer their parent or parent-in-law. Wives caring at a distance reported fewer times late to work or leaving work early than the women caring for a parent who lived within one hour's travel time, but there were no differences with respect to number of days missed for either husbands or wives. This finding, which differs from that in the MetLife (MetLife Mature Market Institute, 2003) study, may be due to the study's fairly high minimum care requirement (at least 3 hours of parent care per week) for all couples, regardless of their distance from the aging parent. As revealed below, additional factors, too, may have affected these relationships.

More detailed analyses of the effects of distance involved grouping respondents from this same data set into seven distance categories (co-resident, < 5 minutes, 5–9 minutes, 10–14 minutes, 15–29 minutes, 30–59 minutes, and 60+ minutes away). These analyses revealed more complexity in the results (Neal et al., 2003). For example, for husbands, there was a clear linear relationship between distance and self-rated performance as a caregiver, with husbands living with their parent or parent-in-law reporting the highest ratings, and those living at a travel time of 60 minutes or more reporting the lowest. This relationship held regardless of whether the parent was the husband's own parent or a parent-in-law. In contrast, husbands caring for a parent-in-law who lived with them reported more concern about their effectiveness at work than husbands caring for their own parent who lived with them. However, as distance increased, this changed, with husbands more likely to worry that they were working less effectively at work when they were caring for a parent, as opposed to a parent-in-law. This finding is probably due to the greater amount of assistance that husbands were providing to parents-in-law who lived with them, compared to that provided for co-resident parents.

Among wives who were caring at greater distances from the aging parent or in-law, those caring for a parent-in-law reported higher levels of positive spillover from work to family than did wives caring for their own parents (Neal et al., 2003). Apparently, characteristics of their employment and their job skills were of particular assistance in caring for a parent-in-law. Interestingly, among wives caring for their own parents, positive spillover from work to family was greatest for those at the middle distances and lowest both for those living with the parent and for those living farthest away. This latter finding provides an example of one of the nonlinear relationships found between distance and outcomes, with co-resident and long-distance caregivers sometimes more similar to each other than to caregivers who live near or relatively near, but not with, their aging parent or in-law. These findings suggest that the boundaries between work and family for long-distance carers may differ depending on the amount of geographic distance involved. For deeper understanding of the boundaries between work and caring, they indicate that it is important to consider (a) the gender of the caregiver, because the pattern of effects of distance appears to differ for men and women; (b) whether the care recipient is a parent or a parent-in-law; and (c) possible nonlinear effects of distance.

Conclusions

Long-distance caregivers who are employed have multiple responsibilities that can make everyday life especially complex and demanding. This chapter has highlighted some of the unique challenges faced by these carers, including effects on their work (e.g., missed time or poorer performance), finances (e.g., additional out-of-pocket expenses for care of or travel to the older adult), and levels of stress (e.g., due to guilt at not being nearby and able to easily provide care).

Most large employers that provide eldercare programs to support employees who are caregivers are aware that many employees provide care at a distance. Programs offered typically include resource and referral services that are national in scope, thus providing information about services available in other parts of the country (Neal & Wagner, 2001). The irony is, however, that despite these work-based eldercare services, few long-distance carers use them, preferring instead to rely upon friends and family who live near the older parent or other family member to help them build a network of support.

Low utilization rates of workplace-based services and lack of satisfaction with community-based services suggest that some changes may be needed in the nature of services provided if these supports are to aid long-distance carers in their attempts to negotiate their intersecting work and family lives. Additional research to develop and evaluate new support options must be conducted, and the resulting programs must be widely and regularly publicized to assure that employees are aware of them.

For example, employers might better address the needs of long-distance carers by instituting a policy that permits employees to access the Internet and/or make calls from work using company phones to contact distant relatives and/or arrange care. Another option is to establish a pool of frequent flyer miles for use by long-distance caregivers on a shared, as-needed basis. Yet another is to set up an online peer support group for caregivers. Clearly, because many caregivers have little information about available formal services when they start helping an elder, increasing access to such information through the workplace is a good place to start the development of a relationship between the carer and this network of services. Because family care is a dynamic and ever-changing situation, it is likely that, at some point, formal services will be necessary, and advance information could make this transition easier for both the elder and his or her family caregiver, whether care is being provided at a distance or not.

Employers also can support long-distance carers by ensuring that those who need to take time off from work are able to do so without unnecessary barriers, whether this time off is paid or, as is more common in the United States, unpaid. Work schedule flexibility, the ability to use paid sick leave to care for ill family members, and managers and supervisors who are sensitive to employees' family needs are additional key components of a workplace that is supportive of working caregivers, whether proximate or long distance (Neal & Hammer, 2007).

Because most long-distance carers help with the arrangement and management of care, increasing access to geriatric care manager services, either through provision directly by the employer or by providing subsidies to employees who contract privately with such services, could be especially supportive of these caregivers.

Although some employers have developed this option, the majority of those with workplace supports for caregivers continue to provide only information and referral services on an as-needed basis. As we saw in our illustrative case of Mr. Anderson, however, a geriatric care management service funded by his employer helped ensure that his parents' health and living arrangements were professionally evaluated, and their need for more supportive housing was met by the professional care manager working directly with the parents to make all of the necessary arrangements for relocation. This service allowed Mr. Anderson to continue to be productive at work and preserve his relationship with his parents.

Community agencies could aid both long-distance and proximate employed caregivers by having information regarding service options available online and/or accessible by telephone 24 hours a day. Having a system in place that would allow long-distance carers to communicate via e-mail with service professionals and also with peers, for support, would be helpful as well, as would flexible hours of service that do not require caregivers to make contact during their own working hours.

The phenomenon of long-distance caring and, in particular, the blurred boundaries between paid work and unpaid care to relatives living at a distance still are not well understood. Considerable work remains to be done to identify and address the needs of this important, but overlooked, group of carers.

References

Baldock, C. V. (2000). Migrants and their parents: Caregiving from a distance. *Journal of Family Issues, 21*, 205–224.

Brody, E. (1985). Parent care as a normative family stress. *The Gerontologist, 25*, 19–29.

Chen, Y. P. (2003). Funding long-term care: Applications of the trade-off principle in both public and private sectors. *Journal of Aging and Health, 15*, 15–44.

De Jong, G. F., Wilmoth, J. M, Angel, J. L., & Cornwell, G. T. (1995). Motives and the geographic mobility of very old Americans. *Journal of Gerontology: Social Sciences, 50B*, S395–S404.

DeWit, D. J., Wister, A. V., & Burch, T. K. (1988). Physical distance and social contact between elders and their adult children. *Research on Aging, 10*, 56–80.

Frankel, B. G., & DeWit, D. J. (1989). Geographic distance and intergenerational contact: An empirical examination of the relationship. *Journal of Aging Studies, 3*, 139–162.

Glaser, K., & Tomassini, C. (2000). Proximity of older women to their children: A comparison of Britain and Italy. *The Gerontologist, 40*, 729–737.

Gottlieb, B. H., Kelloway, K., & Fraboni, M. (1994). Aspects of eldercare that place employees at risk. *The Gerontologist, 34*, 815–821.

Greenwell, L., & Bengtson, V. L. (1997). Geographic distance and contact between middle-aged children and their parents. *Journal of Gerontology: Social Sciences, 52B*, S13–S26.

Joseph, A. E., & Hallman, B. D. (1996). Caught in the triangle: The influence of home, work, and elder location on work-family balance. *Canadian Journal on Aging, 15*, 393–412.

Katz, D., & Kahn, R. (1978). *The social psychology of organizations* (2nd ed.). New York: John Wiley.

Kolb, K. N. (2002). *Long-distance caregivers and stress.* Unpublished master's thesis, Oregon State University, Corvallis.

Lee, G. R., Dwyer, J. W., & Coward, R. T. (1990). Residential location and proximity to children among impaired elderly parents. *Rural Sociology, 55*, 579–589.

Lee, E., Spitze, G., & Logan, J. R. (2003). Social support to parents-in-law: The interplay of gender and kin hierarchies. *Journal of Marriage and Family, 65*, 396–403.

Lin, G., & Rogerson, P. (1995). Elderly parents and the geographic availability of their adult children. *Research on Aging, 17*, 303–331.

Martin-Matthews, A. (1999). Canada and the changing profile of health and social services: Implications for employment and caregiving. In V. M. Lechner & M. B. Neal (Eds.), *Work and caring for the elderly: International perspectives* (pp. 11–28). Philadelphia: Brunner/Mazel, Taylor & Francis Group.

Mercier, J. M., Paulson, L., & Morris, E. W. (1989). Proximity as a mediating influence on the perceived aging parent-adult child relationship. *The Gerontologist, 29*, 785–791.

MetLife Mature Market Institute. (2003). *The MetLife study of sons at work: Balancing employment and eldercare.* Westport, CT: Author. Retrieved August 27, 2007, from http://www.metlife.com/WPSAssets/18221098271172586517V1FSonsatWork2007.pdf

MetLife Mature Market Institute. (2004). *Miles away: The MetLife study of long-distance caregiving.* Westport, CT: Author. Retrieved April 30, 2006, from http://www.caregiving.org/data/milesaway.pdf

Meyer, M. H., Herd, P., & Michel, S. (2000). Introduction: The right to—or not to—care. In M. H. Meyer (Ed.), *Care work: Gender, labor and the welfare state*. New York: Routledge.

National Alliance for Caregiving (NAC), & American Association of Retired Persons (AARP). (1997). *Family caregiving in the U.S.: Findings from a national survey*. Washington, DC: Authors.

National Alliance for Caregiving (NAC), & AARP. (2004). *Caregiving in the U.S.* Washington, DC: Authors.

Neal, M. B., & Hammer, L. B. (2007). *Working couples caring for children and aging parents: Effects on work and well-being*. Mahwah, NJ: Lawrence Erlbaum.

Neal, M. B., Hammer, L. B., Bonn, K. J. B., & Lottes, J. (2003, November). The effects of geographic distance among working, sandwiched caregivers: An exploratory study. In K. N. Kolb and M. B. Neal (Co-chairs), *Caregiving from afar: Does geographic distance matter?* Symposium conducted at the annual scientific meeting of the Gerontological Society of America, San Diego, CA.

Neal, M. B., & Wagner, D. L. (2001). Working caregivers: Issues, challenges, and opportunities for the aging network (Program Development Issue Brief). Washington, DC: Administration on Aging, U.S. Department of Health and Human Services. Retrieved April 30, 2006, from http://www.aoa.gov/prof/aoaprog/caregiver/careprof/progguidance/background/program_issues/special_caregiver_pop.asp

Niles, K. (2002, November). Long-distance caregiving: A look at gender and utilization of formal and informal support mechanisms. Paper presented at the annual scientific meeting of the Gerontological Society of America, San Diego, CA.

Organisation for Economic Co-Operation and Development (OECD). (2002). OECD economic survey: United States health system reform. *OECD Economic Surveys, 2002*(18), 257–358. Retrieved March 21, 2007, from http://titania.sourceoecd.org/vl=434888/cl=24/nw=1/rpsv/~3805/v2002n18/s6/p257

Parker, M. W., Call, V. R. A., Dunkle, R., & Vaitkus, M. (2002). "Out of sight" but not "out of mind:" Parent contact and worry among senior ranking male officers in the military who live long distances from parents. *Military Psychology, 14*, 257–277.

Schoonover, C. B., Brody, E. M., Hoffman, C., & Kleban, M. H. (1988). Parent care and geographically distant children. *Research on Aging, 10*, 472–492.

Select Committee on Aging. (1987). *Exploding the myths: Caregiving in America* (Committee Publication No. 99-611). Washington, DC: Government Printing Office.

Silverstein, M. (1995). Stability and change in temporal distance between the elderly and their children. *Demography, 32*, 29–45.

Smith, G. C. (1998). Residential separation and patterns of interaction between elderly parents and their adult children. *Progress in Human Geography, 22*, 368–384.

Spillman, B., & Black, K. (2005). *Staying the course: Trends in family caregiving.* Washington, DC: AARP Public Policy Institute.

Stern, S. (1996). Measuring child work and residence adjustments to parents' long-term care needs. *The Gerontologist, 36*, 76–87.

Szinovacz, M., & Davey, A. (2001). Retirement effects on parent-adult child contacts. *The Gerontologist, 41*, 191–200.

U.S. Census Bureau. (2004). *Geographical mobility: 2002-2003* (Current Population Reports, p20-549). Washington, DC: U.S. Department of Commerce.,

Vladeck, B. (2003). Universal health insurance in the United States: Reflections on the past, the present, and the future. *American Journal of Public Health, 93*, 16–19.

Wagner, D. L. (1997). *Caring across the miles: Findings of a survey of long-distance caregivers.* Washington, DC: National Council on the Aging.

Wagner, D. L., & Hunt. G. G. (1994). The use of workplace eldercare programs by employed caregivers. *Research on Aging, 16*, 69–84.

Wagner, D. L., Hunt, G. G., Mathews, S., & Niles, K. (2005, November). The efficacy of workplace eldercare programs. Paper presented at the annual scientific meeting of the Gerontological Society of America, Orlando, FL.

Wolf, D., & Longino, C. (2005). Our "increasingly mobile society"? The curious persistence of a false belief. *The Gerontologist, 45*, 5–11.

7

Working Carers in New Zealand

Zones of Care and Contested Boundaries

Sally Keeling and Judith Davey

Introduction

Location clearly constrains practical arrangements for caregiving, but the dynamics and histories of particular families also shape the development of care networks, and the capacity for shared care. Caregiving roles are also placed at the boundary of informal care and public-sector service delivery. This chapter draws on a study of public sector employees in two large city councils in New Zealand and takes a comparative perspective on the intersection of formal and informal care, examining the concept of "zones of care" and gaps in the continuum of care. The experience of the working carers involved in this study suggests that gaps and boundaries between "public" and "private" care and support systems for older people are contested, sometimes permeable, and regularly blurred.

Mapping Conceptual Boundaries

New Zealand shares with other Organisation for Economic Co-operation and Development (OECD) countries the experience and implications of population aging (OECD Health Project, 2005). Similarities and differences in cultural and social policy expectations and assumptions can be derived from an analysis of how New Zealanders talk about their experiences of combining paid work and informal eldercare. This highlights recent changes in the social construction of work and care, as expressed in both policy and personal discourse.

Social policy analysis in New Zealand has used the language of *gap* (rather than *boundary*) to describe the interface between informal care and public and community services. This is implied in Opie's 1992 book title, *There's Nobody There*. Novitz, as early as 1987, used the phrase "bridging the gap," referring to the relationship between paid work and family care. McManus wrote in 2005 of "minding the gap" in her critique of how New Zealand social policy constructs the field where state and family care meet (or, more commonly, fail to meet). The New Zealand Families Commission, established in 2003, identified a focus on "older people in families, contributions and care," in their "gap analysis" of local policy development and research relating to the shifting boundaries between the state and family care and support (New Zealand Families Commission, 2005, p. 24).

In contrast, the language of writers in the United States, following Estes and Swann's work (1992), has been commonly couched in terms of *zones* of care. New Zealand policy discourse, particularly in health, brings the language of zones and gaps together, using *integration* as a key word, to counteract gaps in service coverage and "patch protection" generated by the introduction of market models in health policy (Gauld, 2003; McManus, 2005; Novitz, 1987). The growing use of spatial terms, such as *zones*, *gaps*, and *boundaries*, to describe and analyze patterns of caregiving reached New Zealand following Twigg and Atkin (1994) and has been applied most recently by Milligan (2006). Earlier, Milligan (2000) had presented Scottish work on the personal geographies of carers, noting that as care moves increasingly from institutional to community settings, "it may be creating a blurring of the boundaries between what has traditionally been public/institutional space, and the homespace" (p. 49). Analyzing New Zealand carer narratives relating to their experiences of older people's admission to residential care, she noted the increasing references to a "blurring of the boundaries between formal and informal caregiving" (Milligan, 2006, p. 320).

New empirical data to further these debates are provided by a New Zealand study that documents the nature and extent of eldercare responsibilities among the workforce of the Wellington and Christchurch City Councils (Davey & Keeling, 2004). The study was designed to partially replicate a UK study (Phillips, Bernard, &

Chittenden, 2002), and to build comparative understandings of the interface between work and eldercare. The study was further positioned against a backdrop of research on older workers, workforce change, and work–life balance in New Zealand's social policy context. The particular focus of this chapter, however, is on insights arising from focus groups carried out with working carers. The analysis and interpretation of the focus group transcripts were clearly influenced by Finch and Mason's (1993) formative perspectives on the negotiation of family responsibilities.

Outline of the New Zealand Study: Combining Work and Eldercare

Two local authorities representing major cities, one in the North Island and one in the South Island, were chosen as the sites for this study and readily cooperated in the research. They gave us access to a workforce of 3,809, mixed in terms of occupation, age, sex, and patterns of workforce participation. The research was funded through a contract between the New Zealand Institute for Research on Ageing (NZiRA) at Victoria University of Wellington and the Future of Work research fund (New Zealand Department of Labour, n.d.). The study then proceeded in parallel, with a researcher in Wellington (Judith Davey) and one in Christchurch (Sally Keeling).

A screening questionnaire asked all employees to indicate whether or not they provided informal care to an older person or persons; this was defined as "looking after or giving care to anyone over the age of 65—family members, friends, neighbours or others—because they have long-term physical or mental disability or problems related to old age." Employees who answered yes were sent a self-administered questionnaire to collect basic information about the carer and care recipient; the type, duration, and frequency of care provided; and how they balanced work and caring. The questionnaire also asked the respondents if they were willing to participate in follow-up group discussions. At each stage of the study, response and participation rates were comparable with those reported elsewhere. The screening questionnaire validated our estimate, based on British experience, that 10% of employees were currently providing eldercare.

Women predominated among the working carers who took part in the study. They were mainly well educated and working full-time in professional, technical, and clerical roles (Davey & Keeling, 2004). Parents or the parental generation predominated among care recipients: Mothers made up 43%, fathers 19%, parents-in-law 12%, and aunts and uncles approximately 5%; grandparents accounted for just over 8%, and "friends" for nearly 9%. The type of care provided was most commonly social and emotional support (provided by 92% of the working carers), household assistance (87%), administrative support (72%), and personal care (47%). Female working carers provided higher levels of care, provide care over longer hours, and provided care on a more frequent basis than their male counterparts. Few of the working carers in this study provided very long periods of care: 84% provided less than 10 hours per week. In addition to full-time work and personal or domestic commitments, this is significant. Although 75% of the carers said they had *help* with eldercare (from other family members, and/or from health professionals and community services), only 21% described the *responsibility* for eldercare as shared.

The predominant method of coping with eldercare demands during work hours was to take annual leave, followed by flextime, time in lieu, and sick or domestic leave. Having to provide crisis care in the 6 months before the study was reported by 63% of the working carers, with half of them reporting more than one crisis. Over a third took time off work to deal with crises: The older the care recipient, the more likely the working carer was to have taken time off from work.

There was an inverse relationship between hours of eldercare provided each week and positive attitudes to care. Those who give the longest hours of care report higher rates of negative attitudes, as measured in the survey. These attitudes were also explored in the discussion groups, along with the stresses and satisfactions of providing care, the use of formal care services and levels of satisfaction with them, and plans for the future. Participants shared strategies that assisted in juggling work and care on a routine basis and in crisis situations. The discussions show that the most commonly reported strategies for eldercare management are community and family based, rather than related to their workplace or working conditions.

Boundaries: Negotiation and Responsibility

The following discussion is based largely on qualitative data recorded and transcribed from the eight focus groups and analyzed thematically in discussion between the two researchers. These group discussions involved 32 respondents (representing 24% of postal questionnaire respondents). They followed a common outline of open-ended questions: Group members were asked to describe how their caregiving situation had evolved, then to talk about how they managed their work and eldercare roles, and finally to discuss how they saw their futures as working carers.

Themes emerging within each group, as well as across groups, relate to the concept of "blurred boundaries" in the field of work and eldercare. Finch and Mason's (1993) work on the negotiation of family responsibility provides a significant conceptual foundation for this kind of analysis. Similarly, and more recently, Keating, Otfinowski, Wenger, Fast, and Derksen (2003) considered the patterns of change emerging from analysis of large quantitative databases, as larger and more dispersed support networks become smaller and more focused, and they raised questions about the "behind the scenes" invisible negotiations that appear to be taking place. In particular, the discussion groups explored the caring capacity of family networks in response to increased care needs of older members. Within families, particularly sibling groups, how does one person, usually a woman, become "the carer"? Although this question was not put to the groups in quite such terms, the participants' opening descriptions of themselves usually took a retrospective view, asking, "How did I get into this?" "Well, it just kind of happened…." said one man, before proceeding to describe the steps that he has taken, along with his parents, to manage their declining health.

A leading New Zealand researcher in the field of informal care (of older people with dementia) speculated about the family negotiations that might have preceded the assumption of "primary caregiver" roles by specific individuals. Opie (1992) claimed that these negotiations merit investigation by researchers and service providers in relation to the roles played by "secondary caregivers" or wider participants in the family and social support network.

A further significant theoretical and conceptual challenge has been made by Fine and Glendinning (2005), who claimed that recent work has "led social theory, research and policies to separate the worlds of 'carers' from those for whom they 'care'" (p. 601). Although this chapter discusses the boundaries of these worlds, it is not intended to further entrench the segregation, but rather to address and explore it, in order to show how blurred it is in everyday life and in social theory.

Factors in family negotiations can be summarized as location, sibling relationships, wider family relationships, and experiences of problem solving. Underlying these factors are clearly individual and shared histories, as well as cultural principles of reciprocity, affection, duty, and obligation.

The Boundary Between Working Lives and Eldercare Roles

In the discussion groups, the carers acknowledged shared features in the balance between working lives and caring roles regardless of the age of the people being cared for. Eldercare roles differ from childcare roles in being largely unplanned and developing either gradually or with a sense of crisis. Eldercare demands can also be episodic, but, in common with childcare, a prevailing concern is time management (Stewart & Davis, 1996).

The participants discussed how family-friendliness relates to the culture of each organization. All saw the councils as "good public sector employers." They noted ways in which formal leave mechanisms could be used to assist eldercare. In descending order of frequency of use (in the previous 6 months), these were annual leave (taken by 48% of respondents), time in lieu or flextime (used by 31%), and sick leave and domestic leave (used by 27% and 22%, respectively). Using leave without pay was mentioned by 9% of the working carers. In practice, unit managers and team leaders have some discretion in allowing leave for caring and crisis situations, although neither council has any explicit policies on eldercare.[1] Participants in the focus groups agreed that their employers were consistently supportive and responded flexibly and appropriately in crisis situations. Even though institutional and personal attitudes toward eldercare responsibilities may be generally supportive, the reality is commonly described as a juggling act, which is seldom publicly disclosed. Talking about eldercare when discussing weekend activities in the tea room could be a "conversation stopper." Increased public support for childcare and after-school programs helps working parents, but participants wondered when assistance for those caring for older parents might become more widely available.

When adjustments are needed, the study illustrated how both caring and working arrangements may change. Some group participants talked about adjusting their work hours down to help them cope with caring commitments: "I am fortunate enough to have an employer who recognises the importance of work and life balance; however, if this were to become a difficulty, I would reassess my work commitments." A part-time library worker said an awareness of family commitments underlay her professional choices about job changes, but "if a real crisis comes I might actually have to give it up." Another carer had cut her working hours down to 4 days a week, seeking time to herself, to balance the increasing time she was spending supporting her mother.

Others showed how "coping" had impinged more on caring than on their work: "My hours of care and support have reduced, as I wasn't coping. We have arranged a house cleaner and someone to mow lawns fortnightly. I am unable to keep both homes going."

Many people who need to take time out from work for eldercare were clearly aware that work "piles up." "Catching up at the weekend" was commonly mentioned, although the ability to do this depended greatly on the nature of the work. Council workforces clearly span the whole spectrum from office-based workers, who might have this option, to people in frontline roles, such as staffing enquiry desks, or team-based activities in parks and recreational facilities, where colleagues may have to support each other whilst managing fluctuating and erratic demands for eldercare.

Negotiating the Boundaries Within Family Networks

Mothers, fathers, mothers-in-law, and fathers-in-law were the main care recipients. None of the respondents gave their spouse as the recipient of care, which was a surprise to the researchers. It is possible that people caring for their spouses are underrepresented in the workforce. They may be older people who have already ceased paid work. Alternatively, caring for a spouse may not be seen as "eldercare" in the minds of employees. One woman (a 62 year old working part-time) mentioned caring for her 67-year-old husband. But she had come into the study on the basis of caring for her 85-year-old mother. This was also the only person who mentioned financial issues relating to caring. She and her husband were reliant on her part-time earnings, as her husband's earning power had been significantly affected by his illness, and he had taken early retirement due to ill health.

Geographic distance represents a clear boundary, which either limits or promotes care links between older and younger family members. Keeling (2001), in her study in a South Island community, explored the significance of "relative distance" in how older people handle the separations that families commonly experience. Ideas of personal and geographic distance featured in the discussions with the working carers, referring to their eldercare roles and other family relationships.

Relationships with siblings, in terms of who supports working carers, were widely discussed in the groups. Several participants expressed this in terms of their being "the responsible one." One woman said that, to her mother, "I have become the one who is asked for advice and is called on for support even though my siblings live close by." How care was shared, particular between siblings, gave rise to heated conversations in all the groups, with language of marked emotional intensity. These discussions were couched in terms such as "fraught," "they don't get an idea that it is as bad as it is," "real trouble," and "real vicious stuff" (Davey & Keeling, 2004, pp. 27–28).

Women carers were more likely to say they had the "main responsibility for care"—41% compared to 30% of the men in the study. In the context of sharing care between siblings, it is not always easy to separate the significance of gender from general patterns of behavior, in terms of societal and familial expectations. The study findings, and the focus groups in particular, indicated that male working carers were contributing significantly to eldercare, but it was not always clear whether these men are the only siblings living in the same city as their parent or parents. Several women carers referred to brothers who "help out regularly"; a son carer includes his three daughters in the network to keep his parents company, and they help in other practical ways. One Christchurch woman indicated that she and her sister do most of the carework, and her three brothers "don't have much to do with it, apart from the one who flies over from Australia in emergencies." But she also acknowledged that none of the brothers live in the South Island. Grounds for exemption from family care seem to relate partly to gender, partly to distance, partly to personality factors, and partly to conflicting family and work commitments. One participant accepted the limited support her brothers give their mother, on the basis that "[t]hey have young families and their own businesses" (Davey & Keeling, 2004, p. 31).

Another participant found it hard to evaluate what a "fair share" of family responsibility was, and was unsure of what other family members might reasonably expect from her: "An additional stress is caring for someone who has relatives out of town: do they approve of what I'm doing? Am I going too far in what I do? Should I be allowing her to be so reliant on me?"

In a further example, a woman had previously worked only part-time and had lived very close to her mother. Now she was working more, and her sister was also in town, but her mother's needs had increased, so she tried to renegotiate the sharing of care roles. However, her five siblings could not understand her concerns, which caused her some resentment.

Family relationships often involve more than two people at any point in time. Intergenerational links extend from younger to older and from older to younger. Several three-way relationships were described, in which the working carer provided support to two people, who were often sharing a household, such as parents or parents-in-law. At times of accidents or health crises, the needs of the two elders can diverge, and the working carer is called upon to mediate between, or weigh up the changing needs of, two people. Sometimes, a sibling is part of the negotiation around who cares for whom. One group participant spoke of how she supported both her sister and their mother. After their father's death, the mother had lived for some years with the sister, who had a mental health condition that could include episodes of violence and abuse, so the working carer was used to evaluating what might work for each and both of these women.

Often relations with the people being cared for are complex and difficult. Many people spoke with genuine ambivalence about their parents' continuing refusal to accept assistance. They acknowledged that such resistance was a sign of independence and autonomy. But they could also see the irony in that their parents' wish for independence made things harder for them as carers. At other times, reciprocity was the explicit rationale for care: "I provide care for my father and his wife as they would do for me were they able." Mutual support on a daily basis was described by one carer and her relatively young mother (aged 71). The mother had several medical conditions and needed morning assistance to "get her up and about." By the afternoon, the mother was fully mobile and able to provide care for her grandchildren: "[T]he kids walk there from school and spend after school time with her—it's very mutual."

Family relations can become attenuated or disrupted by disuse or past rifts. Confronting shared dilemmas in family care can be an occasion to reestablish contact. One Wellington carer had renewed contact with a sister following their mother's admission to hospital.

Some eldercare situations were perceived as particularly stressful. One group participant spoke of how hard she found the "one-way" part of dementia care. Although she spent only one hour each day visiting her mother, who was now in a hospital-level dementia care unit, she continued to feel drained and sad after each visit. Although these responses are commonly found within families, they become particularly relevant when the focus moves to services available beyond the family—across the next border.

Eldercare Roles at the Boundary of Informal Care and Public-Sector Service Delivery

This boundary received attention in the group discussions at three levels: first, where information flows (or in some cases doesn't flow) across the invisible boundary; second, where families and households work with community- and home-based services; and, finally, when the older person enters long-term care.

The information needs of family carers and how information is shared emerged as clear and consistent themes in all the discussion groups (Davey & Keeling, 2004):

> It's a problem to find out how to access these things—even the doctor didn't talk to us about the state mother was in—I had to find out by asking the neighbours.... The doctor just ignored the whole situation, which was pretty bad, because my parents had no food in the house and the doctor didn't tell us (or know?) the situation was that bad. We finally got someone to help three times a week, but really had to fight for it. (P. 40)

Questions about information included the following: Who needs to know what, what is available, how can information be accessed, and who is eligible for which services? "No one tells you what services you can get paid for, so you end up paying for everything yourself."

This carer clearly took matters into her own hands, whereas another turned this around, putting the onus on health-sector workers to inform families, saying, "Medical professionals should alert the families more." But other group members suggested that families should initiate information sharing, using phrases like, "The specialist had no idea of how mum was coping." When one carer asked, "Whose job is it to liaise?" the group concluded that both sides share this responsibility, in theory, but not often in reality.

There was a strong call for coordinated information on service options for supporting older people in local communities. This may reflect rapid change in New Zealand health delivery structures in recent years and a corresponding lack of clarity for older people and their carers, who find it difficult to keep up with "how the system works" or, as Gauld (2003) put it, "continuity amid chaos."

Community support groups, such as Stroke Club, Alzheimer's Society, Age Concern, and local church groups, were mentioned, usually in positive terms. Their services were seen as practical and accessible for both the carers and their older family members (Davey & Keeling, 2004, p. 17). Public health services (family practitioners, acute hospitals, and specialists) received a "mixed" response. Respondents were ambivalent in terms of information flows and at times were disaffected by a perceived lack of understanding of the everyday lives of older people and their carers (Davey & Keeling, p. 29). But the respondents were, at the same time, appreciative of the clinical care provided. One group member noted (and others affirmed)

> a sense of pressure, like the speed of the decision to discharge Mum that day. It feels like the system itself is ambivalent—at times they seem to withhold information, at others they are pushing you to get more involved, drop everything.

A phrase used more than once was "stepping in—to fill the gap," as if the system can always "count on the family to step in."

Group members expressed a view that many older people and their families consider admission to residential care as a "last resort," making comments such as "She is terribly worried that we will stick her in a home." However, others expressed relief when a carefully chosen residential care placement was working for both family member and family carers. Some participants were providing quite high-level care (daily visits, personal and emotional support, and care planning) to family members in rest homes or long-term hospitals. This pattern had previously been described in Belgrave and Brown (1997).

On the basis of these discussions, it is clear that planning and managing residential care admission comprise a time of very high stress for all family members, and very mixed feelings were described about how such decisions are made. Milligan (2006) threw further light on these situations in a New Zealand study exploring family decision making relating to residential admission, and there are other local projects in this field, such as Jörgensen (2005). Milligan's analysis relates to blurring the boundaries of care, which in her study is "manifest in an increased penetration of informal caregiving within the semi-public space of the residential care home" (2006, p. 320).

One carer had made a written complaint following a hospital discharge of her mother ("sent home in nightie and bare feet in a taxi"), and others talked of their concerns that ranged from mistrust to dissatisfaction. Looking ahead, one person said her mother would be willing to go to a rest home, but knew this would not mean an end to her concerns as a carer: "You have to watch them all the time." Those who cared for family members in residential care facilities gave examples of crisis care and the management of medical problems. Others talked about dealing with personal shopping, buying clothes, as well as continuing to provide "oversight," to ensure that their family members were being well cared for. "You still have to go in every day and make sure everything is all right." Another carer visited her mother in a long-term hospital daily, taking personal washing home and returning it the next day: "I don't have complete faith in those who run, and work in, these places—night care, especially, worries me."

Key issues when examining the blurred boundary between informal and/or family care and public sector services for older people therefore include access to information and quality assurance, in the sense of public confidence in the services being provided. When their older family members become consumers or recipients of services, family carers continue to care *about* the quality and type of these services, even though they have discontinued their care *for* their elders to some extent.

Public and Private: Zones of Care

Consultation documents used in the development of the New Zealand *Health of Older People Strategy* included a diagram with a series of concentric circles surrounding an older individual (New Zealand Ministry of Health, 2001, p. 7). This provides a way of conceptualizing "zones of care" and the "integrated continuum of care" model. The family circle or network is the zone closest to the older person, the most immediate and implicitly the first preference. Beyond this, in "onion ring" fashion, are friends and support groups, then agencies, organizations, and institutions.

Rossler (2004) has pointed out that two semantic models in everyday language underlie the use of the terms *public* and *private* and that these two models are at odds with each other (pp. 6–7). The first model is the "onion ring," in which the layers imply spheres of activity occurring on a spectrum from private-personal-familial to fully public. The second model, and the source of blurring in the family–public discourse, implies independent action of individuals (such as a personal decision to attend a religious ceremony), but it cannot operate as if private and personal spheres are describable as spaces. Thus, the confusion recorded in the discussion groups echoes the conceptual model embedded within a significant public policy document, by implying that there could be virtual boundaries rather than permeable membranes between these circles or rings. In other words, the New Zealand policy framework implies that these zones are clearly bounded as spaces or zones, whereas families experience the boundaries as blurred.

A unique boundary issue arose in one group, concerning the way New Zealand deals with accidental injury through the Accident Compensation Commission's (ACC) social insurance program (ACC, 2006). In most cases this adopts a "no-fault" approach to service delivery. Nevertheless, members of the discussion groups offered their experience of anomalies and gaps in ACC service coverage. One carer's mother had had a fall in Australia and struggled to meet the costs of physiotherapy on her return to New Zealand. Others commented on their confusion when ACC support for accidental injury seemed more generous than health benefits relating to disease conditions, such as arthritis.

New Zealand research, exploring the border territories between the public–work and family–care realms, which could offer contextual or comparative perspectives on the findings reported in this chapter, is limited. This study covered the perspectives of working carers in two workplaces, but did not systematically seek employer, union, or policy perspectives.

In her feminist analysis of recent New Zealand changes in social policy, McManus (2005) described "the reworking of the care boundary brought about by changes to women's and men's participation in paid employment." Other New Zealand work in this area explores and scopes public and private definitions underlying the provision of care and support for older people. Lilley (2004) for instance, posed the question "Whose role is it anyway?" and scoped policy responses to the challenges of implementing family-friendly workplaces. This literature review cited six barriers to family-friendly workplace practices from the workers' perspective: the corporate culture, career advancement, social pressure, the male work ethic, coworker resentment, and the "long hours" culture.

Principles of Negotiation in the Work–Care Boundary

This chapter highlights the perspectives of working carers who took part in the Wellington and Christchurch study and places these experiences in the context of theories about boundaries and zones of caring. Comparisons can be made with earlier work by Keeling (1998) in the Mosgiel Longitudinal Study of Ageing, which explored the perspectives of older people as active managers of their family and social support networks. Narratives from that study show that older people manage access to care and support from their families through negotiation, and in ways that serve their pragmatic and philosophical desire to maintain their independence, on their own terms. They also adopt the principle of exemption (also seen in Finch & Mason, 1993), whereby elders exempt family members from increasing their support on the ground that "[t]hey've got their own lives to lead." The same principle clearly operates in the Wellington and Christchurch material, as siblings share care or exemption from care, as noted above. A further principle is one of payment. If an elder buys (i.e., a financial transaction is involved) a service, he or she retains control or keeps the exchange reciprocal. Some of the working carers also talked about "buying" care, although mostly in terms of "public-sector" activity or task-specific services, such as gardening, not as a substitute for family care.

The carers' discussions also covered principles of negotiation, which featured in the Mosgiel study (Keeling, 1998), particularly in terms of "surveillance and routinisation," where patterns of regular contact within families provide consistency as well as monitor change. Central principles evident in the Mosgiel analysis, from the viewpoint of older care recipients, resonate in the way that the working carers talk about negotiating the boundaries that lie hidden along the continuum from independence to dependency.

Milligan's comments on blurring the boundaries of informal and residential care have already been mentioned (Milligan, 2006, p. 320). She also demonstrated the limitations of the concentric rings model as related to care provision. Two other New Zealand researchers have used spatial analogies in their descriptions of informal care. Schofield (1996) drew on anthropological approaches to the management of liminality to describe the transitions in caregiving that accompany the admission of an elder to residential care. Family members talk about their sense of a "no-man's-land" between family-based informal care and the roles played by care workers in residential homes. Applying similar analytical approaches to how older people experience the increasing intensity of informal home-based care, Hale (2003) reported a sense of invasion, using the expression "It's not my home any more" to convey this changed sense of space (pp. 253ff). She, like Wiles (2003), highlighted concepts of mobility, routine, and scale. Hale paid particular attention to boundaries, which appear in her interviews clearly as doorways and thresholds.

Wilson (2000, pp. 115ff.), taking a global perspective, critically examined the continuum that runs from duty to love, and from paid to unpaid work, and asked, "[W]here does the family begin and end?" In positioning themselves along this continuum, the New Zealand working carers acknowledge that their thinking is in a state of flux. The 1990s saw a major "rolling back of the welfare state," as Kelsey (1993) put it. This led many people to question and reconfigure their understanding of the roles they play in their daily lives, as individuals, family members, community participants, volunteers, employees, and citizens. It has also changed expectations of how the state might be able to support an aging population, both at present and in the future.

The results of the city council studies cannot be generalized to other New Zealand workforce situations. It would be well worthwhile to extend this study into a wider variety of workplace settings, for example into manufacturing or primary industries. Such work would help to further develop an understanding of linkages and potential "border disputes" between workplaces and patterns of eldercare. This should be part of initiatives to plan actively for long-term economic and social sustainability in the context of an aging society and an aging workforce.

Note

1. A bill, sponsored by Sue Kedgeley of the Green Party, is being considered in the New Zealand Parliament that would provide employees with young or disabled children with a statutory right to request flexible working arrangements and place a legal duty on employers to consider any such request seriously. In March 2006, on behalf of the New Zealand Institute for Research on Ageing, Judith Davey made a submission to the Transport and Industrial Relations Select Committee that such provisions be extended to workers with eldercare responsibilities. An amended bill with this extended provision is progressing through the Parliamentary Process in late 2007.

References

Accident Compensation Commission (ACC). (2006). *Accident Compensation Commission*. Retrieved April 29, 2006, from http://www.acc.co.nz

Belgrave, M., & Brown, L. (1997). *Beyond a dollar value: Informal care and the Northern Region case management study*. Auckland, New Zealand: North Health, Massey University and Waitemata Health.

Davey, J., & Keeling, S. (2004). *Combining work and eldercare: A study of employees in two city councils who provide informal care for older people*. Retrieved February 22, 2007, from http://www.dol/govtz.nz/futureofwork/workforce-elder-care.asp

Estes, C. L., & Swann, J. H. (1992). *The long term care crisis: Elders trapped in the no-care zone*. New York: Sage.

Finch, J., & Mason, J. (Eds.). (1993). *Negotiating family responsibilities*. London and New York: Tavistock and Routledge.

Fine, M., & Glendinning, C. (2005). Dependence, independence or inter-dependence? Re-visiting the concepts of "care" and "dependency." *Ageing and Society, 25*, 601–621.

Gauld, R. (Ed.). (2003). *Continuity amid chaos: Health care management and delivery in New Zealand*. Dunedin, New Zealand: University of Otago Press.

Hale, B. (2003). "It's not my home any more": A critique of in-home care. In R. Gauld (Ed.), *Continuity amid chaos: Health care management and delivery in New Zealand* (pp. 253–264). Dunedin, New Zealand: University of Otago Press.

Jörgensen, D. (2005). Factors and decisions surrounding entry into residential care (abstract for paper presented at Symposium for Postgraduate Students Working on Topics Relevant to Ageing and the Well-Being of Older People in New Zealand). Retrieved April 29, 2006, from http://www.vuw.ac.nz/nzira/downloads/seminar/2005/abstracts2005.pdf

Keating, N., Otfinowski, P., Wenger, C., Fast, J., & Derksen, L. (2003). Understanding the caring capacity of informal networks of frail seniors: A case for care networks. *Ageing and Society, 23*, 115–127.

Keeling, S. (1998). Ageing and independence in a New Zealand community: A three dimensional view. Unpublished Ph.D. thesis, University of Otago, New Zealand.

Keeling, S. (2001). Relative distance: Ageing in rural New Zealand. *Ageing and Society, 21*, 605–619.

Kelsey, J. (1993). *Rolling back the state: Privatisation of power in Aotearoa/New Zealand*. Wellington, New Zealand: Bridget Williams Books.

Lilley, S. (2004). *Whose role is it anyway? Implementing family-friendly workplace practices in New Zealand*. Report, Summer Studentship Programme, Social Science Research Centre, University of Canterbury. Retrieved September 19, 2005, from http://www.ssrc.canterbury.ac.nz/research/reframing/care/whoserole.shtml

McManus, R. (2005, March). Minding the gap. Paper presented to 1st International Conference, "Community, Work and Family: Change and Transformation," Manchester University, UK.

Milligan, C. (2000). "Bearing the burden": Towards a restructured geography of caring. *Area, 32*(1), 49–58.

Milligan, C. (2006). Caring for older people in the 21st century: "Notes from a small island." *Health & Place, 12*, 320–331.

New Zealand Department of Labour. (N.d.). *Future of Work fund*. Retrieved February 22, 2007, from http://www.dol.govt.nz/future ofwork/worklife/asp

New Zealand Families Commission. (2005). *Statement of intent 2004/2005*. Retrieved February 22, 2007, from http://www.nzfamilies.org.nz/publications/strategic.php

New Zealand Ministry of Health. (2001). Health of older people strategy: Health sector action to 2010 to support positive ageing (draft for consultation). In New Zealand Ministry of Health, *Ministry of Health 2002 Health of Older People Strategy*. Retrieved February 22, 2007, from http://www.moh.govtz.nz/publications/hops

Novitz, R. (1987). Bridging the gap: Paid and unpaid work. In S. Cox (Ed.), *Public and private worlds: Women in contemporary New Zealand* (pp. 23–52). Wellington, New Zealand: Allen and Unwin/Port Nicholson Press.

Opie, A. (1992). *There's nobody there: Community care of confused older people*. Auckland, New Zealand: Oxford University Press.

Organisation for Economic Cooperation and Development (OECD) Health Project. (2005). *Long-term care for older people*. Paris: OECD Publishing.

Phillips, J., Bernard, M., & Chittenden, M. (2002). *Juggling work and care: The experiences of working carers of older adults*. Bristol, UK: Policy.

Rossler, B. (Ed.). (2004). *Privacies: Philosophical evaluations*. Stanford, CA: Stanford University Press.

Schofield, V. (1996). *A fragile sort of balance: Careguardianship as a phase of caregiving for people with dementia*. Unpublished Ph.D. thesis, Victoria University of Wellington.

Stewart, J., & Davis, S. (1996). *Striking a balance: New Zealand women talk about career and family*. Auckland, New Zealand: Penguin.

Twigg, J., & Atkin, K. (1994). *Carers perceived: Policy and practice in informal care*. Buckingham, UK: Open University Press.

Wiles, J. (2003). Daily geographies of caregivers: Mobility, routine and scale. *Social Science and Medicine, 57*, 1307–1325.

Wilson, G. (2000). *Understanding old age: Critical and global perspectives*. London: Sage.

8

Boundaries Blurred and Rigid at the Front Line of Care

Care Workers and the Negotiation of Relationships with Older People

Jane Mears and Elizabeth A. Watson

Those in management positions in community agencies, who oversee the work of paid care workers working directly with older clients, can adopt very different positions in relation to "blurred" boundaries and the defining of what is acceptable and unacceptable professional practice. In an interview conducted in a Sydney agency, one of the care workers describes the very different reactions of two coordinators, on two separate occasions roughly a year apart, to a very similar circumstance. The care worker describes the situation in which she found herself, the contrasting responses from management, and how these different reactions elicited a very different response from the worker herself.

In each case an elderly client of the care worker was in hospital for an extended period of time. In the first case the worker describes how she found out about the difficulties this client was facing and her own response to them.

> There was another lady in the ward with her that I also know. She told me that this lady was turning her underwear inside out to wear, because the hospital doesn't do washing. She was bed-bound. She couldn't get up and rinse her underwear herself ... so I took them home and washed them. And I got in so much trouble.

The worker had some understanding of her manager's perspective but felt that she had no option but to deal with this situation in her own way.

> Now I understand where she [the manager] was coming from because there's protocol involved—disease control, [or] her saying I took 10 pair of underpants when I only took 3, all that sort of thing. I was prepared that if that was the case I'd go out and buy her another pair of 7 underpants if that was what it was going to boil down to.

A year later the same circumstance arose, and the care worker decided to "get in first."

> The coordinator rang me this morning and asked me if I'd been to see this lady in hospital. I said, 'No, I'm going to go this afternoon'. And I thought, 'Oh well, I'll try it, while she's on the phone.' I said, 'Have you got a problem with me taking home any clothing that she's got to wash?' And she said to me, 'No, and if you haven't got time to do it, drop them into the office this afternoon and I'll take them home and do them'. So it was a completely different story.

The care worker felt far more comfortable about the second response and also felt that her own judgment and decisions were being vindicated and supported.

> It just makes you feel so much better. I mean you're not worried about ringing the coordinator. I'm not going behind her back doing things. Before I was doing things on my own and thinking, 'I'll just take the consequences when they come'. But now I'm not frightened to do that. I find it very easy.

Introduction

This account of the interactions between paid care worker and coordinator highlights the contested nature of boundary marking and monitoring in the paid care industry. It is a worker's account, and it is workers who, by the nature of their work, find themselves, on a daily basis, confronting issues of personal and professional boundaries and the need to make decisions concerning appropriate behavior. Regardless of whether they deliberately choose to overstep the mark or do so inadvertently, it is more likely that the consequences of those actions and decisions will be experienced more directly by them, and be more likely to result in some form of censure or loss of professional autonomy. Nevertheless, for coordinators and managers in the industry, issues of boundary demarcation, how to apply rules, and how best to monitor them are of even greater concern, even if they are dealing with these issues at arm's length. They, too, seek to ensure that the elderly client group is provided with high-quality and attentive care. But they carry a responsibility as well for the well-being of the care workers whom they manage.

Our interest in paid care workers and in the ways in which they carry out their work and negotiate its particular demands was first explored in a research project we conducted in the mid-1990s. The sample for that research was comprised of working carers. We interviewed 40 women who were carrying a major responsibility for the care of a family member while also undertaking paid caring work of one kind or another (Watson & Mears, 1999). Not all of these women worked as paid care workers, but, among those who did, almost all spoke of the close relationships developed with clients, especially when that association had extended over some time. It was this feature of "hands-on" carework, together with the sense that what they were doing made a palpable difference to the lives of others, that made such work rewarding and, indeed, enjoyable. They also spoke of how difficult it was to draw a line between what was defined as permissible carework and what was not "part of the contract," or to exit from a client's home immediately when the contracted time was up. We were struck by the passion with which the care workers spoke of their work as well as their awareness that sometimes a decision to do something extra for a client, or continue "outside hours," was perceived not just as overstepping the line but also as a breach of "professional" conduct and that their coordinators or managers (almost always) took a very different view from their own about how these "problems" ought to be negotiated. From the point of view of care workers, these apparent "breaches" were deemed essential for the sake of their clients and "good care."

These particular issues became an important focus in a second project undertaken more recently by one of us as part of doctoral study (Mears, 2006), and it is this research that forms the basis for this chapter. Here the focus has been on paid carework. The workers interviewed in this study were all employed by the Benevolent Society of New South Wales, a large, not-for-profit, welfare agency based in Sydney, Australia. The in-depth interviews with 20 care workers and 10 managers and coordinators were taped, transcribed, and coded. The software package NVivo was used to order and organize the coded data and facilitate analysis.

The care workers, managers, and coordinators in this sample were mostly women, aged from 30 to 60 (the average age being the mid-50s). About a quarter were sole breadwinners. They had worked for periods ranging from 3 months to 10 years; most had worked as care workers for at least 5 years. The majority of the care workers were employed as permanent part-time workers, working up to 20 hours per week, and a few were employed as casuals, called to "fill in" when the permanent part-time care workers were sick or unable to work. All the care coordinators and managers were employed full-time. The participants were based in four offices in metropolitan Sydney. For many, this was a job they had come to later in life. A significant proportion of the care workers were "older workers," over 45, when first appointed. This was not a "first job" for any of the people interviewed for this project. They came with a wide range of previous work experience, both paid and unpaid.

We begin our chapter with the reasons for becoming care workers and then move to a consideration of the nature of the work and its particular rewards. Finally, we explore the issue of boundaries, how these are conceptualized and the circumstances in which they become blurred or difficult to maintain, and the notion of professionalism and professional relationships in carework.

Why Did They Choose to Do This Work?

These care workers had chosen to work in this area because they wanted to work with older people.

> Just a liking for elderly people. To enjoy elderly people and to like that kind of work.

They spoke respectfully of the older people they worked with.

> They've got a life of experience, a world of experience, and they're interesting. They're all go, their sense of humour and they are all different characters.

But most of all, they wanted to do a job where there was the opportunity to make personal contact with people.

> I like people and I like meeting them. And I like helping them. And I like getting paid for it too which is lovely.... I love the people. And they are all different and you just respect the differences and enjoy it.

A number of the participants had taken on carework because they had become disillusioned with their previous jobs. They had been working in nursing homes, as human resource managers, and as managers in the finance industry, and spoke scathingly of the effects of reduced funding and cost cutting and the consequent loss of personal contact. They wanted to work in a "caring environment," doing something that was useful and constructive.

> I worked for a bank for a long time and I got sick of being told to sell fries with that, to sell more and more services, when people came in for their withdrawals. I just got tired of that. I wasn't interested anymore. I have always had a liking for the older people.

One participant described doing carework as a chance "to give something back," to make a meaningful social contribution, after one of her adult children was badly injured in a car accident. This was a job where she felt she could make a difference to someone's life. Indeed, doing work that "made a difference" to people's lives was important to most of those interviewed.

> I ended up being manager of a building society. Then my daughter was nearly killed in a car accident. Very touch and go. And it changed my life. It just did, it changed. Up until then my job was the most important thing to me, but then after the accident I reassessed everything and I thought, 'I don't want to do this anymore. I want to do a job where I'm appreciated, where I can help other people more'. I know it probably sounds stupid, but it was like giving thanks for us getting her life back. I don't know, part of it's guilt maybe, or part of it's you want to give something back.... So that's how I started out.

And some had become care workers after informal caring responsibilities had ceased.

> I cared for my mother-in-law when she was dying.... And when she passed away, I thought, 'That is a job I think I might like to do'.

Rewarding Work

Carework, for these women, was immensely rewarding. The care workers spoke at length about the intrinsic rewards of the job; they really enjoyed "working with people." Every day was different; new pleasures were discovered, and new challenges tackled.

> To me this is just the most rewarding job that anyone can have.... I just love my job.... I am so lucky because I have got beautiful, beautiful clients. I thank God for this opportunity to be able to do this kind of work. I really believe that this is what I was put on this earth for. And I do a damn good job. And I just get so much pleasure out of it. There is not a day where I wake up and go, 'Oh no, I've got to go to work today'. I get up and I'm ready to go. I just love it. I absolutely love it.

Much of the time, the care workers worked alone and unsupervised, using their own judgment to make decisions about what needed to be done. This freedom was greatly valued.

> We've also got a lot of freedom. We are out on the road and we like it. We don't have someone on our backs, breathing down our throat. In the bank ... they are there all the time watching you.
>
> There's a lot of trust put in us, and a lot is left up to our own discretion. We have to know our guidelines and we have to know what we can do, but most things, within reason, we can do.

Professionalism and Boundaries: Care Workers

The relationships between the care worker and older person are central to these accounts. The work involved in sustaining those relationships and maintaining the independence of the older person was a prominent theme. But this also prompted comment on professionalism and what this meant in the context of carework. There was constant discussion about where boundaries might need to be drawn. Was the care relationship too close, and how was one to assess that? This was depicted as a delicate balancing act negotiated each day, requiring different strategies depending on the circumstances. Sometimes these strategies were judged successful, and other times less so.

In talking to both the coordinators and the care workers, it was clear that firm, carefully laid down rules, across the board, did not necessarily work; and, indeed, all the workers spoke of some inevitable and (what they saw as) reasonable breaches of the rules. They argued that they broke and stretched the rules in the best interests of the older people. Nevertheless, this is a difficult terrain to negotiate. Setting care worker and coordinator accounts side by side, the contradictory messages become plain. Care workers were employed because they care, yet urged not to care too much. They were encouraged to be flexible and use their own initiative, but not to take this too far. They were encouraged to form good relationships and respect the wishes of the older person, but not to "allow" the older person to become too dependent on these relationships, or too dependent on one particular care worker.

The relationship between the care workers and the older people receiving care is a "professional" relationship based in a "familial" context. There are many parallels with the actions and decisions required in informal, family care but also important differences. The emphasis on ensuring that the relationship not become too close was one such difference.

> The bosses tell you, 'You're not their mother, don't get personal', but it's pretty much impossible really. I try to do it where I can, but ... we're more personal care. When you shower somebody and you see somebody in the nude, you can't help but feel that trusting, relationship with them.

For a small number of care workers, maintaining "distance" and "boundaries" did not appear to be a big issue.

> And you've just got to be very careful with your perimeters that you don't overstep the mark and this is what you do with them. Build up the confidence with them.

The rules can also be used as a guide to good practice, an aid in helping prevent problems from occurring.

> Sometimes you tend to go very much by the book, follow the rules.... The guidelines that we've been given ... strongly emphasise the problems that could be caused if you go outside the boundaries, outside the guidelines. So I do everything I can within the boundaries. I don't want to step outside them.

However, over time and with experience, some of the issues around boundary setting, which had been so fraught at the beginning, became less so.

> When I first started I wanted to do everything for everybody. But now, four years later, I've learnt that boundaries are very important. You've got to stop somewhere. I've learnt the hard way. When I first started, I thought about the job all the time, but you realise that you can't take care of everybody, or solve everyone's problems.
>
> I think you do learn to put up barriers ... and I think as I've lost a client—I hate calling them clients, they're my people—as you lose one, I think the next one that comes in you try and just keep that little tiny tissue paper between you. Not a wall, but just a little tissue paper there:

> you do try. And you've got your own family and you've got your own problems. You do have to draw a line in certain things.

Transgressing the Boundaries: Breaking the Rules

The difficulty of maintaining boundaries between a professional and personal relationship was a perennial concern for the majority. All the care workers had "broken the rules" at one time or other.

> The coordinator talks about being professional and keeping it on a professional basis. It is very hard when you are dealing with people's spirits and their emotions, to keep it clinical. So yes, I do step over that border sometimes.
>
> Sometimes it is really hard to try and keep it on a professional level. Actually I find it almost impossible.... How I am with them, that's how I am in my own home.

In the following excerpt, the care worker saw her ability to form good relationships as a "weakness." This particular care worker was recruited, personally, by one of the managers. She had been a carer, and when her mother moved to a nursing home, she needed work. The manager was particularly impressed by her caring skills. Her exact words were that "she has a calming presence," and, in her own interview, the manager described her as one of the best care workers on her staff. The judgments being made by each party are the opposite of what you would expect.

> Forming relationships is problematic. I find that one of my weaknesses is that I tend to make friends.

Workers were aware that they were pushing the boundaries and breaking the rules, but continued to do so. They saw these transgressions as "little things" that they felt enabled them to better do their job.

> We are never supposed to give our home numbers out to people. But of course we all break the rules and there are certain people we will give the number to and there are certain people you won't. The genuine people will never ring you unless they have to.... It is awful really when you are told not to give your number out to anybody. And then as I've said to one coordinator, 'You've got my home number. You ring me on my home number. What is the difference?' Because it may only be, 'Could you pick me up a bottle of milk or something'? And how much easier and time saving is that?
>
> Nothing major. One lady, I do her washing and hang it out on Thursday. Now if the weather's bad, raining, naturally I can't put her washing

> out, so I'll take it home and put it in my dryer and bring it back to her the next day. Little things like that.

And then there were emergencies, where the care worker felt she had behaved in a responsible manner, but had broken the rules. In the following case, it was her client's daughter who needed the assistance.

> She hurt her foot and couldn't drive her car down to the doctor's. I didn't have to take any extra work time and I just rushed her straight down to the doctor, got her foot fixed and took her back. I put it in my notes. I thought, 'OK I'll be honest. I'll put it in my notes'. Then I got told off, called in and told off. They said, 'Look you should have rung before you went down to the doctor'. And I said, 'Well I know that', but I was trying to do everything within my time and in the five minutes it took me to make the call, I thought, 'I can just rush her down'. So that's annoying.

The emphasis on drawing strict boundaries between work and family lives often proved very difficult in practice.

> Like on a Saturday I might just sit down with a cup of coffee and phone up Mrs B.... Because I know she is sitting there all on her own with nothing to do. See that is another thing. I go home and I think about these people. I do. It doesn't matter what I'm doing, I could be in the shower washing my hair and I'm thinking of this poor old woman by herself. And they don't leave my mind.

The vignette with which this chapter begins is a particularly telling example of the difficulty in drawing boundaries between one's professional and personal life, but it also underlines the problems faced by managers in specifying what constitutes appropriate professional behavior and the different judgments they may make.

Managers and Care Coordinators

The "frontline nature" of carework—the complex, unpredictable nature of this kind of work—was acknowledged by managers and coordinators. It was not simply that many coordinators had themselves been employed as care workers before moving into office-based management jobs, but also that a particular understanding of the nature of carework had been adopted by the organization. This understanding was built into everything that related to this work—recruitment advertisements, job specifications, policy, and protocols. The "official" understanding of carework in the Benevolent Society has been one that emphasizes the importance of the monitoring and observation role of care workers and of trusting them to take initiative so as to ensure that quality care can be delivered. Arguably, this emphasis is as significant a part of the official view of carework as the emphasis on maintaining professional boundaries, or "distance" in professional relationships, and ensuring that workers are neither exploited by clients nor overworked in their effort to do the right thing by vulnerable older people.

> But there are times when they will need to make decisions for themselves and how they follow a care plan.... That is very hard.

The inherent tension in the position of manager arises directly from the dual responsibilities of this position—the need to ensure both that the older people receive high-quality care and that care workers are well supervised and supported in their work. In many cases, care coordinators spoke in terms of the competing rights, interests, and needs of clients, on the one hand, and care workers, on the other. They knew how difficult it was for many workers to draw boundaries and stick to them.

> Some people have very good caring hearts, but there are always boundary issues which get in the way. It is very difficult to separate being a friend from being a worker.... The boundary issues are difficult for a particularly caring person. They go in and they see this person on their own, who maybe has no family and they are lonely and they want to go and visit them on the weekend. And you can't, because they need to separate from their job.

The interviews with coordinators and managers revealed how much thought they had given to ways of negotiating what they called *professional boundaries* to ensure that both the care workers and the older people were protected from potential exploitation, while at the same time developing appropriate professional relationships.

> Everybody struggles with this in this field because you are going in every single day of the week and of course you develop a relationship. We are looking for people who have this ability to be able to be empathetic, understanding, be warm in what they do without actually giving completely of themselves. That is a very difficult balance. I probably have three staff members who do that amazingly well and if I could bottle it I would because you see the others will struggle with it. And that is how we sell ourselves as a relationship based service. And that is the dilemma.

But to the worker interacting day by day with a client, the question of where you draw the line and how you stick to this understanding remained unclear. If you were unable to develop and sustain a relationship with those you cared for and to feel for them and their circumstances, you couldn't do the job properly.

> There seems to be this dilemma that is not settled. How can you actually be human and be emotional, but still cut people off at a certain point without burning out? People are either throwing themselves completely into it or doing an unnatural thing where they are not feeling for people, because they are too scared that they are going to cross those boundaries.

The care coordinators expressed the dilemmas succinctly: The care workers are employed because they care, but they didn't want the care workers to care too much.

> The relationship between a client and a care worker is a very fine line. You walk over the line and you've pushed the boundaries away, you've thrown them away. Trying to educate care workers in where that line is, is sometimes very hard. They don't understand it. And the problem for us is we employ people who care. We employ people who care but we don't want them to care too much. We have a problem. It is educating them. Educating the carers as to why they should never go over that line.
>
> So it is a huge skill to professionally care for someone in a way that is loving and compassionate and then extricate yourself. And that is what we are asking people to do.

What to Do

Although a numbers of strategies were employed to help prepare workers for the difficult decisions they would confront "in the field" and to reinforce this learning, managers emphasized the importance of regular training. Training provided opportunities to work through and deconstruct the care workers' motivations, to reinforce notions of "professional boundaries," and to discuss how a degree of distance between client and care worker might be sustained.

> I remind them about that idea of rescuing and how often we get caught up wanting to help other people, because we've got needs of our own that we're having to fulfil and we do that by feeling good about what we are doing in helping another person. Which isn't a bad thing in itself, but it does create these dilemmas. The way we are managing it at the moment is consistently reminding them about the importance of not doing it. And maintaining separateness from the client. Not doing things out of hours,

> checking in with us if they are doing anything extra, moving them out of the situation, though that is tricky.

Sometimes when the coordinators suspected the relationships were getting too close, they would remove the care worker. It was "a tough call" to work out whether or not a relationship was "too close" and had the potential to harm client or worker or both.

> I've got clients who say, 'I can't have anybody except her'. Then I come in a little bit heavy. I speak to the care worker and I say, 'Look, you have to get out of there, this is becoming too deep. It's too deep. Not only is the client over-involved, but she sees you now as her only support in life. Without you where does she go?' That's bad. That's really bad. So I gently ease the worker out. I say to the worker, 'You need a change. You need to do something different. You've got to start rejuvenating yourself. You've been doing this for too long, the same thing over and over, so you've got to think of yourself'.

In the following excerpt, the coordinator describes how she removed a care worker from a situation she judged "unhealthy." This extract also illustrates the diplomatic negotiating skills demanded of the care coordinator.

> My strategy for dealing with it would depend on the client. I am thinking of a situation, in particular, where the client just would not have anybody else and hated change. I introduced somebody else slowly. So rather than pull the care worker out of the house, devastated, I put in two care workers and split them, so one of them went in for three days and the other went in for two days. I introduced other people for transport, so they were used to other people doing other things for them. It also meant that the care plan was easier to keep. You need a very clear care plan with different people going in. The tasks have to be clear too, as to who is doing what. And then eventually we just pulled them out. So we just slowly pulled her out.

One coordinator felt that the care workers themselves were actually the best people to sort out this issue. If the experience turned out to be a negative one, then, she argued, they would learn from that. She felt that transgressing the boundaries was always going to happen, and there was only so much a supervisor could do.

> I would rather not know about it. Unless I think that they are really wrong, I mean then you find that they have gone too far down the track. I would clearly be reluctant to pull somebody out of a care situation, if it is working, just because the client is saying, 'I like this person'. I think if it is working and most of our care workers, well they are not young. They are middle aged. They are fairly sensible. I think I'd give them the benefit

of the doubt. They usually find the first time, they've given a phone number and they have a client who is calling them in the middle of the night. They learn. It is the best way to learn on that way. You are never going to stop them anyway.

Discussion and Conclusion

How are we to characterize carework and "good care," and is it possible to draw boundaries around "good care" in a way that will be clear and acceptable to all? When paid care workers talk about their work and attempt to explain the nature and demands of that work to others, the complexity and contradictory nature of care and caring work, and the ways we think about caring and enact it, come to the fore. What is particularly prominent in these accounts is the difficulty in defining when a boundary is breached and in reconciling different positions and perspectives on professionalism and what doing the job in a professional way means in practice.

Care is embedded in relationships, and caring describes a relationship: The model for caring work is a familial model. In a similar way, paid carework is also bound up with relationships, those formed between care workers and the older persons for whom they care.[1] These relationships are clearly important to worker and older person alike, and building and sustaining these relationships are what make such work satisfying and rewarding. Furthermore, establishing trust between worker and client is seen as a mark of "success" in one's work and, together with empathy and a good understanding of the client's needs and individual preferences, is viewed as essential to "good care." At the same time, this is a professional relationship and one that requires that boundaries be put in place, boundaries that limit the degree of emotional involvement and the nature and extent of the caring work that is "allowed." Yet this professional caring relationship is being developed in a "familial" context. These workers use the imagery of "family" and speak of the experience of making good friends and developing lasting friendships.

Carework, whether informal or paid, has always entailed more than simply the action and decision making associated with attending to a person's physical needs: It requires emotional labor (Craib, 1995; Duncombe & Marsden, 1993; Jackson, 1993) and the application of what has come to be known as "emotional intelligence" (Goleman, 1995). Needless to say, this is not unique to carework, but it is an especially prominent feature of this work. Workers spoke of how establishing trusting personal relationships had enabled them to perform a range of caring activities that would be difficult without an intimate knowledge of the older person they were caring for. These activities included the less tangible and quantifiable goals of the caring enterprise such as improving and maintaining the emotional and psychological well-being of the client and ensuring that he or she retained as much independence as possible. Emotional labor is itself complex and is not always recognized or taken into account in defining work and its demands. As Twigg (2000) observed, "It is labour that is only partly visible … emotion is not part of the rational, bureaucratic account" (p. 173).

Furthermore, emotional labor is often seen to equate to care: The components of emotional labor—careful thinking about and attentive listening to others, the work required to sustain their emotional well-being, attention to their needs and preferences, the remembering and celebrating of milestones and achievements in the lives of others, the effort involved in being empathic and responding empathetically, and so on—are what we name as *care*, and, when speaking of caring, it is this activity, thought, and effort we have in mind. Some theorists have stressed the importance of viewing care as a practice (although they also emphasize this is not to the exclusion of dispositional aspects; Tronto, 1994, pp. 118–119). This study lends support to that argument but at the same time reminds us how difficult it can be to separate out the emotional or dispositional components of carework; to specify where, in exercising these elements of care, the line should be drawn; or to draw clear and explicit boundaries around what constitutes good care practice. Theorists of care have also pointed to the "unbounded element in carework that derives from the importation into it of an ethic of love that derives from the primary bonds of family" (Twigg, 2000, p. 178). Here is the potential for considerable tension and conflict: It is built into the ways in which we conceptualize carework. Care workers in this study and others "self-identify with being caring persons, and indeed are perceived to be such by employers also," even though, as Twigg pointed out, "such recognition does not translate into the formal work contract" (p. 177). Furthermore, setting limits and drawing boundaries are always likely to be more difficult in relation to emotional components (when is a relationship "too close"?) than in relation to actual actions—specifying what actions, exercised with what frequency or in what circumstances, constitute a problem. These problems are likely to be especially acute when, as in the contemporary context,

> workers find themselves caught between the personalised demands of this ethic of care—reinforced by the emotional bonds that develop over time, particularly in response to dependence—and the conditions of wage labouring in an increasingly hard-nosed and cost-pressured sector. (Twigg, p. 178)

But, as this study reveals so clearly, the tensions and conflicts that arise directly from the ways in which we understand carework were not confined to those at the front line of care. In the accounts of managers and coordinators, we found these same tensions and some additional ones. They, too, were aware of the importance of emotional labor. Most of them had worked as care workers before moving into management roles. They understood the importance in carework of empathy and trust, of having a detailed knowledge and understanding of the habits and idiosyncrasies of the older person. In deciding whether or not to employ someone in this capacity, these were the qualities and skills that they looked for. But in their managerial role, they had taken on an additional set of concerns and priorities. Both workers and managers stressed the primacy of the interests of the client, and both expressed the belief that this principle should direct the decisions taken by both care workers (in their "hands-on" carework) and the Benevolent Society (in its planning and priority setting). But, for the coordinators and managers, a commitment to and responsibility for the well-being of their workers was also an important consideration, and in some circumstances this took precedence over that of the clients (at least in terms of immediate actions taken). Managers and coordinators spoke of professionalism and professional behavior and were committed to the "professionalization" of carework: They wanted to raise the status of this sector and see the requisite skills, capabilities, and knowledge properly recognized. It is also important to note that they had to manage the provision of good care under circumstances of increasing demand without a comparable increase in funding.

The role of manager in these circumstances is not straightforward, and it is not surprising that there were some marked inconsistencies among this group in their response to difficult issues around boundary setting and what constituted stepping over the mark or what was seen to be inappropriate action or flawed judgment. Interestingly, there was a higher level of consistency in relation to actual *statements* about roles and clear boundaries and the importance of setting limits and saying "no," than is revealed in the *actions or decisions* that were taken when confronted with a potential breach. And in this organization, as in most care provider agencies, there are well-established policies that spell out what constitutes professional behavior; and, not surprisingly, in their accounts it was often the language of policy that was called upon and an official position that was enunciated. Nevertheless, listening to their accounts it seemed to us that the language of managers and coordinators could be characterized as more instrumental.

The very fact that boundaries are blurred, and that firm or immovable limits are difficult, if not impossible, to set (except in relation to the more extreme instances), suggests the need to keep revisiting and questioning and critiquing care practice and the notions of professional behavior that apply in the context of carework. It also suggests the importance of ensuring that this critique is informed by both what workers tell us about the experience of engaging in carework and what their supervisors see as causes for concern. We can be sure that this will not guarantee that there will be a happy meeting of minds, a middle ground, or an easy compromise, but it will ensure that the communication channels are kept open for both to voice their concerns and to hear what the other has to say.

Note

1. We might add that these relationships are being established and sustained within an organizational context that is also comprised of relationships, especially those between worker and manager, and that the imagery of (one big) family is sometimes drawn on in this larger context as well.

References

Craib, I. (1995). Some comments on the sociology of emotions. *Sociology, 29*(1), 151–158.

Duncombe, J., & Marsden, D. (1993). Love and intimacy: The gender division of emotion and "emotion work": A neglected aspect of sociological discussion of heterosexual relationships. *Sociology, 27*(2), 221–241.

Goleman, D. (1995). *Emotional intelligence: Why it can matter more than IQ*. New York: Bantam.

Jackson, S. (1993). Even sociologists fall in love: An exploration in the sociology of emotions. *Sociology, 27*(2), 201–220.

Mears, J. (2006). *The world of care work*. Sydney: Benevolent Society of New South Wales.

Tronto, J. (1994). *Moral boundaries. A political argument for an ethic of care*. New York: Routledge.

Tronto, J. (2004). Care as the work of citizens: A modest proposal. In K. Waerness (Ed.), Dialogue on care (pp. 91–118). University of Bergen, Norway: Centre for Women's and Gender Research.

Twigg, J. (2000). *Bathing: The body and community care*. London: Routledge.

Watson, E., & Mears, J. (1999). *Women, work and care for the elderly*. Aldershot, UK: Ashgate.

9

Sharing the Work

Care Networks of Frail Seniors in Canada

Norah Keating, Donna Dosman, Jennifer Swindle, and Janet Fast

> Mary Knowles is 82 years old. She and her husband, George, have lived in the same suburban bungalow for 50 years. Though the neighborhood has changed, the couple still has a few close friends who live nearby. The Knowles have a daughter, Sharon, who is married and living in the same town, and a son, Rick, who is divorced and lives in a community about one hour away. Each has two children. Sharon, her husband, and Rick are employed full-time. Mary and George have two grandchildren and several nieces and nephews. Each has one remaining sibling. In the past 5 years, Mary has had a series of strokes that have left her incontinent and have affected her ability to manage the everyday household tasks she always had done.

The situation of the Knowles family is not unusual. Like many other older couples, Mary and George have a small number of close kin but a more extensive extended family network. None of their family members lives with them, though there are strong connections among them. They have long-standing relationships with neighbors and friends in the area, though the numbers of these relationships are declining with age. Mary and George's children are middle aged and engaged in the labor force; younger family members are beginning their employment careers. Mary's family is concerned about her declining health and ability to manage at home.

In this chapter, we address the question of the intersections of families and work among families caring for an older adult. Through a focus on families, rather than individuals, we ask not about tensions or boundaries between families and work, but about how families organize the "work" of employment and caring. We use the Knowles family as an example of how this set of family members might find different ways to manage their employment and caregiving roles, considering the various intersections between these two family work spheres. Like other families with an older member with chronic health problems, the Knowles family must attend to both their caring work and their labor force involvement.

Employment and Caregiving

The children of Mary Knowles are typical of those in many developed countries where most adults are employed. There has been considerable documentation of the workplace difficulties experienced by these caregivers such as reduced workplace productivity, opportunities for advancement, and employment income and benefits (Duxbury, Higgins, & Coghill, 2003). There also is evidence that people providing care to a frail older family member make workplace accommodations such as reducing their hours of work, moving from full-time to part-time, turning down a job or promotion, or leaving employment altogether in order to provide care (Cranswick, 2003). It's not surprising, then, that we have turned our attention to the question of how families can manage both of these demanding jobs, and the intersections between them.

Later life caring presents particular life course challenges in managing family and employment work roles. For example, whereas the main carers of young children usually are parents who live with them, carers of an older person may be adult children who have responsibilities to family members in their own households as well as to elderly family members living at a distance. For the latter group, their caring challenges may include travel time and running two households in addition to the other demands of care.

In this chapter we consider how families manage their paid and unpaid work responsibilities. A family perspective moves us away from thinking about how individuals juggle caregiving and employment roles. It is useful to know what Sharon Knowles might do given the high demands of her job as well as the increasing care needs of her mother. However, focusing on her family allows us to better understand how the group of people closest to the frail older adult garners its human resources to provide care, the strains they may experience, and the outcome for care recipients of this management of work demands. Does Sharon leave work in order to provide care? Do other family members assist in caregiving? Do Sharon and Rick share the caring among them while retaining their jobs? Does George assume all of the caregiving of his wife?

Who's the family when it comes to care for a frail older adult? The Vanier Institute of the Family (2004) defines *families* as

> any combination of two or more persons who are bound together over time by ties of mutual consent, birth and/or adoption or placement, and who together assume responsibilities for physical maintenance and care of group members ... distribution of goods and services, and affective nurturance-love. (P. xii)

Especially for older adults, *families* and *households* are not synonymous. George and Mary Knowles live alone. Yet they have a broad network of same-generation and younger-generation relatives with whom they have family ties.

Who are the people from this family group who provide the goods, services, and emotional support to older members with chronic health problems? We call this group a *care network* (Fast, Keating, Otfinowski, & Derksen, 2004). The care network for Mary Knowles likely will be drawn from the group of relatives mentioned in the vignette and perhaps also from close friends and neighbors.

Families might find different ways to manage their employment and caring depending upon the resources on which they may draw. Caring alone while being employed may differ considerably from caring with others. The configuration of family caring resources also may have a significant impact on those receiving care. If employment is a competing demand to caregiving, then families in which all carers are employed may provide less care or fewer high-demand, hands-on tasks such as personal care. Other characteristics of networks such as the proportion of women, of close kin, or of proximate members in the network also may influence care receiver outcomes. For example, networks of employed carers who live near the cared-for person may be able to orchestrate employment and care responsibilities more easily than networks at a distance. Networks that are predominantly women may have more familiarity with gendered tasks of meal preparation and personal care.

Three main questions related to employment and caring in families are considered in this chapter. First, what are the employment profiles of families who provide care? Little is known about how families might differ in their apportioning of responsibilities for care to a frail older member and for earning a living through labor force participation. This question is important if we are to better understand not only how families do what they need to do (in this case, providing care to an older member) but also how they provide financial support to family members. Care networks with high labor force involvement of their members may be stretched in terms of their ability to provide some types of care such as the hands-on daily tasks related to personal care. Those with no labor force involvement may have less access to a broad network of coworkers and others who have skills and knowledge useful in navigating the formal care sector. This may be especially true if carers become isolated because of high levels of caring responsibility that result in their becoming disconnected from others.

Second, do caregiving families with different employment profiles also differ in other family resources that may enhance or constrain their ability to provide care? For example, does living close to the cared-for person allow employees to juggle employment and caring responsibilities that would not be possible if they lived at a distance? Finally, we ask whether networks with different employment profiles also vary in the amount and type of care they provide. Given that both employment and caregiving can be time consuming, we anticipate that networks in which no members are in the labor force might provide more care and do more demanding care tasks than networks in which some or all members are employed.

Employment and Care of Older Family Members

Problematizing caregiving is a common theme in the contemporary discourse on employment. Good employees are viewed as those for whom the paid job is their most salient role, requiring them to take on the attitude of "work first" over "care first" in order to remain employed (Appelbaum, Bailey, Berg, & Kalleberg, 2002). From this perspective, there should be strict boundaries between work and family life. If "work first" is the rule, employed caregivers may be more productive and their family members best cared for if employed family members are in networks that have a high proportion of members outside of the labor force.

Do families resolve dilemmas caused by the need to fulfill paid and unpaid work demands by apportioning the jobs among a number of people? Employment does reduce the chances of becoming a caregiver (Dautzenberg et al., 2000), suggesting that the first call on care responsibilities within families may be to those who are not employed. Yet many caregivers are in the labor force. Phillips, Bernard, and Chittenden (2002) found that among a sample of employed carers in the United Kingdom, 44% said that they had primary responsibility for care, 26% shared caring duties equally with one or more others, and a further 30% helped provide care but took less responsibility. Many were concerned about the impact on their own health. Such negative impacts of caring despite assistance from others may be an indication of the difficulty of managing caring and employment even with multiple carers.

Other Family Resources and Care for Older Family Members

Resources such as having close kin available to care, more women, or carers who live close by can make a difference in the ability of families to provide care.

A common finding in research on individual carers is that the majority are women (Barrett, 2005; Morris, 2001). Among care networks of frail older adults in Canada, half are composed entirely of women, and 28% entirely of men; 22% have a mix of women and men (Fast et al., 2004). Women and men carers are not equally distributed across employment statuses. In Canada in 2001, 93% of men carers and 72% of women carers age 45–64 were employed full-time (Cranswick, 2003). This is comparable to the United Kingdom (Phillips et al., 2002) and the United States (Barrett), where a higher number of male carers are in full-time work. These 2005 findings suggest higher proportions of men in networks in which all members are employed because women may reduce their labor force involvement in order to provide care (Dautzenberg et al., 2000).

Relationship and age composition also may be related to labor force profiles of caregivers. Most individual caregivers are close kin of the care recipient (Li, 2004). At the network level, findings are similar, although approximately 20% of care networks contain at least some neighbors and friends (Fast et al., 2004). Over the course of a lengthy caregiving career, those with weaker ties to the cared-for person may adhere to the "work first" imperative, leaving their unpaid job of caregiving rather than reducing their employment. Friends, neighbors, and extended kin are most likely to make these choices. If they are outside of the family of the frail older adult, they have fewer obligations to engage in the work of that family. Boundaries around families can provide legitimate excuses. Families may not have the capacity to accommodate close kin in the same way because these family members may be needed to provide caring and financial support to the family. In other families there may be little labor force involvement among close kin members such as spouses of frail seniors who likely are past labor force age (Brewer, 2002). Spouse caregivers may have limited connections to others, making it difficult to recruit help. They are most likely to be part of small, one- or two-person networks; to be living with their frail husband or wife; and to be providing high levels of care (Carpentier & Ducharme, 2003).

Proximity is an important family resource given the time requirements of both paid work and caregiving. Given their age and life course stage, many employed carers may have responsibilities for their own spouses and children and live in separate households from the cared-for person. A recent study of caregivers in the United States found that carers who lived with the care recipient were less likely to work full-time (39%) than carers who lived more than an hour away (63%) (Barrett, 2005). This suggests that networks with high levels of employed members may be typified by commuting carers who add travel time to their caring responsibilities. Middle-aged caregivers may predominate in care networks in which everyone is employed because younger people may have more family demands, less job flexibility, and thus reduced ability to provide care.

Given these relationships between employment and other family resources, we would expect that care networks in which all members are in the labor force would have more members who are middle-aged, close kin, and living nearby. In contrast, networks in which no one is employed are more likely to have high proportions of older people, especially spouses; high proportions of women; high proportions of live-in caregivers; and fewer members.

Employment Patterns and Care Outcomes

Do different employment patterns in care networks result in different amounts or types of care provided to the older family member? Is it better from the care receiver's perspective to have several carers who are not in the labor force? Or, do those in the labor force have better access to knowledge about supports and services or to direct services such as family care leaves, so that a mixed-employment profile works better for the frail senior?

There has been little research that directly addresses these questions. However, research on individual carers suggests that here, too, employment status is an important care network characteristic. Two thirds of working carers spend fewer than 10 hours per week helping care receivers (Phillips et al., 2002), though care time of employed carers is highly gendered. Women caregivers provide more hours of care (Morris, 2001), reducing their employment hours rather than their family care hours in order to meet both paid and unpaid work demands (Doty, Jackson, & Crown, 1998). Depending upon their resources, networks may be able to compensate for the time crunch of employed carers. Care receivers of employed carers receive significantly more hours of help from other sources compared to those receiving care from caregivers who are not employed (Doty et al., 1998).

Proximity of network members and network size also are associated with higher hours of care (Fast et al., 2004). It's not clear how these characteristics interact with the employment composition of networks. Based on existing findings, our main expectation would be that networks in which all carers are employed will provide more hours of care if most or all network members are women. As caring competes with labor force engagement and productivity, so it seems likely that labor force engagement may reduce time available for care (Pavalko & Artis, 1997).

Employment profiles of networks also will influence the types of care tasks provided. Frail seniors may need a number of care tasks to support them at home such as housekeeping, outside maintenance of their home, transportation to appointments, or personal care. It may be extremely helpful to a care receiver to have someone assist with tasks that can be done in the evening or on weekends, such as picking up groceries or doing some gardening. However, having someone available to get care recipients to appointments during the day, make lunch, or organize care may also be critical (Rosenthal, Martin-Matthews, & Keefe, 2007).

A consistent finding in caregiving research is that women and men provide assistance with different care tasks (Ekwall, Sivberg, & Hallberg, 2004). Yet, employment may dampen the effect of gender, with employed carers doing tasks that they can manage within the constraints of the employment workday (Rosenthal et al., 2007). Fewer than one in four employed carers helps with the time-consuming daily tasks of eating and feeding, toileting, and nursing care (Phillips et al., 2002).

Together these findings suggest that families in which all carers are employed full-time provide fewer hours of care and a more limited range of tasks. It is unclear whether employment profiles directly influence the amount or types of care, or whether other network characteristics such as gender mediate this relationship.

Care Networks of Older Adults in Canada

Data for this chapter came from the 2002 Canadian General Social Survey (GSS) on aging and social support (Statistics Canada, 2002). We use information from the 2,407 adults aged 65 years or older who said that they had received assistance during the previous year from a family member, friend, or neighbor because of their long-term health or physical limitations. Because our interest is in families and care, we focus on the care networks of these older people, that is, the family members (as well as any friends and neighbors) identified by them as having assisted them with one or more care tasks in the previous year because of that respondent's long-term health or physical limitation.

We know several things about members of these networks, including age, gender, relationship to the older adult, and geographic proximity of each network member. From this information on individual members of networks, we developed network measures that were used in our analyses of family caring resources. These are employment status composition (proportion of network members employed) and network size (total number of people who provided assistance). Other network characteristics included gender (proportion of women in the network), relationship (proportion of close kin, extended kin, and nonkin such as friends and neighbors), age (proportion under age 25, 25 to 44, 45 to 64, and over age 65), proximity (proportion in the same household and outside the household), and duration of care (caring for less than 1 year, 1 to 2 years, and more than 2 years).

Older adults in receipt of care also were asked to report on how frequently each of nine care tasks was performed by each network member and how much time was spent on each occasion. Total care time provided by individuals for each task was aggregated to the network level by adding care time provided by each network member. All analyses were weighted to ensure that estimates are representative of the Canadian population.

Three sets of analysis were conducted to address questions about employment profiles and the caring resources of later-life families.

1. What is the employment composition of care networks? Employment composition of networks was categorized into three groups or profiles (all members employed, mixed employment, and no members employed). Then the proportion of all networks with each of three employment composition types was calculated.
2. Do networks that differ in their employment profiles also differ in other characteristics? Frequencies of other network characteristics—that is, family resources (size, gender composition, relationship composition, age composition, proximity composition, and duration of care composition)—were calculated by the three employment profiles.
3. Do networks that differ in employment profiles differ in the amount and type of care they provide? That is, within families, are there trade-offs at the intersections of employment and caring work? To determine the relationship between employment profile and amount of care, number of care tasks, and likelihood of the network providing the care task, the following calculations were done for each of the three employment types: total hours of care per week provided[1] by the network, mean number of types of tasks provided by the network, and proportion of the networks within each of the three employment profiles that provided each of the care tasks. Tests of significance were calculated controlling for key characteristics of the recipient (marital status, gender, and health status).

Organizing Employment and Care: Family Resources and Employment Profiles

Are families like the Knowles able to organize care so that there is a mix of employed and not unemployed caregivers to share in the paid and unpaid work? For the majority of families, the answer is no. The largest proportion of networks are those with no members employed (44%). In the Knowles family, George may be the sole carer, believing that he can manage and not wanting to burden his children. The second largest groups of care networks were those in which all members are employed (37%). An alternate solution for the Knowles family may have been for Sharon and Rick to share the caring responsibilities while retaining their jobs. Finally, 19% of the networks had some members in the labor force and some not employed. A mixed-employment network in the Knowles family might include Sharon, Rick, Rick's former wife, and George and Mary's next-door neighbor.

Family care networks with these different employment profiles have diverse sets of resources and demands as well (Table 9.1). Among networks in which all members are employed, the highest proportion of network members are entirely close kin, are age 45–64, live outside the household, and have been caring for more than 2 years. These networks have the highest employment demands as well as the highest proportion of networks that have been caring for more than 2 years. There are potential strains here as these groups of carers attempt to organize their paid and unpaid work and negotiate the intersections between them. Unfortunately, we know only about the outcome of any negotiation, not the process by which families come to the "solution"—a particular set of people in a care network. The majority of all-employed networks have commuting caregivers who live in the surrounding area, adding travel time to their caregiving. There appears to be a high level of commitment among these network members who provide care for long periods of time. Networks with mixed employment (some members employed, and some not) are diverse. Fewer than half are entirely close kin. In fact, over half of the networks have members who are entirely nonkin or a mix of close and distant kin, friends, and neighbors. Being able to draw on friends and neighbors to assist is a resource that is more available to these networks than to those that have other employment profiles. Most have a mix of women and men, supporting the contention that employment smoothes out gender differences. Networks with carers of different ages predominate in this employment profile. They may be able to negotiate care among themselves to accommodate their specific fam-

TABLE 9.1 Network Characteristics by Employment Profiles

Network Characteristic	All Network Members Employed (%; N = 901)	Mixed-Employment Status (%; N = 447)	No Network Members Employed (%; N = 1,059)
Gender			
All women	33.2	18.7	44.5
All men	48.7	12.3	45.2
Mixed women and men	18.0	69.0	10.3
Relationship			
All close kin	71.9	44.3	66.1
All distant kin	7.9	3.4	10.8
All nonkin	12.6	5.4	16.4
Mixed relationships	7.6	46.9	6.6
Age			
All < 44 years old	31.5		13.3
All 45–64 years old	51.9	17.2	25.9
All 65+ years old	4.0		52.4
Mixed ages	13.0	77.8	9.2
Proximity			
All same household	24.1	14.9	54.4
All outside household	67.4	36.7	38.5
Mixed proximity	8.5	48.5	7.1
Duration			
All caring for < 1 year	8.8	3.8	8.8
All caring for 1–2 years	5.4	4.0	11.7
All caring for 2+ years	82.4	67.0	75.8
Mixed duration	3.4	25.2	3.7
Mean network size	**1.4**	**2.6**	**1.2**

Note: All proportions and means are significantly different across the three employment types.

ily life cycle and employment demands. These networks also have the most members, with an average network size of 2.6 people.

Overall, mixed-employment networks have a variety of resources that may be an excellent basis for providing higher levels of care and diverse care tasks. However, they also have the lowest proportion of networks that have been caring for more than 2 years. It may be that these networks are made up of people who are not sufficiently connected to the cared-for person to sustain caring over a lengthy period of time.

Networks with no one in the labor force also are distinct in their resources. The highest proportion of these networks is entirely women, is over age 65, and lives with the person for whom they are providing care. These networks are small and intense, averaging only 1.2 members. Some may be lone spouses who themselves are elderly. More than one quarter are entirely distant kin or friends and neighbors who live nearby. These networks are very focused on the tasks at hand and may not be able to gain access to a variety of other resources that would be helpful to them. There are concerns about the fragility of these networks despite the lack of competing demands of employment because of the small size, potential isolation, and later-life family stages.

Organizing Employment and Care: Care Provided by Networks with Different Employment Profiles

Patterns of care provided by the three types of networks illustrate how their different sets of family resources are used to provide care. The amount of care associated with the three employment profiles and the types of care provided by members of these care networks differ considerably (Table 9.2).

Networks with all members employed provide the fewest hours of care (6 hours per week) of all networks and the narrowest range of care tasks (2). Only house maintenance and outside work are provided by the majority of these networks. It is not surprising that these care tasks are the most common among employed networks. Neither task requires daily involvement, and both can be scheduled outside of regular employment hours. In contrast, fewer than 20% of these networks do daily tasks such as meal preparation, laundry, or personal care. When the demands of employment and carework compete, these employed carers appear to give priority to employment. Those with sufficient income may have some opportunity to purchase services to assist them. However, it also is possible that the people for whom they provide care do not need assistance with these daily activities. A relatively small proportion (14%) of people

TABLE 9.2 Amount and Type of Care by Employment Profiles of Care Networks

Network Characteristic	All Network Members Employed (%; N = 918)	Mixed-Employment Status (%; N = 723)	No Network Members Employed (%; N = 956)
Mean hours of care per week	5.5	15.1	8.9
Mean number of tasks	2.1	3.6	2.9
Proportion Providing the Following Tasks			
Meal preparation	18.4	43.4	40.9
Laundry	17.8	40.6	36.3
Housekeeping	16.3	51.7	44.1
House maintenance	42.6	53.5	28.5
Outside work	50.5	60.2	33.2
Grocery shopping	40.2	66.4	49.7
General transportation	40.2	65.0	48.0
Bill paying and banking	32.3	48.4	43.1
Personal care	13.4	34.7	33.7

Note: All proportions and means are significantly different across the three employment types.

receiving care from employed networks has severe levels of disability. Alternately, families in which all carers also are in the labor force may not have the time to provide higher levels of care that might be required by those who are very frail.

Mixed-employment networks provide substantially higher hours of care (15 hours per week) and the largest number of care tasks (4). Because of their combination of income and time resources, these networks may be in the best position to manage the work of caring and the work of employment through sharing of these work roles. The majority of these networks provide four tasks: house maintenance, outside work, grocery shopping, and general transportation. Smaller proportions also do more intense daily activities. Proportions of network members doing these tasks are higher than in all-employed networks, suggesting as well that these networks have the best resources to manage family work. The variety of employment statuses, age, gender, and proximity differences, and the larger network size, means that tasks can be divided according to the time and skill of caregivers. Having some members who are relatively new to caregiving may be a source of support to those who have been caring longer. These networks do have the highest caring demands. Among seniors for whom they provide care, 24% have a severe disability.

Networks with no employed members fall between the other groups in average hours of care (9) and number of tasks (3). They appear to have the fewest resources because they are small and mostly over age 65. Fewer than half provide each care task. Yet for the intense daily tasks of meal preparation, laundry, housekeeping, and personal care, their patterns of care are similar to those provided by mixed networks. The main commonality among these two network types is having at least one person who is not employed. In comparison, rates of engagement in these tasks are lower among the all-employed networks. Having network members who are not employed is a real asset when it comes to a network's ability to provide daily, face-to-face contact with the cared-for person, though the small size of these networks and potential isolation also make them vulnerable. In contrast, involvement of not-employed networks in outdoor tasks such as yard work and in maintaining the house is much lower than among networks with some labor force involvement. This may be because members of these networks are older or because they simply cannot manage all of the tasks needed to support the family member for whom they are caring. In some cases, such tasks may not be relevant because of the setting in which the older adult is living or because of his or her level of disability.

A Family View of Family Work

Across the life course, families have paid and unpaid work responsibilities. Yet paid work most often is considered outside of a family context, whereas most unpaid work such as the care of young children or older family members with chronic health problems is seen as being solidly within the family's purview. We believe that these conceptual boundaries between family and work are not part of families' lived experience. Families must earn an income to support themselves, care for one another in times of need, and find the time and other resources to manage their various work commitments. They must do this work across the family life course as family resources and work demands ebb and flow.

We have taken a network perspective to better understand how families undertake two work roles: employment and care to frail seniors. Our interest lay in whether families incorporate into care networks members who are both inside and outside of the labor force and who have a variety of other characteristics, in order to manage their various commitments. The profiles of the networks of these caregiving families suggest that only a small subset of family members provides care.

Among all three types of care networks, relatively few family members are actively involved in providing care for the frail older family member. Why is it that, for example, from a family network of 21 people (spouse, 4 children and children-in-law, 2 grandchildren, 12 nieces and nephews, and 2 siblings), so few members of the Knowles family are involved in Mary's care? Do the demands of employment and care to other family members mean that families simply are too stretched to do more family work? Do expectations about who should be responsible mean that extended kin or older siblings are not expected to do this kind of family work? Do divorces mean that family connections are more tenuous? Because we did not have an insider view to the dynamics of families such as the Knowleses, we are unable to address these questions directly. The ways in which groups of people negotiate the boundaries around "who's family" will result in more or fewer people from the Knowles family available to do this family work. Some family care networks are rich in employment resources but stretched in terms of caregiving time. All-employed networks manage intermittent tasks and low levels of care but may not be able to sustain caregiving over the long haul. Most are midlife networks at high-demand times of their employment careers. We wonder whether such families are able to purchase formal services for hands-on care or whether, over time, one or more members might leave the labor force to do the daily caregiving required by seniors with high levels of disabilities.

Other family care networks have time resources but do not have the benefit of employment income or the linkages that come through interacting with others in the workplace. Not-employed networks are the smallest of the care networks and thus lack the depth of caregiving resources available in other network profiles. These family networks often are not networks at all but consist only of older caregivers, often spouses like George who are isolated in their households with the person for whom they are caring.

However, these networks are most likely to be entirely nonkin, suggesting that friends and neighbors play an important caregiving role, at times replacing family caregivers. As well, some of these not-employed networks may have caregiving resilience because they have younger members. Almost 40% have all members who are under age 65. These may represent adult children or others who have left or forgone labor force involvement in order to provide care. If caregiving responsibilities are such that employment is not feasible, then these families may be severely constrained in their ability to access financial resources to assist them in providing care.

Mixed-employment networks are the richest in caring resources, with the largest numbers of caregivers and diverse membership. They provide the greatest hours of care across the broadest set of care tasks to seniors with the most severe health problems. Members cut across life cycle stages, bringing with them a variety of skills as well as differences in patterns of time availability. This network configuration seems ideal from the point of view of those receiving care as well as families managing demanding work roles. We wonder, then, why it is that only about one third of family care networks have this mixture of employment and other caregiving resources.

Mixed-employment networks may reflect the evolution of all-employed networks who reach the limit of their caring resources. Networks with all members employed may be able to manage if the person they care for does not need a high level of care. However, access to formal services is difficult in many jurisdictions even for those with financial resources. If needs for daily care and for care management increase, these families may find that they need at least one member who takes on these time-consuming tasks. In some cases, such members may be recruited from among family members who are not employed; in others, someone may relinquish employment.

Networks with no employed members might have a different care trajectory. They may evolve into mixed-employment networks if care needs escalate and if there are younger family members with high levels of commitment to caring who can be incorporated into care networks. However, not-employed networks already provide care to seniors with fairly high levels of disability. It may be that rather than recruit younger members into caregiving, these small networks may provide care as long as possible, using nursing homes or other residential facilities as an option if care needs exceed their abilities to provide care.

Profiles of family caring networks provide a basis for targeted supports to families providing care to a frail older adult. Their support needs may differ considerably. Families with high labor force demands might benefit from workplace policies that allow caregiving leave or flexible work arrangements. Those without employment might receive most assistance from income security programs or social programs to assist with home maintenance or other tasks that cannot be managed by small, elderly caregiver groups. Further exploration of the interaction of employment status and other network characteristics might assist with fine-tuning such interventions. For example, within the not-employed networks, network members in midlife might benefit most from support for reentry into employment after caregiving responsibilities have finished.

Finally, we believe that considering the work of families is a useful approach to understanding life cycle differences in the ways in which families manage their work lives. We have illustrated how a family like the Knowleses may find different solutions to their caregiving responsibilities. However, we know little about those who do not assume caregiving roles. Are later-life families similar to young families in that care to dependent family members is seen as the responsibility of a small group of family members? Are caregiving responsibilities in families "assigned" regardless of other work demands such as employment? Should public policies be targeted to facilitate the concurrent caring and employment that appear to be part of the everyday lives of many families?

Further work needs to be done to follow families over time as they take on and move through paid and unpaid work roles, as they share work across generations, and as they care for members, young and old, who need support. Just as employment and caregiving are processes, so too do families change over time in resources, membership, and commitments to their family work.

Note

1. Amount of care provided is determined from the perspective of the care receiver. We estimate that hours of care in some task areas such as shopping or care management may be underrepresented if they are not visible to the care receiver.

References

Appelbaum, E., Bailey, T., Berg, P., & Kalleberg, A. L. (2002). *Shared work, valued care: New norms for organizing market work and unpaid care work*. Washington, DC: Economic Policy Institute.

Barrett, L. L. (2005). *Caregiving in the US* (research conducted for the National Alliance for Caregiving and the American Association of Retired Persons). Retrieved September 13, 2005, from http://assets.aarp.org/rgcenter/il/us_care giving_1.pdf

Brewer, L. (2002). Families that care: A qualitative study of families engaged in the provision of elder care. *Journal of Gerontological Social Work, 39*(3), 41–56.

Carpentier, N., & Ducharme, F. (2003). Care-giver network transformations: The need for an integrated perspective. *Ageing and Society, 23*, 507–525.

Cranswick, K. (2003). *General Social Survey Cycle 16: Caring for an aging society*. Ottawa: Statistics Canada.

Dautzenberg, M. G. H., Diederiks, J. P. M., Philipsen, H., Stevens, F. C. J., Tan, F. E. S., & Vernooij-Dassen, M. J. F. J. (2000). The competing demands of paid work and parent care: Middle-aged daughters providing assistance to elderly parents. *Research on Aging, 22*(2), 165–187.

Doty, P., Jackson, M. C., & Crown, W. (1998). The impact of caregivers' employment status on patterns of formal and informal eldercare. *Gerontologist, 38*(3), 331–341.

Duxbury, L., Higgins, C., & Coghill, D. (2003). *Voices of Canadians: Seeking work-life balance*. Ottawa: Human Resources Development Canada.

Ekwall, A., Sivberg, B., & Hallberg, I. R. (2004). Dimensions of informal care and quality of life among elderly family care givers. *Scandinavian Journal of Caring Sciences, 18*(3), 239–248.

Fast, J., Keating, N., Otfinowski, P., & Derksen, L. (2004). Characteristics of family/friend care networks of frail seniors. *Canadian Journal on Aging, 23*(1), 5–19.

Li, L. W. (2004). Caregiving network compositions and use of supportive services by community-dwelling dependent elders. *Journal of Gerontological Social Work, 43*(2/3), 147–164.

Morris, M. (2001). *Gender-sensitive home and community care and care giving research: A synthesis paper. Final report.* Ottawa: Health Canada, Women's Health Bureau.

Pavalko, E. K., & Artis, J. E. (1997). Women's caregiving and paid work: Causal relationships in late midlife. *Journal of Gerontology: Social Sciences, 52B*(4), S170–S179.

Phillips, J., Bernard, M., & Chittenden, M. (2002). *Juggling work and care: The experiences of working carers of older adults.* Bristol, UK: Policy Press and the Joseph Rowntree Foundation.

Rosenthal, C. J., Martin-Matthews, A., & Keefe, J. (2007). Care management and care provision for older relatives amongst employed informal caregivers. *Ageing & Society, 27*(3), 1–24.

Statistics Canada. (2002). *General Social Survey: Social support and aging.* Ottawa: Author.

Vanier Institute of the Family. (2004). *Profiling Canadian families III.* Ottawa: Author.

10

Financial Payments for Family Carers
Policy Approaches and Debates

Janice Keefe, Caroline Glendinning, and Pamela Fancey

Introduction

Most primary caregivers of older people living in the community are family members. Because this carework is largely unpaid, this contributes to substantial economic advantages for the long-term care system. In fact it has been suggested that without the central role of family, the system would be unable to meet the care needs of its older citizens. Yet, falling birth rates, the increased participation of women in the labor force, changes in households due to increasing divorce rates, and increased geographical mobility challenge the continuing availability of family carers, an assumption upon which most long-term care policy is based (Pickard, Wittenberg, Comas-Herrera, Davies, & Darton, 2000). Moreover, many studies demonstrate that informal caregiving for family members can have adverse impacts on personal physical and mental health (Cannuscio et al., 2004; Cranswick, 1999; Hirst, 2003); family and social obligations; and economic status, including employment income, savings, household expenditures, and, in the longer term, pensions (Carmichael & Charles, 1998; Ginn & Arber, 2000; Glendinning, 1990; Keating, Fast, Frederick, Cranswick, & Perrier, 1999; Keefe & Medjuck, 1997). Unless a range of services and other support for family members are included in long-term care policy, these costs and consequences may only result in a redistribution of expenditures in both the shorter and longer terms. Thus, the issue of payment for family care is at the heart of endeavors to create economically and politically sustainable policies for community-based long-term care. Such policy raises questions about the commodification of family care and the blurring of boundaries between care provided by family that is typically unpaid and that provided by formal (paid) care providers (see Ungerson & Yeandle, 2006).

Countries have different approaches to supporting family caregiving. These approaches tend to reflect the wider social welfare regimes within which they are embedded. In some countries, particularly Scandinavian, older people have access to relatively extensive publicly funded formal homecare services (Wiener, 2003). The care of older people is viewed as a predominantly state responsibility, and formal services help to reduce reliance on family and friends, particularly for very intensive or intimate personal care. At the same time, formal homecare services for the care recipient may provide some relief for family carers. In other countries, such as Australia, "support for family caregivers sits comfortably within the ambit of its [Australian] approach to social policy, based on mutual obligation between the state and other sectors, including individuals and families" (Howe, 2001, p. 111). Here, there has been an increasing amount of support for carers, including the right of access to services and the right to a carer's allowance to help cover the cost of caring (Howe, 1994, 2001; Office for Public Management, 2005).

In a number of countries, policies to support community-based care include the provision of financial payments for care services. They may be paid directly to the care provider or transferred to the care provider through entitlements made to the care receiver. These payments may be accompanied, to a greater or lesser extent, by other measures such as services targeted to the carer and/or the older person needing assistance; and social protection measures such as safeguarding the pension entitlements of those whose caregiving responsibilities prevent them from remaining in the workforce. Such measures further blur the boundary between the employment status of carers and care provided within families. The rationales underpinning financial payments for family caregiving are varied. They may be intended to replace forgone earnings or maintain the incomes of carers who experience reduced, delayed, or interrupted labor force participation; to provide additional resources with which family carers and/or caregiving households can purchase formal services to complement family care; or to offer compensation (again to individual carers or to caregiving households) for additional expenses incurred in the consumption of care-related goods and services. Most financial payments also have an important symbolic intent, in offering societal recognition of the valuable work done by family carers. Financial payment options for carers reinforce the intersections between private and public, professional and personal, and paid and unpaid work.

Based on a content analysis of existing financial compensation policies in selected countries, four specific models or approaches to offering financial support to carers emerge. The models presented in this chapter are consumer-directed personal budgets that allow older people to employ their carers; care allowances paid to the older person, who has complete freedom as to how these are used; care allowances paid directly to the family carer; and payments to family carers that substitute for formal service provision (Glendinning, 2006; Glendinning, Schunk, & McLaughlin, 1997; Jenson & Jacobzone, 2000; Lundsgaard, 2005). Analysis of these financial support options considers several "boundary" issues such as the relationship between caregiver and care receiver, family and state responsibility, monetarizing family care and implications for professionalization, and money for care and its relationship to paid employment. Select evaluative criteria such as adequacy, suitability, and gender are applied in the critique of the models. The results suggest that financial compensation as a support option is complex at both the micro and macro levels, blurring the boundaries between paid and unpaid work, formal and family care, and market and nonmarketized relationships. Indeed, a central theme of this chapter is that financial payment for caregiving is located within, and has implications for, a number of different policy domains. It is this intersection of multiple policy domains that makes the evaluation of policy options in this area particularly complex and continues to fuel the debates surrounding payment for care.

Payment for Care at the Intersection of Multiple Policy Domains

Long-Term Care

All developed countries are facing growing expectations among their aging populations for better long-term care services, and these pressures are likely to increase as the postwar baby boom generation reaches the oldest age groups (Carrière, Keefe, Légaré, Lin, & Rowe, 2007; Huber & Skidmore, 2003). Not only is the volume of care increasing, but so also is the complexity of the care that is required. Current hospital discharge practices are leading to needs for increasingly complex and intensive home-based care. Greater longevity means both the increased risk of developing seriously disabling conditions and illnesses such as dementia, as well as people living longer with these conditions. There is also evidence of an increasing proportion of carers who are elderly themselves and possibly frail. This is particularly true of older spouses, who constitute a growing proportion of family carers (Hirst, 2001; Milne, 2001).

Given that most primary caregivers of older people are close family members, these trends have implications for how the care needs of the older population will be met, and for the sustainability and longer-term cost-effectiveness of the care provided by families and friends. For example, without adequate support, carers are at risk of experiencing exhaustion, injury, and depression that may lead to the increased utilization of health resources by the carer and potentially the inability to sustain community-based care. Further, unless economic measures can provide meaningful financial support for carers, their economic vitality may be at risk due to increased expenditures and reduced income and savings. These fiscal realities intersect with current public policies for income security and economic policies intended to support citizens in later life.

Labor

Demographic trends result in policy makers grappling with competing policy demands. A growing challenge is to reconcile the demands of the labor market to ensure an adequate supply of workers to support each country's social and economic infrastructure, yet at the same time to satisfy the growing demands for (increasingly intensive) long-term care. More specifically, there is growing concern about the availability of the human resources, both formal and informal, required to meet the demand for long-term care services as populations age (Carrière et al., 2007). As the majority of family caregiving is still performed by women, the dramatic increase over the past generation in industrialized countries in women's labor force participation (Jenson & Jacobzone, 2000) further intensifies these supply–demand pressures. Therefore, strategies are needed to recruit and retain both formal and informal carers (Keefe, Légaré, & Carrière, 2007).

Moreover, many societies have seen a transition from a "one-earner family" model of family policy to a "one and a half-earner" (or even "two-earner") family model (Lewis, 2006) and the corresponding growing alignment of welfare provision citizenship and social inclusion with active labor market participation (Lister, 2003). Consequently, policies for family carers that do not take account of, or that even actively discourage, carers' labor market participation may also have indirect impacts on the wider citizenship status of family carers, and on their social inclusion through reducing carers' access to those rights and benefits secured via labor market participation rather than through universal citizenship rights or through the more traditional dependence on a (usually male) breadwinner.

The introduction of long-term care policy that pays family members to provide care may blur the boundaries of labor market policy. The implications of this are of particular interest in this chapter. Such policies may challenge labor legislation or be counterproductive to other policies that promote the retention of human resources to maintain a healthy labor force. For example, if the state provides payment to family members, to what extent does it become the employer? What obligation does the state consequently have to offer social security benefits and other forms of social protection for these family carers? Moreover, what about the potential loss of a productive member of the labor force that payment for care may encourage? Within this context of intersecting policy domains, the next section outlines the different approaches through which family carers may receive financial remuneration.

Paying for Family Care: Different Rationales and Types of Payment

A number of studies have proposed different typologies of payments for family caregiving (see Glendinning, 2006; Glendinning et al., 1997; Jenson & Jacobzone, 2000; Lundsgaard, 2005). Taken together, these studies allow us to identify four different models of paying family carers. These models reflect different relationships between the giver and receiver of care, and variations in the role of the state in regulating these relationships. These models—and their implications for family caregiving—will be briefly illustrated, using examples from different countries. The aim is not to provide comprehensive accounts of each typology, but to highlight the salient features of the different models and their underlying principles in order to illustrate the blurring of the boundaries between paid and unpaid work, market and nonmarketized relationships, and formal and family care as reflected by each.

1. Personal Budgets and Consumer-Directed Employment of Care Assistants

In several countries, including the United Kingdom, the Netherlands, Flanders (part of Belgium), and the United States, older people needing support can opt to receive a personal budget with which to purchase care, either from a private nursing or care agency or by directly employing a personal care assistant (Organization for Economic Cooperation and Development [OECD], 2005; Ungerson & Yeandle, 2006). In the case of the Netherlands, it allows the employment of a close relative, including a spouse, son, or daughter. When a personal budget is used in this way, a formal employer–employee relationship results between the care receiver and the family caregiver. Personal budget holders have to make formal contracts with their employees and adhere to normal labor market regulations concerning wage levels, taxation, social security contributions, and liability insurance (Pijl, n.d.). In the Netherlands, the administrative tasks associated with employer responsibilities are managed by an intermediary agency. In such circumstances, traditional relationships within the family are blurred by this formal structure, and market values and language dominate relationship agreements.

In the Netherlands' model, the amount of budget is calculated according to the level of home nursing and home help needed by the older person reduced by a standard 25% and capped at the equivalent cost of intensive nursing care. Consequently, the actual level of support provided by a family member employed by a personal budget holder is likely to significantly exceed the funding available. This reflects an artificial invoking of the boundary between work and family—family members may be formally employed as carers but differ from formal paid carers because they often co-reside with the receiver of care (with their workplace then also being their home) and also receive lower pay than the value of the care provided. Nevertheless, the notion of paying family members, including spouses and children, is widely accepted, and about half of all Dutch personal budget holders use the funding to pay informal carers. Older people are more likely than younger budget holders to choose relatives as their service providers (Wiener, Tilly, & Cuellar, 2003).

Alternative examples include direct payments in the United Kingdom and consumer-directed programs in the United States and Canada. The UK direct payment scheme allows a cash payment to be made instead of services in kind. Although it was extended to older people in 2000, take-up has been very slow. In this example, it is not possible to use direct payments to employ a close relative living in the same household. In the United States, consumer-directed programs exist in most states but are extremely varied in the number and range of tasks for which the consumer may assume responsibility. In all but six states, family members may be hired (Friss Feinberg, Newman, Gray, & Kolh, 2004). U.S. consumer-directed programs generally follow one of three models: direct pay (the care recipient has full responsibility for all aspects of the employment relationship), fiscal intermediary (an agency manages payroll and taxes), and supportive intermediary (an agency provides training for carers and assistance with recruitment) (OECD, 2005). In some Canadian provinces, most notably Quebec, consumer-directed programs that are extended to older care recipients have adopted a fiscal intermediary model (Keefe & Fancey, 1998).

2. Care Allowances for the Older Person

In an alternative approach to the formal personal budget, cash payments are made to the person needing care, with no specification or formal requirement as to how this is used; the only obligation on the care allowance recipient is to acquire adequate care. Similar to personal budgets, this approach is intended to enhance choice of control by an older service user. Family carers may also benefit indirectly from insurance-based rights available to the older person. Full or partial amounts of these allowances may be transferred to carers to compensate for direct expenditures or as a token payment for services rendered.

Care or attendance allowances exist in a number of countries, including Austria, France, and Germany. In Germany, the long-term care insurance scheme provides insurance-based entitlements for older people (see Glendinning & Igl, in press). Once assessed as qualifying for long-term care insurance, the older person has the option of choosing between an entitlement to service "assignments" up to a specified value, depending on level of care dependency; a lower value, nontaxable cash allowance that can be spent in any way so long as adequate care is obtained; or a combination of the two. Despite its significantly lower value, the cash allowance option is consistently the most common preference, chosen by between 64% and 82% of beneficiaries (depending on the severity of the disability and level of payment). The vast majority of those choosing the cash allowance are believed to do so because they prefer to receive care from family and friends rather than strangers, but in some instances the benefit is not fully transferred to the carer (Wiener et al., 2003). In addition to the cash allowance, family carers whose relatives opt for the cash benefit are entitled to 4 weeks' respite care each year. This can be in the form of institutional respite services or a cash payment with which to purchase substitute home-based care. Family carers of insured older people who receive (at least some of) their benefits as a cash allowance may also have their pension and accident insurance contributions paid.

The Austrian Care Allowance is a similar unconditional benefit paid to the older person, whose only obligation is to secure appropriate levels of care (Kreimer, 2006). France gives beneficiaries a cash allowance, most of which must be used to pay nonspousal care workers (Wiener, 2003).

In this model, the money enables the receiver of care to have choice in terms of receiving care from the marketplace, the family, or a combination of both options. Consequently, the issue is less about whose responsibility it is to provide care for the older person—state or family—but rather about choice, preference, and, perhaps, availability. If family care is purchased in combination with formal services, it is likely that the boundaries between formal providers and family carers will be blurred further as both will receive payment for the carework they provide.

3. Care Allowances Paid Directly to the Family Carer

In this model, the state makes financial payments directly to the carer. Although eligibility is linked to the health of, or amount of care needed by, the older person, the carer has a direct entitlement to such payments and control over how they are used. The rationale underpinning such payments varies. Rationales include compensation for a loss or reduction in earnings from paid work, support for low-income carers so they are not further economically disadvantaged because of their caregiving responsibilities, and the simple symbolic recognition of the societal importance and value of family caregiving.

Recognizing the Value of Family Care Few countries provide an allowance simply in recognition of the carer's role, but Australia is one example (Howe, 2001). The Australian Carer Allowance is a financial payment made directly to carers who provide full-time care on a daily basis for a dependent child or adult. The rate of remuneration is much lower than Australia's Carer Payment (see below), but it is not income or asset tested, and the payment is nontaxable (Montgomery & Friss Feinberg, 2003). The allowance is not viewed as income support, but rather is intended to help with extra costs associated with caring for a dependent child or adult (Howe, 2001).

Income Maintenance Payments for Low-Income Carers An alternative approach involves paying benefits through a social security system to low-income family carers. It is generally assumed that caregiving responsibilities place family carers at a particular disadvantage in the labor market. The underlying rationale is therefore to sustain a minimum level of income for carers whose opportunity to support themselves financially (through paid work or entitlement to other social security benefits) is restricted because of providing care. Often there are strict income and care provision criteria (for either individuals or households) attached to eligibility for these payments, and often these payments are treated as taxable income.

The most important feature of all these payments made directly to carers is that they explicitly acknowledge the rights of family carers to an *independent* source of income, regardless of the rights, entitlements, or wishes of the older person who is receiving care. Although eligibility is generally linked to the older person's level of disability and/or intensity of care needs, such payment schemes nevertheless do not entail the financial dependence of the caregiver on the receiver of care. In addition, if such payments are located within national social security systems, they are likely to be governed by universally applicable and largely categorical principles of rights and entitlements; they do not involve the kinds of discretionary judgments that are often involved in the allocation of services to either carers or older people. Finally, because of their underlying rationale of financial support for family carers, they generally do not preclude either carers or older people from *also* receiving services—an option denied under the German or Austrian care allowance approach (Glendinning et al., 1997).

Income Maintenance During Temporary Absences From Work Another approach involves publicly funded income support payments for employees who take a temporary leave of absence from work to provide support or care for a critically or terminally ill relative. Such programs exist in Canada, Sweden, Norway, and Ireland. The objective of these payments is to maintain the income and well-being of an employee who has family care responsibilities while at the same time safeguarding his or her place in the labor force.

These programs also reflect the intersection or blurring boundaries between paid and unpaid work for the carer. Often the financial payment is contingent upon the carer's labor force participation and/or relationship to the care recipient. This model reflects the intersection of long-term care policy that "compensates" carers and the rights and entitlements of employees in the paid labor market. In Canada, for example, employment insurance benefits of up to 6 weeks to care for a dying relative are not considered compensation for carework but rather an entitlement of eligible employees. Analysis of most examples in this model suggests that when money is involved, an increasing formalization of the relationship emerges.

4. Paying Carers Instead of Formal Social Service Provision

In the fourth model, family carers are paid as a substitute for formal home–help services; this model operates in a number of Scandinavian countries (Jenson & Jacobzone, 2000; OECD, 2005). Here, family caregiving is formalized within a quasi-employment relationship (similar to the personal budget model described above); however, in this model it is the state (in the form of the local municipality) rather than the care receiver that acts as the employer. This approach reflects the high levels of female labor force participation in Scandinavian countries, alongside continuing relatively high levels of publicly funded formal social services and the challenge of delivering domiciliary services in sparsely populated areas.

In Finland, the Informal Carer's Allowance is awarded on the basis of the older person's needs but paid directly to the carer by the municipality; the carer enters into a contract with the municipality to provide an agreed level of care according to a service plan (Jenson & Jacobzone, 2000). The vast majority of carers employed in this way are spouses or other close relatives, and a third are aged 65 or older (Martimo, 1998). Similar initiatives exist in Sweden and Norway at the local level (Ingebretsen & Eriksen, 2004; Johansson, 2004). Generally, these allowances are lower than the costs of either institutional care or formal homecare services (Sweden is an exception; see Johansson, 2004). In practice, they provide no incentive to begin caring; rather, they are believed to encourage relatives to continue their existing caregiving responsibilities (Kröger, Anttonen, & Sipilä, 2003), thereby enabling the older person to remain at home.

Drawing on specific countries' experiences, the above examples illustrate the range of financial payment schemes that pay family carers (or pay for family caregiving), their underlying principles, and the melding together of traditional conceptualizations of public and private spheres. The personal relationship between carer and care receiver becomes increasingly formalized with the introduction of monetary compensation. This analysis suggests that the context in which financial payment as a policy option evolves is complex, intersecting with other policy domains, formalizing familial relations, and balancing notions of rights and entitlements. What follows is a discussion of the issues and debates that surround financial payment for family carers.

Payment for Care: Blurring the Responsibilities of Family and State

The aims and nature of payments for family carers are key elements of wider policy debates about the best ways of supporting older people now and in the future (Jenson & Jacobzone, 2000; Keefe et al., 2007; Kunkel, Applebaum, & Nelson, 2003–2004). Differing perspectives on the respective responsibilities and rights of families and the state for family caregiving frame these debates. These perspectives also have strong gender dimensions (Lewis, 1992, 2006). Debates around payment for care as a policy option, therefore, continue to focus on its impact on carers (primarily women; Kreimer, 2006), the labor force, and quality of care. There is also concern that payments for family care will erode normal filial obligations of caring for dependent members.

At the core of the "family versus state responsibility" debate is the question of how far unpaid work—particularly that involved in providing care for children, the disabled, and frail older people—is viewed as an entirely private family responsibility or a collective social responsibility, and the consequent role played by the state in supporting and/or compensating family care. Over the past 2 decades, welfare states have increasingly acknowledged the importance of unpaid carework, both for the individuals involved and in sustaining the wider production of care as a welfare good. This acknowledgment is reflected in the introduction of measures such as rights to leave from paid employment for both mothers and fathers, direct and indirect financial transfers, and social rights (such as pension protection) attached to caregiving. However, there remain substantial variations between countries in the extent to which they explicitly attempt to strengthen families' responsibilities or, alternatively, promote the extension of public services to relieve families of some of their caregiving responsibilities (Leitner, 2003). Esping-Anderson (1999) referred to these variations as "familialistic" and "defamilializing" welfare regimes, which are distinguished by the extent to which public policy assumes that households or the state carries the principal responsibility for the welfare of families and their members.

Devaluation of Carework

Embedded in the family or state discourse are concerns about the devaluation of carework. Each of the models of financial payment to family carers may be viewed by some as continuing confirmation of the low value attached to caregiving work and the associated potential to impoverish family carers in both the shorter and longer terms.

First, in most of the countries the cash payment equivalent is not equal to the full value of the carework performed, according to the level of payment for a full-salaried care worker. For example, the level of the financial payment is likely to be at (e.g., the Dutch personal budget) or below (e.g., the UK Carers Allowance) any legal minimum-wage level. This suggests that carework has nominal value in relation to other work. Second, unless the rate of remuneration increases regularly, its value continues to decline. In Germany, the cash allowance has not been increased in 10 years, resulting in an increasing gap between benefit levels and the cost of living (and the costs of formal care services). This is not the case in Australia or the United Kingdom, where allowance programs are part of their respective social security systems and are therefore indexed. Third, the amount of cash allowance is often less than the value of in-kind benefits offered at the same care level, again reflecting an assumption that family care is a low-cost option. In Germany, those who choose the in-kind service option receive benefits at nearly twice the value of the cash payment option. A similar inequity exists in the Dutch personal budget scheme on the grounds that informal care does not carry institutional overheads. Fourth, if payments to family carers are treated as taxable income, their value is further reduced (assuming that carers have sufficient income to reach tax threshold levels). Fifth, cash payments are not always accompanied by other social benefits, although in a few examples some minimum state pension protection for family carers is provided (e.g., in Germany, the Netherlands, and the United Kingdom).

The commodification of this carework inevitably leads to a comparison with the market value of the services rendered. The softening of the traditional boundaries between unpaid carework by family members and paid carework in the formal sector has the potential double negative effect of devaluing family work by setting a low price for which it is compensated and devaluing formal care as a comparative cost to what can be "purchased" from family members. Models of payment that are accessed only through the entitlement of the older person and that depend on the discretion of the latter to pass on the payment to a family carer (as in Austria and Germany) do not appear to offer much choice or social protection for the carer. Moreover, they can detract from societal recognition for carers, who may become financially dependent on the person to whom they give care (Glendinning, 1990).

Reinforcing Gender Roles

Linked to the devaluation of carework is the well-established fact that women are the primary providers of care to dependent older family members, whether spouse, parent, parent-in-law, or other (Campbell & Ikegami, 2003; Hirst, 2001; Keating et al., 1999; Mestheneos & Triantafillou, 2005). However, financial compensation may be a double-edged sword for women. On the one hand, cash payments for family carers do recognize and attempt to ameliorate the direct and opportunity costs associated with caregiving and provide some formal recognition of the caregiving role. On the other hand, these programs can entrap women into caregiving roles by offering financial support in place of other care options. This dilemma was explicitly debated during planning for the Japanese long-term care insurance scheme:

> The arguments in favour were that a cash allowance ... recognizes and rewards the contribution of family caregivers (particularly the daughters-in-law who traditionally provided care) ... Critics of cash allowances, notably feminists, rebutted all these points ... Daughters-in-law need liberation, not recognition. In most households, a cash allowance would not change existing caregiving patterns, which are inherently oppressive. (Campbell & Ikegami, pp. 26–27)
>
> In contrast, the cash-based care allowance approach in Austria has increased neither choice nor gender equity amongst informal carers. (Kreimer, 2006)

The impact of cash payments on gender roles is also affected by patterns of resource control and allocation within households. In societies where men are considered the head of the household, such as Japan and Israel, women's advocates are hesitant to support cash payments because it is expected that these would go to the head of the household, whereas women would still provide care, but without support and recognition.

The impact of cash payments for care on gender roles may be mitigated to a greater or lesser extent if formal services are also available. In Australia and the United Kingdom, it is possible for carers to receive both income maintenance benefits *and* services in kind. In Germany, there is a gradual trend for long-term care insurance beneficiaries to opt for a combination of cash payments and services in kind; in addition, carers of insurance beneficiaries are entitled to 4 weeks of respite care a year (as mentioned above), plus counseling and retraining opportunities. Carers in Finland who are employed as quasi–home helps can convert part of their payment into services in kind, to help reduce the stress of full-time caregiving. Such combinations of payment and services dissolve boundaries between public and private care, and between paid and unpaid carework.

Reconciling Labor Market and Care Policies

As noted above, the rationale and nature of payments for family caregiving need to be compatible with wider labor market policies, particularly the significant recent increases in women's labor market participation and the future supply of labor that will be required to balance changing dependency ratios (Arksey & Kemp, 2006). None of the models of payment for family caregiving described above are high enough, in relation to the level of caregiving work involved, to be viewed as an incentive for family carers to leave the labor force to take up caregiving. For example, only those with low-employment incomes are eligible for the Australian Carer Payment. It is, therefore, not so much an enticement for employees to leave the workforce to take up caregiving, but rather a means of maintaining a minimum income level for those who have already reduced (or are unable to increase) their labor force participation because of their caregiving responsibilities. Even the income maintenance programs during temporary leave from the workplace, such as in Canada and Sweden, offer payments that are lower than the employee's regular earnings. In Sweden, carers are paid only 80% of their regular income, whereas in Canada, only 55% of an employee's regular income is payable.

Even though none of these models of payment for care can be viewed as an incentive to leave the labor force, many carers nevertheless do so either temporarily or indefinitely (Arksey, Kemp, Glendinning, Kotchetkova, & Tozer, 2005; Canadian Study of Health and Aging Working Group, 1994). This puts at risk not only their income but also their entitlement to those social protection policies that are linked with labor force participation, thus potentially further impoverishing carers in both the shorter and longer terms. Membership in retirement pension schemes, entitlement to income when sick or disabled, and accident insurance entitlements all increasingly derive from labor market participation and paid employment roles. So for those carers who do leave the workforce in order to provide care, protection of their pension entitlement through the crediting of contributions is essential, as is the provision of training programs to help carers to reenter the labor market both while caring and after a period of caregiving has ended.

Finally, payments for family carers arguably may have a doubly damaging impact on labor force productivity, in that they may support family carers' premature exit from the labor market and at the same time depress demand for labor in the form of paid care workers for older people. Thus, the costs related to two labor force positions are increased—the family carer who leaves his or her position and must be replaced, and the potential paid carer who might have been hired to assist the person to remain in his or her own home.

Quality of Care

Adding to the complexity of the discussion surrounding paying family carers are issues relating to the quality of care received, the consequences when the quality is inadequate, and the quality of alternative service supports for carers to sustain their role. First, concerns are raised about the quality of care that family carers may provide, given a lack of training and the sometimes complex care required (Keigher, 1987). Conventional quality assurance mechanisms such as professional accreditation, agency regulation, and inspection regimes are absent—and are arguably impossible to design when care allowances are used to purchase care from family members. Indeed, the state may be providing support to a care situation where the carer has little training and is deemed the "right" person solely by virtue of his or her relationship with the client. Moreover, "[P]ublic agencies and disabled individuals have great difficulty disciplining poor performing relatives. It is difficult for government officials to insist that a daughter be fired" (Wiener, 2003, p. 16).

Second, the range, availability, and quality of formal services are fundamental to a comprehensive community care system. To safeguard the quality of care provided by family carers, there needs to be available high-quality formal services that carers can access on an ongoing basis or for a period of respite from their caregiving situation (Keefe & Fancey, 1997). Australian policies to support caregivers and care recipients exemplify this (Howe, 1994, 2001). Formal services are a vital adjunct and complement to family caregiving. It would seem likely that inadequate income or poverty also risks jeopardizing the quality of informal care. However, if the principle underpinning payment for family caregiving is that the latter is intended to substitute for formal service provision, then it may be difficult for older people (and their carers) to receive publicly funded services as well. The lack of alternative formal care services can, in turn, jeopardize the quality of informal care.

Conclusion

This chapter has identified various approaches to payment for family carers and illustrates how such approaches intersect multiple policy domains. Key differences in the approaches discussed here are the different relationships of the care receiver and the caregiver to the financial payment, and the role of the (central or local) state in regulating these relationships. This chapter has identified the ways in which these approaches are distinct. However, they all involve the monetarizing of family relationships, and, regardless of the specific approach or underlying principle, this blurs the boundaries between market and nonmarket, formal and informal, and paid and unpaid work. A transfer of money from the public domain for services provided by the family alters the context in which family care occurs. It blurs the boundary of what is considered family responsibility and what is state responsibility. Publicly funded financial compensation programs explicitly recognize the value of family care to society, and they therefore begin to shift the locus of responsibility for the long-term care of older people from the family to the state. However, the extent of this shift is limited by the fact that in all instances, financial payments are considerably lower than the actual value of the caregiving work that is performed, thereby reinforcing gender roles and inequity. The state thus remains at least partially dependent on the unpaid carework of families.

The complexity of this dependence of the state on family availability as a "more cost-efficient" deliverer of care unveils itself in the blurring of labor policy. Are such family members employees of the state or of the care recipients, and how does this affect the short- and long-term productivity of the labor market? The evaluation of such policies is complicated further by the gendered nature of the work and the potentially increased expectations placed on women to provide such care. When women succumb to these expectations and quit their employment, the long-term result may be economic disadvantage despite the intent of some payment-for-care models to support women's economic well-being.

As governments struggle with the complex issues of aging societies, the accessibility and availability of family and friends to support older persons are primary concerns. There is increasing interest in the utility of financial payment as a support option for carers, particularly if it can strengthen family support in the community and thereby delay more costly care arrangements. However, there are noted costs and consequences for families who engage in substantial caregiving, and additional measures are needed to offset the impact on carers' lives and support them in providing high-quality care. It should be noted that there is no one right way to support carers, but rather "options" should be available. It is also important that the principles underpinning the emerging trend of consumer-directed care are also available to family carers (Arksey & Glendinning, 2007). Although there are commonalities amongst carers, caregiving is not a uniform experience, and neither should be the options designed to support carers. Payment for care as a public policy option is no exception.

In practice, multiple measures are needed to reduce the risks of poverty and social exclusion for family carers and to balance their rights and interests with those of their elderly relatives who receive care. Policies in many countries do include multiple measures—

combinations of payments to caregivers and care receivers, pension protection, workplace-based rights, and formal services. The challenge is to ensure the appropriate balance between these different measures, so that carers are not unduly disadvantaged in the pursuit of sustainable solutions to long-term care. Recognition of the complexity of payment for care options across multiple policy domains is needed. Rather than critique such approaches as contributing to the blurring of boundaries between public and private, professional and personal, and paid and unpaid, we need to accept this complexity and focus evaluation efforts on the outcomes of such policy for the well-being of the carer and the receiver of care.

References

Arksey, H., & Glendinning, C. (2007). Choice in the context of informal care-giving. *Health and Social Care in the Community, 16*(2), 165–175.

Arksey, H., & Kemp, P. A. (2006). Carers and employment in a work-focused welfare state. In C. Glendinning & P. A Kemp (Eds.), *Cash and care: Policy challenges in the welfare state.* Bristol, UK: Policy.

Arksey, H., Kemp, P. A., Glendinning, C., Kotchetkova, I., & Tozer, R. (2005). Carers' aspirations and decisions around work and retirement (Research Report 290). London: Department for Work and Pensions.

Campbell, J. C., & Ikegami, N. (2003). Japan's radical reform of long-term care. *Social Policy and Administration, 37*(1), 21–34.

Canadian Study of Health and Aging Working Group. (1994). Patterns of caring for people with dementia in Canada. *Canadian Journal of Aging, 13*(4), 470–487.

Cannuscio, C., Colditz, G., Rimm, E., Berkman, L., Jones, C., & Kawachi, I. (2004). Employment status, social ties and caregivers' mental health. *Social Science & Medicine, 58*, 1247–1256.

Carmichael, F., & Charles, S. (1998). The labour market costs of community care. *Journal of Health Economics, 1*(6), 747–765.

Carrière, Y., Keefe, J., Légaré, J., Lin, X., & Rowe, G. (2007). Population aging and immediate family composition: Implications for future home care services. *Genus,* LXIII(1-2), 11–31.

Cranswick, K. (1999, Winter). Help close at hand: Relocating to give or receive care. *Canadian Social Trends, 55*, 11–12.

Esping-Anderson, G. (1999). *Social foundations of postindustrial economies.* New York: Oxford University Press.

Friss Feinberg, L., Newman, S. L., Gray, L., & Kolh, M. S. (2004). *The state of the states in family caregiver support: A 50-state study.* San Francisco: Family Care Giver Alliance.

Ginn, J., & Arber, S. (2000). The pensions cost of caring. *Benefits, 28,* 13–17.

Glendinning, C. (1990). Dependency and interdependency: The incomes of informal carers and the impact of social security. *Journal of Social Policy, 19*(4), 469–497.

Glendinning, C. (2006). Paying family care-givers: Evaluating different models. In C. Glendinning & P. A. Kemp (Eds.), *Cash and care: Policy challenges in the welfare state.* Bristol, UK: Policy.

Glendinning, C., & Igl, G. (In press). Long-term care. In G. Naegele & A. Walker (Eds.), *Social policy in ageing societies: Britain and Germany compared.* Basingstoke, UK: Palgrave Macmillan.

Glendinning, C., Schunk, M., & McLaughlin, E. (1997). Paying for long-term domiciliary care: A comparative perspective. *Ageing and Society, 17,* 123–140.

Hirst, M. (2001). Trends in informal care in Great Britain during the 1990s. *Health and Social Care in the Community, 9,* 348–357.

Hirst, M. (2003). Caring-related inequalities in psychological distress in Britain during the 1990s. *Journal of Public Health Medicine, 25,* 4.

Howe, A. (1994, March). Commitment to carers: The Australian experience. *Ageing International,* 54–59.

Howe, A. (2001). Recent developments in aged care policy in Australia. *Journal of Aging & Social Policy, 13*(2/3), 101–116.

Huber, J., & Skidmore, P. (2003). *The new old: Why baby-boomers won't be pensioned off.* London: Demos.

Ingebretsen, R., & Eriksen, J. (2004). Services for supporting family carers of elderly people in Europe: Characteristics, coverage and usage. National background report for Norway (report submitted to EUROFAMCARE consortium). Hamburg, Germany: EUROFAMCARE.

Jenson, J., & Jacobzone, S. (2000). Care allowances for the frail elderly and their impact on women care-givers (Labour Market and Social Policy Occasional Paper 41). Paris: OECD Publishing.

Johansson, L. (2004). *Services for supporting family carers of elderly people in Europe: Characteristics, coverage and usage. National background report for Sweden* (report submitted to EUROFAMCARE consortium). Hamburg, Germany: EUROFAMCARE.

Keating, N., Fast, J., Frederick, J., Cranswick, K., & Perrier, C. (1999). *Eldercare in Canada: Context, content and consequences.* Ottawa: Statistics Canada.

Keefe, J., & Fancey, P. (1997). Financial compensation or home help services: Examining differences among program recipients. *Canadian Journal on Aging, 16*(2), 254–278.

Keefe, J., & Fancey, P. (1998). *Financial compensation versus community supports: An analysis of the effects on caregivers and care receivers* (Report submitted to Health Canada). Halifax, Nova Scotia: Department of Gerontology, Mount Saint Vincent University.

Keefe, J., Légaré, J., & Carrière, Y. (2007). Developing new strategies to support future caregivers of the aged in Canada: Projections of need and their policy implications. *Canadian Public Policy, 33*, S66–S80.

Keefe, J., & Medjuck, S. (1997). The contribution of long term economic costs to predicting strain among employed women caregivers. *Journal of Women & Aging, 9*(3), 3–25.

Keigher, S. (1987, Winter). Point/counterpoint. Paid family caregiving for the elderly: Good for the poor? Market mechanisms gone awry. *Health and Social Work*, 64–65.

Kreimer, M. (2006). Developments in Austrian care arrangements: Women between free choice and informal care. In C. Glendinning & P. A. Kemp (Eds.), *Cash and care: Policy challenges in the welfare state.* Bristol, UK: Policy.

Kröger, T., Anttonen, A., & Sipilä, J. (2003). Social care in Finland: Stronger and weaker forms of universalism. In A. Antonnen, J. Baldock, and J. Sipilä (Eds.), *The young, the old and the state: Social care systems in five industrial countries*. Cheltenham, UK: Edward Elgar.

Kunkel, S. R., Applebaum, R. A., & Nelson, I. M. (2003–2004, Winter). For love and money: Paying family caregivers. *Generations*, 74–80.

Leitner, S. (2003). Varieties of familialism: The caring function of the family in comparative perspective. *European Societies, 5*(4), 353–375.

Lewis, J. (1992). Gender and the development of welfare regimes. *Journal of European Social Policy, 2*(3) 159–173.

Lewis, J. (2006). Care and gender: Have the arguments for recognizing care work now been won? In C. Glendinning and P. A. Kemp (Eds.), *Cash and care: Policy challenges in the welfare state.* Bristol, UK: Policy.

Lister, R. (2003). *Citizenship: Feminist perspectives.* Basingstoke, UK: Macmillan.

Lundsgaard, J. (2005). *Consumer direction and choice in long-term care for older persons, including payments for informal care: How can it help improve care outcomes, employment and sustainability?* Paris: OECD Publishing.

Martimo, K. (1998). Community care for frail older people in Finland. In C. Glendinning (Ed.), *Rights and realities: Comparing new developments in long-term care for older people*. Bristol, UK: Policy.

Mestheneos, E., & Triantafillou, J. (2005). *Services for supporting family carers of elderly people in Europe: Characteristics, coverage and usage. Pan-European background report* (report submitted to EUROFAMCARE consortium). Hamburg, Germany: EUROFAMCARE.

Milne, A. (2001). *Caring in later life: Reviewing the role of older carers.* London: Help the Aged.

Montgomery, A., & Friss Feinberg, L. (2003, September). *The road to recognition: An international review of public policies to support family and informal care givers.* San Francisco: National Center on Care Giving.

Office for Public Management. (2005, March). *Scottish unpaid carers: International case studies.* London: Author.

Organization for Economic Cooperation and Development (OECD). (2005). *The OECD Health Project: Long-term care for older people.* Paris: OECD Publishing.

Pickard, L., Wittenberg, R., Comas-Herrera, A., Davies, B., & Darton, R. (2000). Relying on informal care in the new century? Informal care for elderly people in England to 2031. *Ageing and Society, 20*(6), 745–772.

Pijl, M. (n.d.). Home care allowances: Good for many but not for all. *Practice, 12*(2), 55–65.

Ungerson, C., & Yeandle, S. (2006). *Cash for care in developed welfare states.* Basingstoke, UK: Macmillan.

Wiener, J. (2003). The role of informal support in long-term care. In J. Brodsky, J. Habib, & M. Hirschfield (Eds.), *Key policy issues in long-term care.* Geneva: World Health Organization.

Wiener, J., Tilly, J., & Cuellar, A. E. (2003). *Consumer-directed home care in the Netherlands, England and Germany.* Washington, DC: AARP Public Policy Institute.

11

Economic and Social Roles in Midlife in Britain

Expanding Intersections and Blurring Boundaries

Maria Evandrou and Karen Glaser

Introduction

Recent socioeconomic and demographic changes, such as rising female labor force participation and increases in longevity, have meant that women and men are increasingly likely to find themselves combining a variety of economic and social roles. This is particularly the case in midlife, when the roles of parent, spouse, carer, and paid worker may overlap, blurring the boundaries between work and family life. The increasing possibility of caring for elderly parents whilst still caring for or supporting one's own children has been highlighted by a U.S. Census Bureau report on the "sandwich generation" (Kinsella & Velkoff, 2001). In Britain, 6 million people are providing unpaid care for a family member, and 3 million of these are also in paid work. There is now growing recognition by both government and employers of the importance of supporting individuals in juggling work and family commitments. In 2000 the UK government launched the Work-Life Balance Campaign (Department for Education and Employment [DfEE], 2000), and in 2002 the Employment Act introduced the flexible working law, enabling parents with a child under 6 or a disabled child under 18 to request flexible work arrangements from their employer. As a result of the Carers (Equal Opportunities) Act 2004, from April 2007 the law extended the right to request flexible work arrangements to include carers of adults.

However, despite greater recognition within policy of the intersection between work and family responsibilities, there remains relatively little research in Britain on the *extent* of multiple role occupancy amongst midlife men and women on a national basis, and little examination of how this has changed across birth cohorts. Such evidence is important for planning for the future. Much of the literature on this issue is located in North America. In the early 1980s, research found that multiple role commitments among women were becoming a normative experience (Brody, 1981, 1985). Studies in the 1990s documented that being caught in the middle, in terms of simultaneous caregiving responsibilities to dependent children and frail parents while in paid work, was uncommon (Dautzenberg, Diederiks, Philipsen, & Stevens, 1998; Himes, 1994; Rosenthal, Martin-Matthews, & Matthews, 1996; Rosenthal, Matthews, & Marshall, 1989; Soldo, 1996; Spitze & Logan, 1990). However, some empirical studies indicate that the extent of multiple roles is increasing among younger generations (Moen, Robison, & Fields, 1994; Robison, Moen, & Dempster-McClain, 1995).

This chapter reports on research using British data from a range of nationally representative surveys to examine the occupancy and intersections of four roles: "partner," "parent," "carer," and "paid worker." First, evidence is presented on the prevalence of multiple work and family responsibilities among middle-aged individuals in Britain. The analysis examines both role occupancy and role "intensity," distinguishing individuals with "low" versus "high" role commitments. Second, the factors associated with multiple role occupancy are investigated, documenting how the number of roles occupied in midlife varies by demographic and socioeconomic characteristics. Being "caught in the middle" between competing work and family responsibilities has been found to be a different experience for women compared to men (Brody, 1981). Thus, throughout the recent research, separate analyses are presented for women and men. Third, the chapter examines the experience of multiple role occupancy over the life course using longitudinal data. Fourth, changes in the extent of the intersection of economic and social roles between birth cohorts are explored; and, finally, the implications of occupying multiple roles for individuals' health, leisure, and economic welfare in later life are discussed. The results highlight that the blurring of the boundaries between parenting and caring and the widening intersection between paid work and caring in midlife can have important repercussions in terms of health, social activities, and entitlements to pensions and other welfare benefits in old age.

Economic and Social Roles in Midlife

The Extent of Multiple Role Occupancy

Over the life course, individuals undertake a variety of roles within work and family life, including partner, parent, carer, and paid worker. This reflects the multifaceted and complex nature of modern social and economic life, as well as the wide range of choices and constraints that are faced today. Information from the British General Household Survey (GHS)[1] conducted in 2000 (Office for National Statistics [ONS], 2000) is used to investigate the occupancy of four roles—*partner, parent, carer,* and *paid worker*—amongst women and men in midlife. *Midlife* is defined here as the period prior to retirement (45–64 years old).[2]

Figure 11.1 summarizes how the selected roles are operationalized. The *partner* role variable distinguishes between those individuals who reported that they were living in a cohabiting or marital union and those who did not. The *parental* role variable distinguishes individuals who had children of any age in the household (including adopted children and stepchildren) versus those who did not, in keeping with previous studies (Farkas & Himes, 1997; Penning, 1998; Rosenthal et al., 1996; Spitze & Logan, 1990). The literature indicates that the demands of dependent children are likely to be greater than those of adult children (Bartley, Popay, & Plewis, 1992; Dautzenberg et al., 1998; Reid & Hardy, 1999). Thus, those living with at least one dependent child were defined as having a more "intensive" parental role.

The GHS also collects information on informal care. The *carer* role variable is defined as providing unpaid care for 5 hours or more per week. The intensity of the caring role is captured by distinguishing individuals who provided care for 20 or more hours per week. Previous research has found a significant association between hours of care, employment, and health status (Evandrou, 1996). *Paid workers* are defined as those individuals in either full-time or part-time work, either as employees or self-employed. Paid workers working

Role Occupancy	Role Intensity
Partner Married or cohabiting with a partner	
Parent Children of any age living at home	Living with at least one dependent child *
Carer Providing care to someone who is sick, handicapped or elderly for 5 hours or more a week (unpaid)	Providing care for 20 or more hours a week (unpaid)
Paid worker In any paid work	Working full-time (over 30 hours per wk)

Note: * Dependent children are defined as children aged under 16 and children aged 16-17 in full-time education.

Figure 11.1 Operationalizing role occupancy and role intensity in the GHS.

full-time for over 30 hours per week are further distinguished as having a more intense economic role.

When we examine the combinations of role occupancy within the spheres of caring, paid work, parenting, and partnership found amongst British women and men in midlife in 2000, we found that overall, 26% of women and 18% of men aged 45–64 are caring for someone, 37% of women and 41% of men are a parent, 75% of women and 78% of men are a partner, and 56% of women and 68% of men are a paid worker. Only 8% of midlife women and men occupy none of these four roles, and the majority occupy at least two, highlighting the extent of the intersection of work and family roles. However, only one in 20 (5%) experience the most demanding role configuration, combining all four roles of carer, parent, partner, and worker simultaneously, blurring the boundaries between family care and paid work. The British results support earlier research in Canada and the United States that indicates that only a small proportion of midlifers are in complex role configurations at a given point in time (Dautzenberg et al., 1998; Rosenthal et al., 1996; Spitze & Logan, 1990).

There is little difference in the overall extent of multiple role occupancy by gender, with similar proportions of men and women holding two or more roles. This echoes previous research that indicated that men were equally likely as (or more likely than) women to face multiple roles (Rosenthal et al., 1996; Spitze & Logan, 1990). However, there are significant gender differences in the *distribution* of role combinations, with women being more likely than men to occupy two or more roles when caregiving is one of the roles considered (25% of women versus 17% of men). Conversely, men are more likely to hold role combinations involving paid work.

The Intensity of Role Occupancy

Taking the intensity of the role into account, and excluding the role of partner, significant differences by gender emerge. As expected, although similar percentages of men and women are in paid work, twice as many men are in full-time work when compared with women (62% compared to 30%). Overall 7% of women in midlife are providing care for 20 or more hours per week, compared with 4% of men. Men are more likely to have at least one dependent child at home than women (21% versus 16% respectively). The fact that men in midlife are more likely to have co-resident children than women is confirmed by other studies (Spitze, Logan, Joseph, & Lee, 1994), and largely reflects gender differences in the timing of parenthood (men tend to marry and have children at older ages than do women). The measure of co-residence with dependent children used here is, however, a fairly broad indicator of parental involvement, and does not reflect the level of active participation in the role, which is likely to be higher for women given their greater involvement in family life.

Table 11.1 and Figure 11.2 illustrate the extent to which these intensive roles overlap. The results highlight the fact that holding multiple intense roles is a rare occurrence cross-sectionally, with only 17% of men and 7% of women occupying two or more intense roles. Again, there are significant differences between men and women in the occupation of intensive multiple roles. Not surprisingly, a greater proportion of men have combinations of roles that involve full-time paid work. Women in midlife are less likely to have intensive roles than men, which largely reflects gender differences in full-time paid work.

TABLE 11.1 Percentage of Men and Women Aged 45–64 Occupying a Combination of Intense Economic and Social Roles

Multiple Intensive Role Occupancy	Men	Women	Total
No roles	21	29	25
No intense roles	31	55	43
One Intense Role			
Carer (20 or more hours per week)	2	5	4
Parent (at least one dependent child at home)	5	10	7
Paid worker (full-time)	45	23	34
Two Intense Roles			
Carer (20 or more hours per week) and one other intense role	2	2	2
Paid worker (full-time) and parent (at least one dependent child at home)	16	5	10
Three Intense Roles			
Carer (20 or more hours per week), parent (at least one dependent child at home), and paid worker (full-time)	< 1	< 1	< 1
N	(2,361)	(2,442)	(4,803)

$\chi^2 = 568.32$. $DF = 7$; $p = 0.000$.
Source: Office for National Statistics (2000).

Correlates of Multiple Role Occupancy

The number of roles within the world of work and family life that an individual undertakes is likely to be influenced by various demographic and socioeconomic characteristics. Results of multivariate analyses show a negative relationship between age and the likelihood of holding one or more roles for both women and men (Evandrou & Glaser, 2007). This is in line with a priori expectations. As a person ages, he or she is less likely to be a parent with a dependent child at home. Engagement in the labor market also decreases with age. Thus, although the propensity to provide care rises with age, this is not sufficient to offset the decrease in the probability of occupying the parent and paid worker role, emphasizing the age-bounded nature of multiple role occupancy. Not being married (or cohabiting) also significantly reduces the likelihood of occupying a higher number of roles for both women and men. This is not surprising,

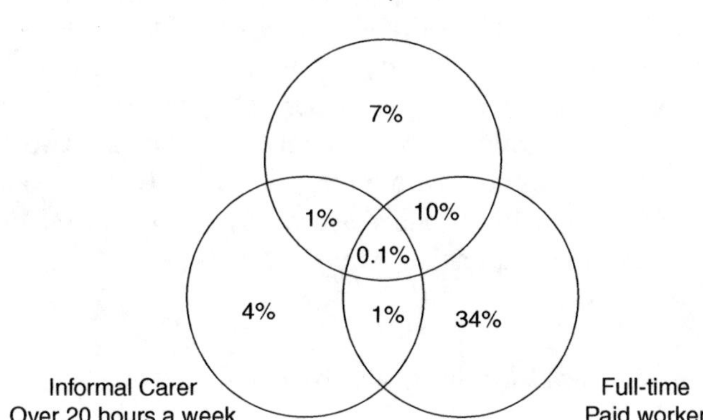

Figure 11.2 Occupying intense economic and social roles. (From GHS, 2000.)

as marital status is correlated with the likelihood of living with a dependent child and hence occupying the parental role.

Being in poor health is also associated with fewer roles. Midlife individuals who report that they had a long-standing illness, disability, or infirmity that limits their activities have a significantly lower probability of holding one or more roles than those who do not. It is likely that poor health may be a barrier to engaging in both paid work and informal caring. However, poor health could also be the result of "role stress" (Goode, 1960). Longitudinal data are therefore needed to unravel the direction of any causal relationship, and this relationship is further examined in the "Changing Economic and Social Roles Across Birth Cohorts" section (below) using such data.

There also appears to be an association between indicators of socioeconomic position and probability of occupying multiple roles. The multivariate analyses show that amongst midlife men, living in public housing significantly reduces the likelihood of occupying a higher number of roles compared to owner-occupiers. This reflects the fact that space is more likely to operate as a major constraint on the ability to co-reside with either an adult child or elderly parent in the social housing sector as well as the relationship between paid work and housing tenure. Housing tenure is not a significant predictor of the number of roles occupied by women; however, education and occupational social class are. Women with no or only limited educational qualifications (such as clerical, commercial, and trade qualifications) are significantly less likely to hold one or two roles in midlife compared to those with higher education (high school graduation and a university or college degree), reflecting the relationship between education and the labor market.

Economic and Social Roles Over the Life Course

So far, the chapter has considered the extent of multiple role responsibilities using cross-sectional data. Longitudinal data from the Family and Working Lives Survey (FWLS)[3] may be used to examine economic and social roles over the life course. Retrospective data on past episodes of caregiving, paid work, and family life have been analyzed to investigate current and past multiple role commitments as well as variations in the number of roles held (Evandrou, Glaser, & Henz, 2002). The operationalization of multiple role occupancy was similar to that used in the GHS (ONS, 2000), presented in Figure 11.1 with some minor changes.[4]

The findings from the FWLS indicate that although the proportion of midlife individuals who currently hold multiple roles is relatively small, when examined over the life course, the proportion is much higher (Evandrou et al., 2002). The majority of men and women have occupied the role of parent and paid worker simultaneously at some stage in their life (73% and 66% respectively; see Table 11.2). Five percent of women and 1% of men had been both a parent and paid worker at some stage and a carer and parent at another stage. What is most striking, however, is that the proportion of individuals in midlife who had ever held all three roles simultaneously at some stage in their life course was substantial: 11% of men and 18% of women. This compares with just 1% of men and 3% of women in the FWLS who had held all three roles at the time of the survey (i.e., cross-sectionally). Thus, although multiple occupancy at any one point in time is not a common experience, once taken over the life course, it is clear that a significant proportion of men and, especially, women have to juggle the demands of being a parent,

TABLE 11.2 Distribution of Midlife Individuals (45–59/64 years old) by Gender and Retrospective Multiple Role Occupancy (%)

	Men	Women	Total
Never had two or more roles simultaneously	13	8	11
Ever Had Two Roles Simultaneously			
Had been carer and parent	–	0	0
Had been carer and paid worker	3	4	3
Had been paid worker and parent	73	66	70
Had been paid worker and parent and (at another time) carer and parent	1	5	3
Ever Had Three Roles Simultaneously			
Had been carer, parent, and paid worker	11	18	14
N	(1,027)	(947)	(1,974)

$\chi^2 = 63.92$. $DF = 5$. $p = 0.000$.

Note: All sample numbers presented are unweighted, whereas percentages given are weighted.

Source: Family and Working Lives Survey (FWLS; King & Murray, 1996); and Evandrou, Glaser, and Henz (2002).

carer, and worker. This highlights the importance of taking a life course approach in understanding the boundaries and intersections of family and work, both for research and policy purposes.

Changing Economic and Social Roles Across Birth Cohorts

It is likely that demographic and socioeconomic changes over the latter half of the last century will have increased the number of roles occupied by men and women in midlife. Analysis reported in Evandrou and Glaser (2002) looked at how the occupancy of the roles of partner, parent, carer, and worker during midlife have changed across those birth cohorts born between the mid-1920s and the mid-1940s (see Figure 11.3).

The research shows there has been little change in the proportions occupying a partner role during midlife between those cohorts born 1926–1931 to 1941–1945. The rising divorce rates of the last 30 years appear to have had little impact on the probability of living in a union in midlife amongst these cohorts, being offset by the lower likelihood of widowhood due to improvements in life expectancy and

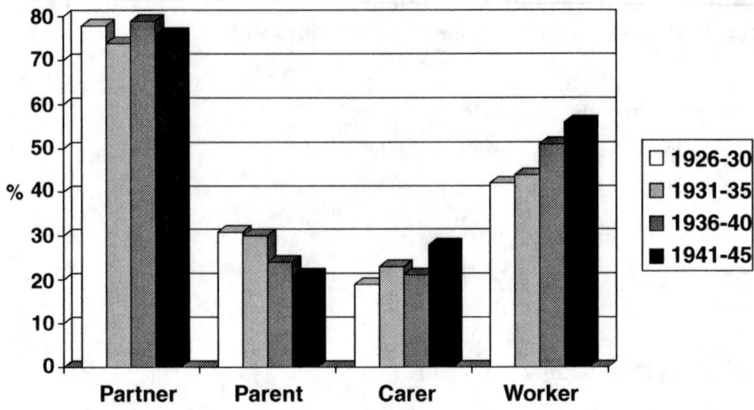

Figure 11.3 Changes in role occupancy amongst mid-life women (aged 55–59) by birth cohort. (From Evandrou & Glaser, 2002, Table 5a.)

by higher proportions marrying and remarrying. The cohort born in 1946 holds the distinction of being the "most married" British cohort since vital registration records began, with 95% of women ever married by age 40. It is anticipated, however, that this will change as the cohorts born in the late 1950s and early 1960s enter midlife as marriage rates amongst these cohorts are considerably lower. Amongst those women born in 1963, the peak of the UK second postwar baby boom, just 81% had married by age 40 (ONS, 2006a, Table 3.36).

The research also indicates that a significantly lower proportion of successive cohorts born between 1926 and 1945 occupy a parental role (i.e., are still living with children) in midlife. For example, at ages 50–54, 39% of women born in 1941–1945 are living with at least one child compared to 44% of those born in 1936–1940 and 51% of women born in 1931–1935. The likelihood of co-residence with children in midlife is influenced by the parental age at completion of childbearing and also the age at which children leave home. The recent trend toward leaving home at later ages and rises in the proportion of young adults returning home (Grundy, 1992) would imply an increase in co-residence with children in midlife. However, changes in the timing of childbearing—with a fall in the average age at last birth across the cohorts of women born between 1926 and 1945—have largely offset the trends in leaving home. Thus women from the 1941–1954 cohort, who had their children at younger ages, are now less likely to have children residing at home in midlife than women from earlier birth cohorts.

It is not clear which direction this trend will go in the future. In contrast to those born in the 1940s, women born in the 1960s have tended to postpone childbearing, and the average age at first birth (within marriage) in England and Wales has risen from 24 in 1970 to 30 in 2004 (ONS, 1985, 2005). Thus, amongst those women in the 1960s cohort who have children, a *higher* proportion are likely to still be living with them in midlife than amongst current cohorts of midlifers. However, amongst women born in 1960, only 82% of women had had a child by age 45 compared with 91% of women from the 1946 cohort at the same age (ONS, 2006b, Table 10.3). Thus in the future, for those with children are more likely to be occupying a parental role well into midlife, but there will also be a significant minority who will be childless and *never* occupy a parental role.

The likelihood of providing intensive care to someone who is sick, handicapped, or elderly during midlife is rising across cohorts. For example, 8% of women aged 60–64 from the 1936–1940 cohort report providing care for over 20 hours a week compared to 5% among the 1926–1930 cohort at the same age (Evandrou & Glaser, 2002). Similar upward trends across birth cohorts are found among men, although the differences are not statistically significant. These trends are in line with previous findings from the United States, where the prevalence of caregiving was found to be increasing across birth cohorts (Moen et al., 1994). In addition, increasing proportions of women are working in midlife; in 2006, 68% of all women aged 50–59 in the United Kingdom were employed, and this proportion has been rising consistently over the previous decade (ONS, 2006c).

The occupancy of a *combination* of roles is particularly important from a policy perspective, emphasizing the intersections and boundaries between different spheres of activity and responsibility. Evidence shows that being "caught in the middle," in terms of simultaneous family and caregiving responsibilities whilst in paid work, currently remains an atypical experience. Only one in nine women born in 1941–1945, and one in 10 men, were found to be occupying all three roles concurrently at ages 45–49 (Evandrou & Glaser, 2002). These findings support earlier research (Dautzenberg et al., 1998; Rosenthal et al., 1996; Spitze & Logan, 1990).

However, although multiple role commitments in midlife tend to be uncommon, there is evidence that the extent of multiple roles is *increasing* among younger cohorts, particularly those roles that combine caring and paid work. For example, 11% of women born in 1941–1945 were occupying the carer and paid worker roles at ages 55–59, compared to 6% of women from the 1926–1930 cohort at the same age. Similar patterns are found among men, although the differences across cohorts are less marked. The changes in patterns of role occupancy between cohorts at ages 50–54 and 55–59 are statistically significant for both men and women. Cohort differences are also significant among women at ages 60–64 (Evandrou & Glaser, 2002).

As mentioned above, there are marked gender differences in the distribution of role combinations, with women being more likely than men to occupy two or more roles when caregiving is one of the roles being considered, whereas men are more likely to hold role combinations involving paid work. For example, among the 1941–1945 cohort at ages 45–49, 16% of women are both a carer and parent compared to 12% of men; in contrast, 56% of men are a worker and parent compared to 41% of women (Evandrou & Glaser, 2002).

It is clear that the boundaries between being a parent and an adult child who is caring for one's own parent are becoming blurred, and increasingly women in particular are taking on both roles simultaneously. Although only a minority of midlifers are currently combining care for the generations both above and below them, with a greater proportion of people surviving into their seventies and eighties combined with a rise in the age of childbearing, it seems likely that more midlifers will do so in the future. Furthermore, the boundaries between paid and unpaid work are also becoming more imprecise, with people being "paid" for caring (i.e., receiving a carer's allowance or direct payments), whereas people in paid work are increasingly expected by employers to participate in work activities on a voluntary basis. The intersection between the roles of carer and worker is widening, with many people having dual roles. The last 30 years have seen a structural shift in both the family and the labor market, with the demise of the single-earner male breadwinner model and the rise of the dual-earner family with women working full-time. Increasing multiple role occupancy in midlife and expanding intersections between family and work have implications for health, leisure, and economic welfare in later life. Research examining each of these is discussed in the next section.

The Impact of Multiple Roles for Leisure and Economic Welfare in Later Life

Leisure

Little research has been carried out on the boundaries in different spheres of life, particularly the relationship between multiple roles and their effects on personal time and leisure activities. Research by Glaser, Evandrou, and Tomassini (2006) used data from the 2000 British Household Panel Survey (BHPS) to investigate gender differences in the association between intensive multiple role occupancy and the level of social activity participation and also the frequency of meeting friends and relatives amongst midlife couples. Analysis was carried out separately for wives and husbands, including variables measuring both their own and their spouse's role occupancy. The results indicated that occupying an intensive parental role (e.g., either living with dependent children or with only adult children, at least one of whom was in poor health, unemployed, or widowed, divorced, or separated) significantly reduces the level of participation in social activities for both wives and husbands (Glaser et al., 2006).

Regarding the extent to which couples negotiate the intersection of work and family roles when boundaries are challenged, particularly when caring responsibilities are intensified, men and women tend not to reduce their involvement in social activities in response to their *own* paid work and caregiver roles. They are, however, significantly affected by their *spouse's* participation in caregiving and paid work. Wives' involvement in social activities is significantly reduced if their husbands are providing care for over 20 hours a week. In contrast, husbands' social involvement is significantly increased if their wives are in full-time paid work. Given that women are consistently reported to have larger and more multifaceted networks than men, and that men tend to maintain close, intimate relationships primarily with their spouses (Shye, Mullooly, Freeborn, & Pope, 1995), the negative effect of husbands' intensive caregiving on wives' social activity may reflect husbands' greater reliance on their wives for support, highlighting the blurring of the boundaries between the partner and carer roles. However, the positive effect of wives' paid employment on husbands' social activities may reflect the greater resources available to the couple, which in turn may facilitate the pursuit of social activities outside the home.

Paid employment significantly reduces the frequency of meeting friends and relatives for both wives and husbands (Glaser et al., 2006). Providing care for 20 or more hours a week had been shown to have a positive significant effect on meeting friends and family for wives, and this finding is similar to other studies that found caregiving to be associated with higher social activity levels among midlife women (Farkas & Himes, 1997; Hoyert & Seltzer, 1992). The simultaneous occupation of the intensive caregiver and parental roles among husbands can have a significant negative effect on both their own and their spouse's frequency of meeting friends and relatives. In addition, the simultaneous occupation of the intensive parental and paid worker roles significantly reduces the frequency of meeting friends and relatives among husbands.

Thus, the main difference between men and women in the effect of family and work roles on the frequency of activity participation lies in the positive effect of intensive caregiving for women, and the negative effect of the intensive parental role for men. Given that women have larger social networks than men (Shye et al., 1995), the findings may reflect gender differences in the ability to draw on these networks for support. It should be noted, however, that contact with friends or relatives may also reflect contact with a non-co-resident dependent family member to whom care is being provided. Thus it is difficult to disentangle contacts for social support from contacts for social care.

The results also show significant gender differences in the impact of the spouses' social roles on the frequency of social activity participation and meeting friends and relatives. Wives' level of social activity participation and frequency of meeting friends or relatives were more likely to be negatively affected by husbands' multiple role obligations than vice versa, reflecting the gendered nature of social relations.

Economic Welfare in Later Life

Economic well-being is an important indicator of quality of life, and British research using longitudinal data has demonstrated the importance of events earlier in the life course on income in later life (Bardasi & Jenkins, 2002). For most people, income security in later life is dependent upon the entitlements to state and private pensions that they have built up *across* their working life. Therefore, multiple role occupancy in midlife may impact upon economic well-being in retirement.

Research analyzing work and caring history data from the FWLS investigated differences in entitlements to the state retirement pension and contributions to occupational and private pensions in Britain according to current and retrospective role occupancy (Evandrou & Glaser, 2003). There was little difference in entitlement to the state retirement pension between groups, once the impact of credits for periods of unemployment and caring responsibility (e.g., Home Responsibility Protection)[5] were taken into account. This suggests that the British social security system provides significant protection for those men and women who are providing care or who are a parent and not in paid employment.

Unfortunately, until very recently no such protection was afforded to second-tier pensions,[6] and significant differences were found according to current role occupancy. In common with other research, women were found to be particularly disadvantaged (Ginn, Street, & Arber, 2001). Fifteen percent of midlife women within the FWLS have made no contributions to either a state or private second pension. This figure was 20% for those currently occupying one role as a parent. Just over half (51%) of midlife women have contributed to an occupational or personal pension compared to three quarters of men (78%). However, among women either occupying a parent role alone or combining parenting with caring, this figure drops to less than a third (28% and 30% respectively). Not only do fewer women contribute toward second-tier pensions, but they also have, on average, contributed for fewer years (13 years compared to 21 years for men; Evandrou & Glaser, 2003).

Efforts to unravel the effect of caring responsibilities upon work arrangements and the likely impact upon pension prospects have also been undertaken. The evidence indicates that combining paid employment with caregiving is *not* an option for a significant minority of women with caring responsibilities. One in five midlife women in the FWLS who have ever had caring responsibilities reported that upon starting caring, they stopped work altogether, and a further one in five reported that they worked fewer hours, earned less money, or could work only restricted hours (Evandrou & Glaser, 2003). The response to caring varies according to the stage of the life course, with both men and women being more likely to stop work altogether if they assume caring responsibilities close to statutory retirement age. However, men taking on caring responsibilities in early midlife (45–49) are more likely to change their working arrangements than others; that is, work fewer hours, earn less money, do a different type of job, or work only on certain days. A reduction in labor market activity is not necessarily matched by an increase once caring responsibilities cease. Just over a third of women who report that their work arrangements have been affected by their caring responsibilities also report that the cessation of caring was not accompanied by any change in their work arrangements.

These trends have important consequences both for carers' welfare today, in terms of reduced income from employment, and also for their future welfare in terms of reduced opportunity to accumulate pension entitlements. A lower proportion of men and women who stopped work as a result of caring were members of an occupational pension scheme than other groups, and among those who were, they had accumulated fewer years of contributions than their counterparts who continued working (Evandrou & Glaser, 2003). This will result in a lower pension income in later life. Second-tier pensions will become increasingly important for maintaining an adequate income in old age as the relative value of the state retirement pension continues to decline. Given these findings, it appears that women who have fulfilled the important social roles of carers and parents look likely to continue to run the risk of being socially excluded in terms of financial resources in later life.

Conclusion

The findings from recent British research studies indicate that being "caught in the middle," in terms of simultaneous work and family roles, remains an atypical experience. However, a higher proportion of midlife individuals have simultaneously occupied multiple roles at some point over their life course than is indicated at a single point in time. In addition, analysis across birth cohorts shows that multiple role occupancy is increasing, and it is likely that the proportion of men and women juggling work and family responsibilities will continue to rise.

The research has also highlighted the potentially negative consequences of multiple role occupancy for health, social activities, and the accumulation of pension entitlements. Living with dependent children or with an adult child who was in poor health, unemployed, or divorced, separated, or widowed both was associated with subsequent poor health and significantly reduced levels of participation in social activities for both midlife men and women. Research shows that adult children moving back in with their parents constitute the fourth largest source of change in living arrangements in later life (Evandrou, Falkingham, Rake, & Scott, 2001). Increasing rates of student debt and rising house prices, combined with higher rates of relationship breakdown and growing career instability, have meant that more adults are returning to their parental home than in the past. A recent survey of more than 3,300 adults found that 27% of leavers return to live with their parents at least once, and one in 10 returns four times before leaving for good (Mintel, 2002). Given this, more research is needed on the impact on quality of life of the lengthening of the period of parental responsibility into and beyond midlife.

Occupying a caring role in midlife has the potential to negatively affect future pension prospects. The new carer's credit for the basic and second-tier state pensions explicitly recognizes the important role of caring. However, this goes only so far, and many carers fail to accumulate rights to earnings-related second-tier pensions that offer greater security in later life. One way to ameliorate this is to support carers in maintaining contact with the world of work (Department of Health, 1999). However, although there has been increased recognition of the importance of supporting individuals in juggling work and family commitments (DfEE, 2000; Department of Trade and Industry [DTI], 2003), most of the schemes funded in Britain have focused primarily on improving the balance between paid work and parenting for young children, with little attention given to the demands of caring for an older dependent. Since 2003, parents of children under age 6 and of disabled children under 18 have had the right to request work flexibility in their current jobs (DTI, 2004), and this right is being extended to carers with adult dependents from April 2007 (Carers [Equal Opportunities] Act 2004). The success of this will critically depend upon the implementation of this by employers.

The role of employers is fundamental in changing workplace culture to permit more flexibility for employees to combine work and family life (Dex, 1999). Research within a health and social care National Health Service trust found that very few of the family-friendly policies available are offered on a routine basis (Phillips, Bernard, & Chittenden, 2002). The status of working carers in the organization, the type of work they are engaged in, and the nature of their work were all found to be important in determining workers' access to policies and benefits. So too was manager discretion and flexibility, as well as their knowledge of the worker's caring and work histories. Working carers tended to make use of familiar, easy-to-access policies (such as annual leave and time off in lieu), which did not stigmatize them as being in need of assistance. Major gaps in knowledge and provision remain. A recent British study on family-friendly employment policies within local government, retail, and retail banking found that 50% of all employees in the study were not aware of the policies offered by their employers (Yeandle, Wigfield, Crompton, & Dennett, 2002). The extent to which government, and society as a whole, recognizes and supports individuals combining their economic and social roles in order to protect their quality of life, both currently and in their own old age, remains a critical issue on the policy agenda in Europe and North America.

Notes

1. The British General Household Survey (GHS) is a cross-sectional survey of individuals living in private households carried out annually by the UK Office for National Statistics (see, e.g., ONS, 2000).
2. The 2000 GHS (ONS, 2000) provides a subsample of 2,442 women and 2,361 men aged between 45 and 64.
3. The Family and Working Lives Survey (FWLS) is based on a nationally representative sample of 9,139 individuals aged between 16 and 69 years in Britain who were interviewed in 1994–1995 (King & Murray, 1996).
4. The caring role included all carers providing care for at least 3 months, and the partner role was excluded from this analysis.
5. Home Responsibility Protection provides coverage for those out of the labor market due to caring for a dependent child or a disabled adult for at least 35 hours a week.
6. From April 2002, carers receiving the Carer's Allowance received a credit for entitlement to the State Second Pension. Currently this applies only to people caring for at least 35 hours a week for a person in receipt of Attendance Allowance or Disability Living Allowance. However, the 2007 Pensions Bill will extend this to those caring for 20 hours or more a week.

References

Bardasi, E., & Jenkins, S. (2002). *Income in later life: Work history matters.* Bristol, UK: Policy.

Bartley, M., Popay, J., & Plewis, I. (1992). Domestic conditions, paid employment and women's experience of ill-health. *Sociology of Health and Illness, 14,* 313–343.

Brody, E. (1981). "Women in the middle" and family help to older people. *The Gerontologist, 21,* 471–480.

Brody, E. (1985). Parent care as normative stress. *The Gerontologist, 25,* 19–29.

Dautzenberg, M. G. H., Diederiks, J. P. M., Philipsen, H., & Stevens, F. C. J. (1998). Women of a middle generation and parent care. *International Journal of Aging and Human Development, 47,* 241–262.

Department for Education and Employment (DfEE). (2000). *Changing patterns in a changing world.* Edinburgh: DfEE Scottish Office.

Department of Health. (1999). *Caring about carers: National carers strategy.* London: Author.

Department of Trade and Industry (DTI). (2003). *Balancing work and family life: Enhancing choice and support for parents.* London: Stationery Office.

Department of Trade and Industry (DTI). (2004). *Results of the first flexible working employee survey* (Employment Relations Occasional Paper). London: Author.

Dex, S. (1999). *Families and the labour market: Trends, pressures and policies.* London: Family Policy Studies Centre and the Joseph Rowntree Foundation.

Evandrou, M. (1996). Unpaid work, carers and health. In D. Blane, E. Brunner, & R. Wilkinson (Eds.), *Health and social organization: Towards a health policy for the twenty-first century* (pp. 204–231). London: Routledge.

Evandrou, M., Falkingham, J., Rake, K., & Scott, A. (2001). The dynamics of living arrangements in later life. *Population Trends, 105,* 37–44.

Evandrou, M., & Glaser, K. (2002). Changing economic and social roles: The experience of four cohorts of mid-life individuals in Britain, 1985–2000. *Population Trends, 110,* 19–30.

Evandrou, M., & Glaser, K. (2003). Combining work and family life: The pension penalty of caring. *Ageing and Society, 23*(5), 583–602.

Evandrou, M., & Glaser, K. (2007). Changing economic and social roles in mid-life in Britain (Centre for Research on Ageing Discussion Paper Series, DP7001). Southampton, UK: University of Southampton.

Evandrou, M., Glaser, K., & Henz, U. (2002). Multiple role occupancy in mid-life: Balancing work and family life in Britain. *The Gerontologist, 42*(6), 781–789.

Farkas, J. I., & Himes, C. L. (1997). The influence of caregiving and employment on the voluntary activities of midlife and older women. *Journal of Gerontology: Social Sciences, 52B*, S180–S189.

Ginn, J., Street, D., & Arber, S. (Eds.). (2001). *Women, work and pensions.* Buckingham, UK: Open University Press.

Glaser, K., Evandrou, M., & Tomassini, C. (2006). The relationship of multiple role occupancy on social participation among mid-life wives and husbands in the UK. *International Journal of Aging and Human Development, 63*(1), 27–47.

Goode, W. (1960). A theory of role strain. *American Sociological Review, 25*, 483–496.

Grundy, E. (1992). Household circumstances and transitions. In A. Warnes (Ed.), *Homes and travel: Local life in the third age* (Research Paper No. 5). Fife, UK: Carnegie United Kingdom Trust.

Himes, C. L. (1994). Parental caregiving by adult women: A demographic perspective. *Research on Aging, 16*, 191–211.

Hoyert, D. L., & Seltzer, M. M. (1992). Factors related to the well-being and life activities of family caregivers. *Family Relations, 41*, 74–81.

King, S., & Murray, K. (1996, March). Family and working lives survey: Preliminary results. *Labour Market Trends*, 115–119.

Kinsella, K., & Velkoff, V. (2001). *An aging world: 2001* (U.S. Census Bureau, Series P95/01-1). Washington, DC: Government Printing Office.

Mintel. (2002). *Marketing to tomorrow's consumers.* London: Mintel.

Moen, P., Robison, J., & Fields, V. (1994). Women's work and caregiving roles: A life course approach. *Journal of Gerontology: Social Sciences, 49*, S176–S186.

Office for National Statistics (ONS). (1985). *Birth statistics: Historical data* (Series FM1 No. 13). London: Author.

Office for National Statistics (ONS). (2000). *British General Household Survey.* London: Author.

Office for National Statistics (ONS). (2005). *Birth statistics* (Series FM1 No. 33). London: Author.

Office for National Statistics (ONS). (2006a). *Marriage, divorce and adoption statistics* (Series FM2 No. 31). London: Author.

Office for National Statistics (ONS). (2006b). *Birth statistics* (Series FM2 No. 34). London: Author.

Office for National Statistics (ONS). (2006c). Labour market review 2006. London: Author.

Penning, M. J. (1998). In the middle: Parental caregiving in the context of other roles. *Journal of Gerontology: Social Sciences, 53B*, S188–S197.

Phillips, J., Bernard, M., & Chittenden, M. (2002). *Juggling work and care: The experiences of working carers of older adults.* Bristol, UK: Joseph Rowntree Foundation and Policy Press.

Reid, J., & Hardy, M. (1999). Multiple roles and well-being among midlife women: Testing role strain and role enhancement theories. *Journal of Gerontology: Social Sciences, 54B*, S329–S338.

Robison, J., Moen, P., & Dempster-McClain, D. (1995). Women's caregiving: Changing profiles and pathways. *Journal of Gerontology: Social Sciences, 50B*, S362–S373.

Rosenthal, C. J., Martin-Matthews, A., & Matthews, S. H. (1996). Caught in the middle? Occupancy in multiple roles and help to parents in a national probability sample of Canadian adults. *Journal of Gerontology: Social Sciences, 51B*, S274–S283.

Rosenthal, C. J., Matthews, S. H., & Marshall, V. W. (1989). Is parent care normative? The experiences of a sample of middle aged women. *Research on Aging, 11*, 244–260.

Shye, D., Mullooly, J. P., Freeborn, D. K., & Pope, C. R. (1995). Gender differences in the relationship between social network support and mortality: A longitudinal study of an elderly cohort. *Social Science and Medicine, 41*(7), 935–947.

Soldo, B. J. (1996). Cross pressures on middle-aged adults: A broader view. *Journal of Gerontology: Social Sciences, 51B*, S271–S273.

Spitze, G., & Logan, J. (1990). More evidence on women (and men) in the middle. *Research on Aging, 12*, 182–198.

Spitze, G., Logan, J. R., Joseph, G., & Lee, E. (1994). Middle generation roles and the well-being of men and women. *Journal of Gerontology: Social Sciences, 49*, S107–S116.

Yeandle, S., Wigfield, A., Crompton, R., & Dennett, J. (2002). *Employers, communities and family-friendly employment policies.* Bristol, UK: Joseph Rowntree Foundation and Policy Press.

12

Clashing Temporalities

Time, Home, and the Bodywork of Care

Julia Twigg

Across the western world, homecare has become the acknowledged ideal for the support of frail older and disabled people, seen as providing the best-quality care, as well as the only feasible form economically, in the context of rising levels of demand. The primary setting for service delivery has, thus, shifted decisively to the home. But we have only slowly begun to address the implications of this for both service delivery and the lives of older and disabled people. Home is familiar territory, so much so, indeed, that it can appear obvious, its complexities glossed over by the assumed and commonsensical. In fact it is a highly complex site in which material, symbolic, social, and cultural constructions mingle and interpenetrate. The coming of care potentially destabilizes and reconstitutes these meanings, refracting them through different discourses, different rationalities. Further complexity is added by the nature of the work within homecare—the fact that it primarily involves the body—so that the symbolic and spatial relations of home and care closely interact with those of the body and bodywork. Service delivery intrudes upon these relations, disturbs these privacies. The challenge of homecare is, thus, how to preserve the nature of this setting and protect the identity of the self in its material and socially embedded form—at ease, at home, located within its own time and space—and yet provide service support in a way that is consonant with the logic of economic production.

In this chapter I explore these discordances through the analysis of time and the rival temporal orderings of body, home, and service delivery. Much of the best recent work on homecare has been concerned with questions of space and place, exploring the ways in which home is both a material and discursive site, in which the processes of care can act to reformulate its nature. This work reflects the wider shift away from an understanding of space as bounded physical territory and toward relational formulations that present it as the outcome of socioeconomic processes (Conradson, 2005; Massey, 1994; Valentine, 2001); and it links to earlier phenomenological work that explored the particular, and symbolically significant, meanings of home (Gurney & Means, 1993; Rubinstein, 1989; Sixsmith, 1990). The coming of care into this space reorders its materiality, so that it becomes, as Dyck and colleagues argued, a negotiated moral landscape in which the ethic of care is constructed though spatial strategies, in complex conditions of materiality, embodiment, fields of knowledge, and social relations (Angus, Kontos, Dyck, McKeever, & Poland, 2005; Dyck, Kontos, Angus, & McKeever, 2005). Rescripted as a workspace for caring, home comes to signify disability and disorder, a key site within which the vulnerable body is interpreted and lived (Dyck, 1998; Dyck et al., 2005; Imrie, 2004; Wiles, 2003). In the context of domiciliary care, home is both a personal dwelling, imbued with meaning and emotion, and a site of complex labor-intensive carework (Wiles, 2005).

The space of home, however, cannot be considered separate from time. Time and space represent two fundamentals of social order. Though distinct, they also interpenetrate and co-constitute each other (Adam, 1995; Crow & Heath, 2002; Urry, 1996), so that spatial relations intersect with temporal ones, to the extent that many theorists present space and time as a unified framework (May & Thrift, 2001). These linkages are carried over into the analysis of the body. Just as the body is the primary medium through which we experience space (Rodaway, 1994; Tuan, 1974), so too is time lived sensuously at the level of the body, its rhythms, cycles, and orderings (Adam, 1995). Time and temporality have, however, received relatively little attention within the homecare literature. It is the aim of this chapter to redress this neglect, and in doing so offer a parallel analysis to one developed earlier in relation to the spatial ordering of care (Twigg, 1999).

A subsidiary aim of the chapter is to contribute to a more general project of shifting the analysis of social care away from its current primary location at the level of organizations and policies, toward the front line of provision. Until recently social care, and homecare within it, tended to be analyzed within a framework that derived from professional or public policy agendas, and that foregrounded rationalist, bureaucratic structures to the expense of the day-to-day realities of care consumption and provision. There is a need to shift the analysis closer to the front line of care, for it is at that level of action and exchange that "care"—the primary product to the care system—is created and consumed. Focusing on time and the lived experiences of time offers one of the ways of doing this.

Lastly, in exploring these clashing temporalities, I want to address the way in which homecare has remained a sector that has proved relatively intransigent to productivity gains. Though greater efficiency has in recent years been extracted from the homecare system, this has largely been achieved though privatization, downward pressure on wages and conditions, and the use of migrant labor. The productivity of carework itself has not, by and large, increased. I want to suggest that this arises not from failure to get to grips with the sector managerially, but from certain essential features of carework, in which the temporal dimension plays a part. In particular I will suggest that efficiency of production is predicated on a particular set of ideas about time. Though these occupy a hegemonic position within western culture, closely linked as they are to the key project of modernity in the form of science and industrial capitalism, they need to be set in a larger theoretical framework that recognizes the plural and multiple nature of time and of time frames. This means that (some at least) of the classic means whereby efficiency is increased—and productivity gains made—are not available in the field of homecare, or are so only through the imposition of alien frameworks that undermine the character of life at home.

New Theorizing in Relation to Time

The last two decades have witnessed a revival of interest in time among social theorists, associated in part with Harvey's (1989) analysis of postmodernity in terms of space–time compression, but reflecting also renewed interest in phenomenological accounts rooted in the experiences of the body. The poststructuralist emphasis on discursive constitution of both the body and the social world has given further impetus to such approaches. The writings of Anthony Giddens (1984, 1991) and Barbara Adam (1995) have been particularly influential here. They argue for an understanding of time as socially embedded, something that is both experiential and structural. Time is, thus, multiple and complex; there is no single time, but rather a plurality of times rooted in distinct social forms and relationships. Time, furthermore, can be cyclic, repeating, folding back on itself—a time of being and becoming. Its tempo and intensity can vary, so that we experience it differently at different times in our lives. This account of time stands in contrast to what is the dominant account within western culture, which derives from clock time and which presents it as abstract, linear, unvarying, and separate from social processes. Adam argued, however, that this account, though it has become naturalized in modern culture, is, in fact, an artefact, the product of the machines—clocks—developed to measure and record it. It is time abstracted, stripped of its organic roots, quantified, spatialized, and rendered unvarying, precise, and endlessly and perfectly repeatable. This reified version of time underpins the development of modernity, informing both the modern scientific worldview and the logic of industrial production. It is clock time that enabled time to be fully commodified, that created the time of capitalist production, time and motion studies, time management and time budgeting, and the world that made time money. So dominant has this account become, Adam argued, that we can scarcely think outside its parameters. Empirical studies reported in Daly (2001) confirm this.

Much recent theoretical work has been concerned to rescue our understanding from this hegemonic account, arguing for the existence of Other Times, other experiences of temporality and chronicity. Among the most interesting work in this vein has been that of feminists concerned to explore the ways in which time is gendered (Davies, 1994, 2001; Hantrais, 1993; Leccardi, 1996; Leccardi & Rampazi, 1993). Davies (2001), for example, argued that the classic linear account of clock time is itself grounded in gendered power relations, growing as it did out of religious, scientific, and economic structures that reflected hierarchical gendered relations. Women's experiences of time, by contrast, are characterized by plurality and interdependence, the product of interweaving and interconnection, and marked by simultaneous activities, overlapping temporalities. Davies (2001) argued that these divergent experiences have their roots in women's caring roles; and she suggested that women's use of time and their temporal consciousness are closely related to the time demands of significant others—as, indeed, is their experience of space—so that where and when women find themselves are determined to a significant degree by the needs of others. For Adam (1995), although such accounts are illuminating, and suggestive of the variety and complexity of time and time frames, their insights should not be limited to women. All people to some extent live their lives in multiple time frames. This applies particularly to anyone whose life is lived outside the dominance of the economy and clock time: the old, disabled, women, carers—the key actors, indeed, in social care. The analytic task is, therefore, to get behind the dominance of clock time to reveal this wider complexity.

I want now to turn to seven ways in which the temporal ordering of the body and domestic life is in conflict with the rationalities of service provision. The first three relate to the nature of the body and its care.

The Body in Time

Carework centers on the body. Though it extends to the material surroundings of the home or the facility, its essential nature is as bodywork (Twigg, 2000a,b; Wolkowitz, 2002). This means that it is closely tied to the needs of the body in both spatial and temporal terms. The body has its own temporality: rhythmic, cyclic, guided not by clock time but by organic processes. As a result, care has to be provided *when* it is needed. The units of time are highly context specific, closely attached to the discrete physicality of the body. They cannot be accumulated in the classic sense that commodified, abstracted time can be. You cannot, for example, save up taking someone to the toilet for a week, and then do it all in one go. This limits the capacity of the service provider to rationalize the labor process on classic efficiency lines. The possibility of economies of scale—one of the basic building blocks of efficient production—is constrained by the nature of the body, its rhythms and needs. Such difficulties apply to the spatial dimension also. Care by its nature has to be provided close to the care recipient: The tasks cannot be separated from the person. Here questions of provision intersect with issues of globalization, and in particular the restructuring of economic production consequent on the compression of space and time associated with the revolution in information technology and its role in creating the postmodern world (Giddens, 1991; Harvey, 1989). Carework, however, is one of the sectors in the new economy that cannot be transferred across traditional spatio-temporal boundaries; its very materiality and closeness to the body mean that it has to be performed locally, close, in the home and on the bodies of recipients. As a result the primary flows in relation to globalization have been ones, not of goods, but of labor, in which poor migrant workers move to rich first world economies to undertake basic service work, often around the body.

The second dimension of conflict relates to the cyclic, repetitive nature of bodytime. Carework centers on the restoration and maintenance of order against the entropic forces of disruption and disorder. Like housework and other related—usually gendered—service work, it is about maintaining a state rather than producing a product. This gives it a hidden quality—something visible only in its absence. At any moment, it can be undone, the activity nullified, the state of order overthrown. For example, the client whom the worker has just got clean and comfortable may vomit up over him or herself as the worker goes out the front door. The work is thus hard to predict in terms of units of activity or time, because it is not about an activity but a state. This presents problems for a service like homecare that is predicated on the temporal commodification of activity in the form of units of workers' time, for this, in essence, is how the homecare is managed. So, though the clock time of economic production within which service delivery exists is linear in nature, and cannot be reversed, the organic, repeating, cyclic nature of bodytime disrupts this linearity, folding back on itself, repeating, recycling, returning the tasks, in ways that disturb and challenge the rationality of production and allocation.

The third interlinkage between the body and time rests on the unpredictability of need, in conjunction with very tight and exacting time demands. This can result in abrupt changes in the intensity and significance of time. For example, falls can occur at any time; they are unpredictable. And yet from the moment of their occurrence, the clock of deterioration and danger starts to run. Time has become of the essence in relation to survival and care. A fall is thus an irruption of crisis time—acute time—into the slow, continuous time, almost nontime, of homecare. For many staff, carework is experienced as a time of monotony, dominated by routine, repetition, and boredom. This is the nontime of care, the eternal present of low-level engagement and endlessly repeated tasks. The tempo of this is radically different from that of crisis time, when urgent intervention is suddenly required. From the perspective of services, this contrast of modes presents significant organizational difficulties, as the tempo switches and as moments of time come to be acutely significant.

The Time of Care

The fourth discordance relates to tempo and speed. It is in the nature of care that it is closely interpersonal, something produced and consumed at the front line, an activity where the quality of the interaction between worker and client is critical. This is what creates the difference between cold, dehumanizing care that treats the person as an object, and high-quality or "real" care where there is a full acknowledgment of their personhood, an exchange of human recognition and feeling. Time is relevant to this, however, in that many of the techniques used to increase time efficiency threaten to undermine the quality of the interaction. Care provided as fast, and as efficiently, as possible is care that is instrumental, distant, and cold. As Goffman (1961) showed in the context of the psychiatric ward, it is quicker and more efficient to treat patients as objects—to line them up and deal with their needs collectively—than to respond to them individually. Shutting down the interaction, and keeping up the pace with that of an active younger person, are ways of getting the work done. It is a question of not just tempo, but also instrumentality. Part of the meaning of care is focusing on the present, valuing the time of now, for and of itself. This is the slow time of the mindful present, which recognizes that how things are done can be as important as what is done. Parkins (2004) has analyzed this in the wider context of the slow-living movement in which there is a conscious commitment to occupy time attentively, to remain in the moment, savoring being and doing as much as becoming and achieving, in the attempt to wrest the experience of time from the dominance of modernity with its valorization of speed, action, and achievement. Something of the same task applies to carework, though the economic logic of service provision constantly undermines it.

The interpersonal aspect at the heart of carework relates also to the way in which it is an activity that is—ideally—person centered, in the sense that it is built around the actions and wishes of the person. The care worker is—ideally—secondary, enabling disabled people to do what they want to do, in their own time and at their own time, so that temporal ordering, scheduling, and the pace of the activity are determined by the frail older or disabled person. But the reality of time scheduling in the work context means that all too often the desires of the older person are made subordinate to the requirements of the care system. Care proceeds at the pace and at the times that providers determine.

The Temporal Ordering of Home

The fifth area of tension concerns the temporal ordering of the home and the body. We are familiar with the ways in which the privacy of home is structured spatially in terms of zones of greater and lesser intimacy and closure, in which, for example, bedrooms and bathrooms are spaces of relative privacy in contrast to the more public areas of the hallway or sitting room (Gurney, 2000; Lawrence, 1987; Twigg, 1999). This also occurs temporally, so that home in the evening and at night changes its character, becoming more intimate and private, a territory where strangers are excluded. This is one of the reasons why having care staff in the home at night can be experienced as burdensome and difficult. Their presence can rescript the nature of home and nighttime, introducing an alien, discordant element, at odds with the temporal regime of privacy. Night-sitting services and round-the-clock care are, of course, expensive, and that is a significant factor in their limited use, but relevant also are the challenges that strangers present to the ordering of home. This is often particularly felt by carers who share their home with the disabled or frail person (Twigg & Atkin, 1994). Night sitters may bring the promise of relief and a decent night's sleep, but their presence can be disturbing, a cause of unease; and they tend to be used only in the more extreme or final stages of illness.

Duration of care is also significant in structuring power dynamics. In general, homecare visits do not last long. Even those receiving high levels of input spend the majority of the day not in the company of workers, and not under the temporal gaze of service provision. This gives a tangential quality to their presence in the home. Care is inserted only at distinct moments; and there are long periods of time in which the domestic ordering of the home reasserts itself. This is in marked contrast to the situation in institutions, where care and the presence of care workers extend unremittingly over the full 24 hours so that the time regime of residents becomes wholly that of the institution. This extends even to the level of the body and its functions, as washing, eating, and excreting come under the time regime of the institution.

The domestic ordering of the home intersects closely with that of the body. The body has its own rhythms and regularities, rooted deep within its physiology (Adam, 1995), and these intersect with those of domestic life to structure the daily, weekly, and yearly round. Such embodied patterns play no small part in our sense of ontological security in the world. Domestic life is indeed structured around the care of the body: We get up, get dressed, and wash and feed ourselves, and we do this in patterns that are meaningful. Meals punctuate the day and give it shape: before lunch, too late for tea. Baths and showers similarly act as points of transition between social and bodily states: between the day and the night, between the ordinary life of work and the special event of a party. Body care thus occurs at significant times. It is not randomly embarked upon. Once again, the coming of care potentially disrupts these ordered sequences, imposing different, externally driven ones that derive from the logic of service delivery. For example, the demands of efficient production mean that clients are very often offered baths and showers at radically discordant times: at meaningless moments, such as 11:30 in the morning. Imposing such clock-driven schedules on the body is a weak form of Foucauldian regulation and discipline; and there are parallels here with classic carceral settings such as prisons, workhouses, and schools, where bodies are similarly marshaled and disciplined according to the rigidities of clock time. Accepting the coming of care into the home thus means accepting that the timings and rhythms of domestic life will be replaced by those of the service agency.

Workers too are caught within these competing time regimes of work and domesticity. Though they enter the home as agents of commodified time, they also live their lives in plural time frames. They too are embodied and have time needs that relate to the body and its care—eating, resting, sleeping—and they have domestic and family lives that impose their own forms of temporal order. As a result, the demands of their personal, bodily lives are often in direct competition with those of clients: Workers want their lunch in the middle of the day, they too have to be home to prepare evening meals for families and put children to bed, and they want to spend time in the company of family at home on the dark evenings. From their perspective, at least, their inputs cannot be treated as abstract units of time unlocated within structures of social meaning. Indeed, as Davies (2001) has commented, the lives and times of women are closely constrained by such multiple caring obligations. For these reasons, providing a fully flexible service that fits with the desires of clients—allowing them, for example, to have their meals at normal social times or to be put to bed as late as they might wish—is awkward or costly, achievable only through complex patterns of rostering that may impose difficult and fragmenting time demands on workers.

Economic Incommensurability: The Time of Public and Private

The sixth issue, that of competing temporalities, emerges most clearly in the incommensurability of time as between the paid and unpaid spheres. In the world of work, time is literally money; in the world of old age, it is not. As Adam (1995) noted, different times are accorded different statuses; and times governed by commodified time take precedence over those outside the time economy. Service provision reflects this. Older people—indeed, clients and patients in general—wait upon the time of service providers and professionals. Indeed, waiting in this way systematically reveals patterns of power and status. Thus, lesser workers wait on the time of hospital consultants or senior managers, and patients wait on the time of care workers, nurses, and doctors. As Frankenberg (1988) recorded in his phenomenological account of being a hospital patient, the time of the patient is nontime. Lee and Piachaud (1992) noted how social services do not consider the time costs of clients; indeed, many of the ways in which they work impose time costs on clients and carers, through, for example, cancellations, rescheduling, and abrupt discharge. Attempts have been made to redress this through demands that staff improve their punctuality and give greater weight to the time of clients and carers; and the shift toward a more closely managed homecare service in the United Kingdom has probably effected positive change in this regard, though we noted earlier the difficulties presented to time scheduling by the unpredictable and unstable nature of bodily need.

At a more analytic level, attempts have been made to factor in the interests of clients and carers, through ascribing values to their time inputs as part of a more general evaluation of cost-effectiveness.

Thus, the time spent by patients waiting at the clinic can be factored into estimates of the efficiency of its working. In social care, the most developed work in this vein has been in relation to informal care, where estimations have been made of the time input of carers and of their value in the form of either opportunity costs or a version of shadow pricing (Netten, 1993). The fact that the focus has been on informal carers is, of course, significant. Unlike clients, many carers, at least if they are offspring, are still part of the time economy of work, and time estimations are relevant to the potential opportunity costs and trade-offs made by carers as between caring and working. They are also relevant to the questions of the future availability of care, as well as to wider debates concerning the valuation of nonwaged activity in the economy. But such analyses are rarely if ever extended to the opportunity costs or time losses of clients. Though such approaches can be heuristically useful, they ultimately suffer from the problem of artificiality; and they remain distant from the day-to-day pressures and political realities of the sector.

Time Next to Death

Lastly, some of the low valuation of the time of old people derives from the particular moment in the life course within which their lives are embedded. We noted earlier how the time of homecare can often be experienced by care staff as nontime, an eternal presence of boredom, in which little happens and tasks ceaselessly return—a protracted space of waiting. This sense of marking time is also affected by the potential imminence of death. As Vincent (2003) observed, modern societies are distinguished by the degree to which death is concentrated in old age; and this profoundly affects how old age is perceived and experienced. Modern secular society is largely silent about death; it has little or nothing to say about it; and this silence acts back on the stage prior to it—old age—so that death empties old age, and the time of old age, of meaning. In previous eras, dominated by prescientific or religious worldviews, the time of old age had special significance. An important stage in the pilgrimage of life (Cole, 1992; Katz, 1996), it was a period of preparation and spiritual endeavor at the end of life, but with the decline in the belief of the afterlife, the stage next to death loses its meaning. It content is sucked out, becoming an empty space—an empty time—waiting to finish; and this profoundly affects how it is regarded in the wider culture of which service provision is part.

Conclusion

Homecare cannot be seen separated from the world in which it is embedded—that of home, the body, and domesticity. Much attention has been given recently to the spatial dimension of this world, and to the ways in which the ordered relations of home and the body are disordered and reconfigured by the processes of care. Less attention has been paid to the temporal dimension. And yet, as we have seen, home and body are enmeshed in complex interpenetrating time frames, so that the coming of care potentially disrupts and disorders these in ways that parallel and intersect with spatiality. We saw how the temporal ordering of the home intersects with the daily round of body care, so that domestic life is structured by such rhythms and regularities, and how that in turn helps underpin our day-to-day sense of ontological security. Care disrupts these patterns, intrudes upon these privacies, imposing temporal structures that have their roots in the commodified time of production. There are conflicts between the linear, abstracted, unvarying form of time that underpins economic rationality, and the organic cyclic character of bodily needs, as they present and re-present themselves. Here the task is never finished because it endlessly returns; achievements are never secure, because they are always potentially about to fall back into disorder. Clashes occur also in relation to tempo. The time of care stops and starts in unpredictable ways, shifting abruptly between the slow, endless, almost nontime of day-to-day care and the sharply defined moment of crisis, when time, far from being endless, becomes acutely circumscribed and measured out—the time of life-and-death interventions. We saw how the time of care, with its focus on being rather than achieving, is in conflict with the task-driven nature of service provision, the slow time of the mindful present at odds with the driven instrumental quality of time efficiency. This finds further expression in the divergent tempos of young and old, with the desire of young, fit, often energetic care workers to get on with the job and keep the pace of life up to a tolerable level, and the need of old frail clients to take things slowly, to move carefully, to take their time. Older people at home are time rich, and this can be in marked contrast to the often time-harassed lives of workers with their competing demands of their domestic and family lives. Time is also enmeshed in value, and we saw how the time of old people is commonly treated within the service system as having no value. Partly this reflects their disengagement from the world of work, so that their time—unlike that of professionals and care workers—has no monetary value, except in the rather artificial estimations of cost–benefit analyses (which are in any case rarely extended to older people), but partly it reflects wider societal ageism. The time of old age is a time of cultural disparagement, and part of the reason for this lies in the stage of life that old age represents: that next of death. As such, it is the object of projection and fear, its meaning and value hollowed out in ways that act back onto service provision.

References

Adam, B. (1995). *Timewatch: The social analysis of time*. Cambridge: Polity.

Angus, J. E., Kontos, P., Dyck, I., McKeever, P., & Poland, B. (2005). The physical significance of home: Habitus and the experience of receiving long term home care. *Sociology of Health and Illness*, *27*(2), 161–187.

Cole, T. C. (1992). *The journey of life: A cultural history of aging in America*. Cambridge: Cambridge University Press.

Conradson, D. (2005). Landscape, care and the relational self: Therapeutic encounters in rural England. *Health & Place*, *11*(4), 337–348.

Crow, G., & Heath, S. (Eds). (2002). *Social conceptions of time: Structure and process in work and everyday life*. Basingstoke, UK: Palgrave.

Daly, K. (Ed.). (2001). *Minding the time in family experience: Emerging perspectives and issues*. Oxford: Elsevier Science.

Davies, K. (1994). The tensions between process time and clock time in carework: The example of day nurseries. *Time and Society*, *3*(3), 277–303.

Davies, K. (2001). Responsibility and daily life: Reflections over timespace. In J. May & N. Thrift (Eds.), *Timespace: Geographies of temporality*. London: Routledge.

Dyck, I. (1998). Women with disabilities and everyday geographies: Home space and the contested body. In R. A. Kearns & W. M. Gesler (Eds.), *Putting health into place: Landscape, identity and well-being*. Syracuse, NY: Syracuse University Press.

Dyck, I., Kontos, P., Angus, J., & McKeever, P. (2005). The home as a site for long term care: Meanings and management of bodies. *Health & Place*, *11*(2), 173–185.

Frankenberg, R. (1988). "Your time or mine": An anthropological view of the tragic temporal contradictions of biomedical practice. *International Journal of Health Services, 18*, 1.

Giddens, A. (1984). *The constitution of society: Outline of a theory of structuration.* Cambridge: Polity.

Giddens, A. (1991). *Modernity and self identity.* Cambridge: Polity.

Goffman, E. (1961). *Asylums: Essays on the social situations of mental patients and other inmates.* New York: Doubleday.

Gurney, C. M. (2000). Accommodating bodies: The organization of corporeal dirt in the embodied home. In L. McKie & N. Watson (Eds.), *Organizing bodies: Policy, institutions and work.* Basingstoke, UK: MacMillan.

Gurney, C. M., & Means, R. (1993). The meaning of home in later life. In S. Arber & M. Evandrou (Eds.), *Ageing, independence and the life course.* London: Jessica Kingsley.

Hantrais, L. (1993). The gender of time in professional occupations. *Time and Society, 2(2)*, 139–157.

Harvey, D. (1989). *The condition of postmodernity.* Oxford: Blackwell.

Imrie, R. (2004). Disability, embodiment and the meaning of home. *Housing Studies, 19*(5), 745–763.

Katz, S. (1996). *Disciplining old age: The formation of gerontological knowledge.* Charlottesville: University Press of Virginia.

Lawrence, R. J. (1987). *Housing, dwellings and homes: Design theory, research and practice.* Chichester, UK: Wiley.

Leccardi, C. (1996). Rethinking social time: Feminist perspectives. *Time and Society, 5*(2), 169–186.

Leccardi, C., & Rampazi, M. (1993). Past and future in young women's experience of time. *Time and Society, 2*, 353–380.

Lee, T., & Piachaud, D. (1992). The time consequences of social services. *Time & Society, 1*(1), 65–80.

Massey, D. (1994). *Space, place and gender.* Cambridge: Polity.

May, J., & Thrift, N. (Eds.). (2001). *Timespace: Geographies of temporality.* London: Routledge.

Netten, A. (1993). Costing informal care. In A. Netten & J. Beecham (Eds.), *Costing community care: Theory and practice.* Aldershot, UK: Ashgate.

Parkins, W. (2004). Out of time: Fast subjects and slow living. *Time & Society, 13*(2/3), 363–382.

Rodaway, P. (1994). *Sensuous geographies: Body, sense and place.* London: Routledge.

Rubinstein, R. L. (1989). The home environments of older people: A description of the psychosocial processes linking person to place. *Journal of Gerontology, 44*(2), S45–S53.

Sixsmith, A. (1990). The meaning and experience of "home" in later life. In B. Bytheway and J. Johnson (Eds.), *Welfare and the ageing experience*. Aldershot, UK: Avebury.

Tuan, Y. F. (1974). *Topophilia: A study of environmental perception, attitudes and values*. Englewood Cliffs, NJ: Prentice Hall.

Twigg, J. (1999). The spatial ordering of care: Public and private in bathing support at home. *Sociology of Health and Illness, 21*(4), 381–400.

Twigg, J. (2000a). Carework as bodywork. *Ageing and Society, 20*, 389–411.

Twigg, J. (2000b). *Bathing: The body and community care*. London: Routledge.

Twigg, J., & Atkin, K. (1994). *Carers perceived: Policy and practice in informal care*. Milton Keynes, UK: Open University Press.

Urry, J. (1996). Sociology of time and space. In B. S. Turner (Ed.), *Blackwell companion to social theory*. Oxford: Blackwell.

Valentine, G. (2001). *Social geographies: Space and society*. Harlow, UK: Prentice Hall.

Vincent, J. (2003). *Old age*. London: Routledge.

Wiles, J. (2003). Daily geographies of caregivers: Mobility, routine, scale. *Social Science & Medicine, 57*(7), 1307–1325.

Wiles, J. (2005). Conceptualizing place in the care of older people: The contribution of geographical gerontology. *International Journal of Older People Nursing, 14*(8), 100–108.

Wolkowitz, C. (2002). The social relations of bodywork. *Work, Employment and Society, 16*(3), 497–510.

13

Blurring the Boundaries

Aging and Caring at the Intersection of Work and Home Life

Judith E. Phillips and Anne Martin-Matthews

Over the last 20 years, there has been increasing international interest in the social sciences literature on the subject of boundaries and in particular on shifting boundaries of home and work life. As noted in preceding chapters, this interest has been led by feminist writers on the concept of care, and increasingly in relation to work–life balance. The chapters in this book highlight the imprecise boundaries of work, home, and care life and provide evidence that blurring boundaries is a useful concept to be studied theoretically and empirically.

Conceptual approaches to blurring boundaries in different social, cultural, and economic contexts and in relation to work life and family or home life responsibilities have been continuing themes throughout the book. Based on what can be termed a number of work–life balance studies conducted across the world, we make a case in this concluding chapter for greater integration of the domains of work and care. As previous chapters reveal, the complexities in the boundaries of work and family life are oversimplified in the literature on "balancing" or "juggling" work and care for older people that suggests it is a matter of individual competence in balancing two separate but equal parts of life. Collectively we would argue that this approach provides us with a false dichotomy based on an assumption that the nature of the relationship between work and care in each sphere is totally different. If we concentrate on these spheres as separate entities, then we fail to see the interconnections between them and the important interaction and negotiation in the spaces between them as people develop strategies for managing these boundaries. In conclusion we argue that there is utility in the concept of boundaries to advance our understanding of care provision. The blurred spaces between and around home and work life—which have been termed the "intermediate" domain of care (Cathy Ward-Griffin in chapter 1)—give us a way of reconceptualizing care at the boundaries. As Atiya Mahmood and Anne Martin-Matthews suggest in chapter 2, the permeability of these boundaries forces us to rethink our conceptualization and assumptions that underpin policy and practice on the interface of work and home life.

This concluding chapter draws together the strands of the book to underpin the above argument. It approaches the argument from the perspective of "workers" who are paid employees with responsibilities for caring for elderly members and workers whose jobs involve care of others and who also have responsibilities for care of older people in their personal lives. We highlight four themes and argue that

- the boundaries are becoming indistinct between care and work.
- there are a number of boundary layers.
- working carers experience difficulty at the boundaries, particularly in defining the boundaries.
- there are a number of ways in which people manage the boundaries between work and care.

Each is summarized below.

The first common strand or theme is that the *boundaries between work and care have become indistinct.* Some commentators in the wider literature (Giddens, 1990; Vincent, Phillipson, & Downes, 2006) have argued that boundaries are increasingly blurred through globalization, the increased feminization of the workplace, and technological advances, key features of the postmodern state.

As chapter 6 highlighted, there is an argument that homogeneity results from the global economy. Care is also produced in a global marketplace, with geographical boundaries being indistinct. People are shifting across the world to provide care, making carework a global phenomenon. This is clearly illustrated, although in a different sense of people moving for other work, through the astronaut family outlined in chapter 6, where children leave older people to face what is termed a "double jeopardy"—being alone without care in a foreign environment. Extending the argument, we could argue that such globalization and associated homogeneity have left all care facilities looking similar, with the result that a placelessness or the "space of non place" emerges (Augé, 1995), where the unfamiliar becomes familiar and time and space are compressed.

Feminists, such as Tronto (1993) and Williams (2001), have argued that there should be no boundaries between public and private space, domestic and work space, and male and female spaces; they argue that boundaries need to be broken down if care, and the labor of all those involved in care, is to be valued. The argument is that care pervades all relationships, both at work and at home.

Second, *there are a number of boundary layers.* In relation to boundaries *within* the family, Boss and Greenberg (1984) argued that boundary ambiguity exists; this refers to family members "uncertain in their perception about who is in or out of the family and who is performing what roles and tasks within the family system" (p. 535). Finch and Mason (1993) looked at how people become carers and negotiate care roles and responsibilities within the family. They referred to the lack of fixed obligation and the uncertainty in such decision making. In chapter 9 of this volume, Norah Keating and her colleagues demonstrate that boundaries within care networks also operate—as between the provision of direct help to the care recipient and of indirect help to the caregiver.

A further layer exists *between the family and employment* (work and home life). Nippert-Eng (1996) spoke about placement and removal, integration and segmentation. She argued that work and home can be fully integrated with no distinctions between them, and that all space and time are multipurpose (Nippert-Eng, p. 5). Alternatively, at the other end of the spectrum, home and work are totally separate, "segmented" worlds—there is no ambiguity—it is either work or home with no overlap. In relation to family and employment, however, several chapters illustrate the difficulties of segmentation. Boundary blurring occurs in relation to location as well as role for homecare workers (i.e., within the "home"). Examples in chapters 1 and 2 are drawn from Canada, where research demonstrates that the role of the care worker can blur into becoming one of a friend rather than an employee performing tasks. Care workers also undertake unpaid tasks outside their paid role for the older person.

Cathy Ward-Griffin in chapter 1 illustrates that working carers—who are formal as well as informal, and are called "double-duty workers"—simultaneously participate in the public and private domains of caregiving, using their knowledge in one realm to assist in the other. Within the family, however, they may be earmarked as the responsible one—and this creates subsequent tensions between the boundaries of work and care.

Boundaries are also blurred *between state and family* (Ungerson, 2004). Chapters in the book highlight policies developed to encourage blurring of the state "formal" and the family "informal" caregiving roles, for example domestic maids and filial piety; and direct payments to carers. This is further explored by Janice Keefe and her colleagues in chapter 10 in relation to payments for care, and by Kalyani Mehta and Leng Leng Thang in chapter 3. Such boundaries are social constructions and can be real or virtual.

As Kalyani Mehta and Leng Leng Thang reveal, domestic maids in Singapore are brought in to assist families in retaining their notions of and commitment to filial piety. Here we see the blurring of boundaries of family and nonfamily, of public meeting the private (lives of families), of filial piety and hired carers, of care providers for children and older people, of formal and informal care, and of direct and indirect help—domestic maids helping parents to care for both younger and older generations within the family.

Across countries, people speak about the *difficulties at the boundaries, particularly in relation to defining them.* In many of the studies reported in this volume, people refer to "breaches" and how difficult it is to "draw the line," to maintain the boundaries, and to know when a boundary had been breached, and how easy it is to step over the boundary and to take the consequences when the boundary is breached.

The disputes and contested areas ranged over the following:

- What was implicit and explicit (as when managers didn't inform care workers)
- Zones of care and gaps (what was allowed in what zone)
- No-man's-land between families and care workers (role ambiguity)

Some examples of contested areas around the boundaries relate to relationships and the geography of space and time.

Care is based on a relationship, but only a degree of emotional involvement is allowed by homecare agencies, as illustrated in some of our chapters; it cannot be a relationship of friendship, and yet care involves emotional labor. In the chapters, this is discussed in terms of appropriate professional and personal behavior; despite agency guidance, some care workers talked about how easy it is to slip into a friendship relationship and to undertake tasks outside the agency remit. Conflict often involves isolation (social and geographic) from managers and lack of wider support from peers due to the very nature of the job. For some service users, boundaries are essential to ensure privacy of place and space.

Geographical boundaries also cause negative sentiments and contested areas to emerge. Boundaries are evident in relation to geography, with distance thresholds within which personal care can be performed. But this occurs not only in terms of space but also in relation to *time and distance.* This is illustrated through homecare again but also through examples from employed carers. If we look at work–life studies and the issue of distance (combining space and time), the impact on families, individuals, and work is considerable, causing boundary conflict.

Looking at the temporal dimension here, we also see conflicts across boundaries. Time has multiple and contested meanings, and, as Julia Twigg in chapter 12 argues, where the body is concerned, boundaries and time become even more contested, with different meanings of time for service users and homecare workers. For example, there is clock time and body time, and there are many ways in which time is experienced and understood. This is highlighted in the boundaries evident in the exercise of carework in the home setting. Carework is immediate: a time-bound activity yet one that can disrupt the time and rhythm of the older person. It is closely tied to the needs of the body—it is organic and cyclic. And it is not driven by clock time but by what is needed—care cannot be saved up, and you have to go with body rhythms.

Personal care based on body time is also hard to predict (as it is not an activity but a state) and therefore clashes with the units of a worker's time, which are set. There are conflicts on the boundaries between the commodification of time as experienced by the care worker and the experience of the older person in the form of "non-time"—as care is ever present for the older person. As Julia Twigg illustrates, different time worlds operate.

Yet care has often to be provided in a fast and efficient manner and can be perceived as cold and distant. Person-centered care, therefore, has a different tempo than that prescribed by the care agency; often, it is the older person's time that gets neglected, with baths and bed at 5:00 p.m. to fit in with the worker's and agency's schedule. As Kalyani Mehta and Leng Leng Thang argue in chapter 3, personal space and time are being invaded by care workers' schedules.

Finally, a common theme throughout the chapters centered on how people *manage* the boundaries.

In our studies of care workers, many talk about setting limits—for example, you shouldn't care for your own relatives if you are in care-work jobs—and the private needs to be clearly demarcated; alternatively, workers felt they could use the knowledge they had from their job to make the right connections. Professional standards are often invoked to reinforce boundaries; boundary guidelines differ between professional bodies, and often such bodies create boundaries between themselves. For managers and employers, boundary demarcation in a number of instances is seen as a responsibility of individuals and part of their personal life. This causes difficulty for some care workers.

Others reinterpret or blur the boundaries between home and work as a form of adaptation, sometimes using strategies of segmentation to achieve boundary management (preserve the meaning of home) or integration (treat workers as fictive kin). For employee carers, the segmentation may mean giving up the job or care responsibilities.

As Nippert-Eng (1996) argued, commuting is one way of accommodating and managing boundaries where distance is involved. Commuting is a boundary-spanning demand that can impact on work and family life. In an attempt to be distance-defying or accommodating, carers used commuting as a long-term strategy in Judith E. Phillips and Miriam Bernard's study in chapter 6. Moving the older person nearer or having a long commute to work and care is one way of accommodating the liminal spaces or transitions between work, home, and care life.

Conclusion

The book highlights the diversity of the care–work relationship. We have attempted to demonstrate in the book issues around the following:

- Workers whose places of employment are someone else's home (Atiya Mahmood and Anne Martin-Matthews; Kalyani Mehta and Leng Leng Thang; and Jane Mears and Elizabeth Watson).
- Family members paid for caring for kin (Janice Keefe et al.).
- Particular challenges when distance plays a role and becomes an aspect of the locational triangle between work and family life (Judith E. Phillips and Miriam Bernard; and Margaret Neal et al.).

- Challenging the dyadic nature of the carework relationship (previous literature has focused on the single employee and his or her caregiving responsibilities) and placing the emphasis and level of analysis *from* the dyad *to* the network (Norah Keating et al; and Joanie Sims-Gould et al.).
- A micro focus on the body, time, and links to carework (Julia Twigg)
- A macro focus on the societal, cultural, economic, locational, and policy contexts (Maria Evandrou and Karen Glaser; Kalyani Mehta and Leng Leng Thang; Margaret Neal et al; and Judith E. Phillips and Miriam Bernard).
- The life course approach to work and care. Care is not one-way, but rather is multidirectional; care is not only given *to* older people but also provided *by* older people (Kalyani Mehta and Leng Leng Thang). The older person's home becomes the site of care, not only where care is received (by them) but also where care is provided (by them) to grandchildren.

The importance of flexibility at the boundaries of home and work life is a key feature of this book and runs through all the above issues. Boundaries and intersections are constantly shifting and merging or segregating, depending on the environment. Consequently, we need a more nuanced conceptual and empirical understanding of the work–life balance as it is experienced by carers in a number of contexts—as working carers and care workers. A thorough investigation of these boundaries is one way of better understanding care. As Atiya Mahmood and Anne Martin-Matthews describe, a useful conceptual frame for understanding boundaries is through the concept of integration (in relation to homecare), where workers are treated like family or fictive kin, or the concept of segregation, where strict routines are adhered to and any accommodations are frowned upon, Carers talk about boundaries in their attempts to provide care and paid work. *There is utility in the concept, but it is the contested areas at the intersection of the two domains that have the greatest value in advancing our understanding of paid work and carework.* What Cathy Ward-Griffin has termed the "intermediate domain"—between home and work, and between the public and the private, where carework roles and practices exist along a continuum of integration and segregation (using concepts from Nippert-Eng, 1996)—is the area that provides us with the primary location for intervention. The boundaries are contested yet permeable and blurred, and people employ strategies to move from one domain to the other as needs dictate. Voydanoff (2006) explored this in terms of boundary-spanning resources and demands and drew on work–family border theory (Clark, 2000). Like Nippert-Eng (1996), she "views relationships between domains as a continuum ranging from segmentation to integration" (p. 5). Permeability and flexibility can be high or low and define the ends of the continuum. One of the advantages of the Voydanoff model is that it also includes community resources and demands, not just those within the home or the workplace.

The intermediate domain may be the transitional space from one domain to the other. It is also the space where the rethinking of time and space can occur, where new ways of accommodating work and home can take place, and where policy and practice need to be concentrated.

The book not only provides a theoretical framework for understanding this intermediate domain but also identifies strategies and interventions that are grounded in evidence from across the world. For example, distance is geographically bounded but can be accommodated in a number of ways by adjustments (e.g., commuting or moving) on the boundaries in terms of time and space. Direct payments and the multiple policy contexts in which they operate, as discussed in Janice Keefe et al.'s chapter, provide us with strategies for taking the contested areas forward into policy and practice.

Policy and Practice Implications

As the chapter by Janice Keefe and colleagues illustrates, multiple policy domains operate. Direct payments to carers, for example, blur the boundaries of labor market policies and not just in relation to care policy. However, in many countries, the boundaries between policy domains are segmented and have little crossover, particularly in terms of policies in relation to older people and their carers. Yet the impact in one domain can influence another, as the previous statement illustrates. Boundary blurring is a useful concept to consider in policy terms.

One of the key considerations in policy is the need to challenge where the boundaries are drawn and "policed." Flexibility in policy to respond to more integrated approaches to care is necessary if individuals are to achieve any kind of "balance" or to effectively juggle work and home life with care. Policy can no longer look at separate spheres of care and work activities.

On a more local level, there is the need to develop flexibility in all environments, whether they are in relation to homecare or in an office of employee carers. Such flexibility can come through benefits, services, and policies at the workplace as well as through the policies of care agencies to assist carers and older people.

Given these considerations, there is a further need to focus on the strengths, agreements, and consensus of the boundaries—on a local level, in terms of agreement between individuals in areas of homecare on issues such as duration, timing of visits, and roles and tasks to perform, for example. On a macro level, there is a need for a concerted approach in policy and practice to provide opportunities for women to remain in and return to the workplace while undertaking care but also to provide high-quality funded care if they do so.

In relation to research, there are a number of gaps in our knowledge, and we call for a more planned approach to research in this area across the globe. Such research themes and questions would focus on the liminal or transitional spaces between different domains, whether they be policy or practice spaces; conflicts and ambiguities on the boundary; the quality of care in the intermediate domain; and how choices are made in terms of integration or segregation—are they considered, or do people drift into particular domains? Is boundary permeability easier one way than another, for example to become a carer rather than an employee? What are the constraints to moving across boundaries—are these political, social, cultural, or economic? Similarly, are intensive roles, particularly in relation to the emotional aspects of "intense care," played out in these intermediate domains?

Finally, public and private, and professional and personal, are not separate entities as they are treated in policy on work–life balance but rather are interconnected through the provision of care and acted out in spaces between and around boundaries in what can be termed an *intermediate domain*. "Care is not conducted in a vacuum but in spaces imbued with meaning for carers, care workers, and older people" (Mahmood and Martin-Matthews). The globalization of care and work, highlighted by Michael Creedon in the foreword, will have considerable impact on the debates around work and care, not only in the United States but also across the world. We trust that this book has filled some of the gaps in our knowledge to take these debates further.

References

Augé, M. (1995). Introduction. In *An anthropology of supermodernity.* London: Verso.

Boss, P., & Greenberg, J. (1984). Family boundary ambiguity: A new variable in family stress theory. *Family Process, 23*(4), 535–546.

Clark, S. C. (2000). Work/family border theory. *Human Relations, 53,* 747–770.

Finch, J., & Mason, J. (1993). *Negotiating family responsibilities.* London: Routledge.

Giddens, A. (1990). *The consequences of modernity.* Cambridge: Polity.

Nippert-Eng, C. (1996). *Home and work.* Chicago: University of Chicago Press.

Tronto, J. (1993). *Moral boundaries: A political argument for an ethic of care.* New York: Routledge.

Ungerson, C. (2004). Whose empowerment and independence? A cross-national perspective on "cash for care" schemes. *Ageing and Society, 24,* 189–221.

Vincent, J., Phillipson, C., & Downes, M. (Eds.). (2006). *The futures of old age.* London: Sage with the British Society of Gerontology.

Voydanoff, P. (2006). *Work, family and community.* New York: Laurence Erlbaum.

Williams, F. (2001). In and beyond New Labour: Towards a new political ethics of care. *Critical Social Policy, 21,* 467–493.

Author Index

A

B

C

D

E

F

G

L

M

S

T

U

V

W

Y

Z

Subject Index

N

O

P

R

S

T

U

V

W

Z